# WESTMINSTER ABBEY
## ITS WORSHIP AND
## ORNAMENTS

KING HENRY III

ALCUIN CLUB COLLECTIONS
No. XXXIV

# WESTMINSTER ABBEY
## ITS WORSHIP AND ORNAMENTS

*By*

JOCELYN PERKINS
M.V.O., M.A., D.C.L., F.S.A.
SACRIST OF WESTMINSTER ABBEY

VOLUME II

OXFORD UNIVERSITY PRESS
LONDON : HUMPHREY MILFORD
1940

OXFORD UNIVERSITY PRESS
AMEN HOUSE, E.C. 4
LONDON EDINBURGH GLASGOW NEW YORK
TORONTO MELBOURNE CAPETOWN BOMBAY
CALCUTTA MADRAS
HUMPHREY MILFORD
PUBLISHER TO THE UNIVERSITY

PRINTED IN GREAT BRITAIN

# NOTE

IN addition to those to whom I have already expressed my thanks in the Preface I must add the names of others who have rendered me equally valuable assistance in connexion with this second volume.

First and foremost is the Right Reverend the Dean of Westminster who has been good enough to permit the reproduction of Canaletto's fine painting of a Procession of the Bath, one of the many treasures of the Deanery.

I am much indebted to one of our old Choristers, Mr. H. V. Abbott, A.R.I.B.A., who has made the three plans of Henry VII's Chapel, the Roxburghe Society, the Master and Fellows of Corpus Christi College, Cambridge, and the Syndicate of the Cambridge University Library who have courteously allowed me to reproduce some illustrations in certain manuscripts belonging to them.

JOCELYN PERKINS

W.A.M. = Westminster Abbey Manuscripts

# CONTENTS

# ILLUSTRATIONS

The MS. from which this picture is taken is the best copy of the shorter *History* of Matthew Paris known as *Historia Anglorum* (British Museum Royal MSS. 14 C. VII, f. 9*a*).

The picture of Henry III is the last of a series of Kings, four in a page, seated beneath a horseshoe arch with ornamental spandrels within elaborate frames. Each king is holding the model of a church of which he was the founder.

From Dart, *Westmonasterium*, vol. i.

J. Cole sculpt.

This is the oldest full-length view extant of the nave of the Abbey. In the far distance can be seen the Classical Altar-piece erected in 1708. A projection on the north side of the choir indicates the organ played upon by Purcell, Blow, and Croft. Abbot Islip's screens separating the spaces beneath the two towers are still intact.

T. Bowles delin., T. Bowles sculpt.

This picture indicates the extensive changes which occurred between 1710 and 1740. In the immediate foreground Abbot Islip's stone screen beneath the south-west tower is still *in situ*, though destined soon to give place to the huge monument in memory of Captain Cornewall, who perished in the naval battle off Toulon in 1743. On the north side, the ancient screen appears to be standing, but an incongruous classical monument, since removed, has been erected in front of it.

The floor portrayed in this picture and its predecessor is probably the original pavement. It will be seen that it was carefully designed to facilitate the passing of processions. The destruction of this ancient landmark, partly by renewal and partly by the introduction of tombstones mainly in the nineteenth century, is a great loss.

From *The History of Westminster Abbey*, vol. ii, by R. Ackermann.

T. Uwins delt., J. Blück sculpt.

The splendid wrought-iron gates are a prominent feature of this picture, while further eastward can be seen the ascent of three steps into the choir which latter was unfortunately lowered in 1848. Still further eastward, though not clearly indicated, is the Classical Altar-piece. Above appears the lower portion of Shrider's organ case.

Reproduced by permission of *The Times* newspaper.

borne by four beardless men. The King is met by two mitred and coped bishops and an abbot, all three carrying croziers. 'Sequebatur conventus Westmōn cum abbatibus et monachis quos longum esset enumerare festive vestitis et canentibus et classico magno pulsato.'

British Museum, Royal MSS. 14 C. VII, f. 146.

This is another of the marginal drawings inserted in his *History* by Matthew Paris. It represents the *Passus Christi* given to the Abbey by Henry III. The lower part of the Saviour's figure is seen ascending into the clouds. His right foot is touching the ground, leaving a footmark, which was the relic acquired by the King.

The original of this picture is said to have been painted by Max Emanuel Ain Miller in the year 1851. The photograph from which the reproduction has been made formed part of a collection belonging to the Crown Prince Ruprecht of Bavaria. It will be noticed that the grate at the entrance to Henry V's Chantry is lacking. The beautiful pavement and its relation to the Shrine (though the details of the latter are not wholly accurate) are delineated with great skill and should be carefully noted.

From the *Inventory of the Historical Monuments of London*, volume i, *Westminster Abbey*, Pl. 42. Published by the Royal Commission on Historical Monuments.

(*a*) The Nobles swearing allegiance to Queen Emma.

(*b*) The Coronation of King Edward.

(*c*) The Divine Child appearing to King Edward during Mass.

Ibid., Pl. 43.

(*a*) King Edward giving his ring, as an alms, to a beggar outside his palace at Havering-atte-Bower.

(*b*) St. John giving the ring to two pilgrims from Ludlow on a road not far from Jerusalem.

(*c*) The pilgrims returning the ring to King Edward.

Talman designavit, G. Vertue sculpt.

As indicated by the Latin inscription, this beautiful print was made at the expense of the Society of Antiquaries in the year 1724. Apart from the charm of George Vertue's workmanship it possesses the special interest of being the oldest print extant of the Confessor's Shrine.

Its accuracy, however, is open to question. The upper portion of Abbot Feckenham's wooden feretory almost certainly suffered injury at an earlier date, whereas here it is represented as being intact. Probably the third stage, as it appears in this picture, has been evolved out of Talman's imagination. It is doubtful also whether the twisted column on the right-hand side was occupying this position in 1724. On the whole, however, this picture (though probably representing in some measure what Talman thought the Shrine *ought* to be) gives a fairly good idea of its appearance from the time it left the hands of Abbot Feckenham down to the nineteenth century.

Undercroft, while the shield and saddle are attached to the heavy wooden bar above, which unites the two eastern pillars of the apse.

It will be noted that the aumbry on the north side still possessed its doors in 1786. To-day only the hinges remain.

## THE VESTIBULE OF HENRY VII's CHAPEL, THE AMBULATORY, AND THE METAL BARRIER ENCLOSING THE TOMB OF HENRY V.
*facing page* 146

From *The History of Westminster Abbey*, vol. ii, by R. Ackermann.
Thompson delt., J. Blück sculpt.

The massive cage of wrought iron with which the fifteenth-century Convent endeavoured to protect the tomb of the victor of Agincourt did not prevent a gang of burglars from rifling it in the reign of Henry VIII. The cage was removed by the Dean and Chapter in the reign of George IV, and sold at so much a hundredweight together with the greater portion of the metal-work in their possession.

## HENRY VII BESTOWING THE INDENTURES OF HIS NEW FOUNDATION UPON ABBOT ISLIP AND THE CONVENT OF WESTMINSTER
*facing page* 149

British Museum, Harleian MSS. 1498, No. 59.

This picture is one of four in a large volume containing the various indentures drawn up between the Most Christian and Excellent Prince Henry VII on the one hand and Abbot Islip, the Prior, and the Convent of St. Peter of Westminster on the other, on July 16th, 1506. In the principal letter the King, robed and crowned and holding a sceptre, is seated upon a throne, over which is suspended a canopy. In front kneels the Abbot who is holding a crozier (Westminster being a mitred abbey) and supported by a group of monks in the Benedictine habit. The border which is painted on a gold plan contains the Tudor Royal Arms with the dragon and greyhound supporters, together with portcullises and red roses with sprigs of rose leaves on either side.

## THE PROPOSED CHANTRY CHAPEL OR MONUMENT OF HENRY VI
*facing page* 152

British Museum, Cottonian MSS. Aug. II. 1. Artist unknown.

## GROUND PLAN OF HENRY VII's CHAPEL     *pages* 155, 157, and 159
Drawn by H. V. Abbot, A.R.I.B.A.

(*a*) As intended by the Founder, (*b*) as completed by Henry VIII. Based on a drawing left by the architect John Thorpe and preserved in Sir John Soane's Museum, probably of early seventeenth-century origin, (*c*) as existing to-day.

## THE TWO HOUSES OF CONVOCATION IN SESSION AT WESTMINSTER ABBEY     .     .     .     .     . *facing page* 166
A contemporary broadside published by Thomas Jenner, now among the Historical Prints in the British Museum.

This remarkable picture is described in the following terms:
'Venerable aspect of both the Houses of Convocation of the Reverend

Prelates and Clergy of the Province of Canterbury assembled by his Majesties authority the first in St. Paul's London February 13th 1623, thence removed to Westminster, and there yet continuing this 23rd of April.

'Whereof the Upper House consisted of the Most Reverend Metropolitan and the Right Reverend Bishops of the Province now assembled in Henry the Sevenths Chappel in Westminster; and the Lower House of the Deanes, Archdeacons, and Clerkes of the Diocesses and Chapters of that Province, is assembled in another distinct place on the north side of Westminster Church.'

It will be noticed that on the left-hand side of the foreground of the picture appear several bishops who belong to the Province of York. They are attired in the episcopal habit, unlike their brethren who are depicted wearing their synodical robes. This distinction is made in order to indicate the fact that the York Bishops are simply visitors from another province. Archbishop Abbott is in the chair, supported by George Montaigne, Bishop of London, and Lancelot Andrewes, Bishop of Winchester.

The 'distinct place on the north side of Westminster Church' was the eastern aisle of the north transept, which was divided by the thirteenth-century builders into three chapels separated from the rest of the building by stone screens of great beauty. To-day it is filled with tombs, monuments, and tablets, but in the seventeenth century there appears to have been sufficient space available to provide a meeting-place of some dimensions. This arrangement was still in existence at the end of the seventeenth century, according to Keepe.

'This Chappel (St. Michael) with part of the Chappel of St. John the Evangelist and St. Andrew are now taken up and the monuments almost covered by scaffolds placed here, being made use of at present for the lower Convocation House for the Deans, Prebends and Doctors &c., as that of King Henry VII is for the Archbishop and Bishops when the Parliament sits at Westminster.' (Keepe, _Monumenta Westmonasteriensia_, p. 172.)

The actual building is completely hidden by the curtains which surround the seats, but immediately behind the Prolocutor (John Young, Dean of Winchester) some iron railings are visible, which possibly form part of the Norris monument.

From _A Genealogical History of the Kings of England and Monarchs of Great Britain_, by Francis Sandford, Lancaster Herald.

This volume was published in 1677, therefore this picture would have been drawn about thirty years after the destruction of the altar by the representatives of the Long Parliament. It was probably copied by some unknown artist from an older picture which has disappeared.

Its details do not altogether tally with those laid down in the contract drawn up between the executors of Henry VII's will and Pietro Torrigiano, nor yet with some of those visible in the earlier illustration. It may be assumed, however, that it gives a fairly accurate representation, save for the absence of the frontals which were definitely ordered in Henry VII's will.

From the _Inventory of the Historical Monuments of London_, vol. i, _Westminster Abbey_, pl. 107.

The medieval consecration cross above the north door should be noted.

The Chapel of King Henry VII at the beginning of the Eighteenth Century *facing page* 185

T. Schijnvoet ad vivum fecit.

In all probability this is the oldest picture extant showing the interior of Henry VII's Chapel as a whole. Its chief interest lies in the fact that it enables us to realize the very considerable changes subsequently made with the establishment of the Most Honourable Order of the Bath in 1725.

The stalls occupy three bays only instead of four as to-day. Their remarkable domical tops are completely visible and with charming effect, whereas to-day they are hidden by the helmets, swords, and lambrequins of the members of the Order. The substalls are confined to one bay only. Their companions were added in 1725.

The stone screens which enclosed four of the eastern chapels, two on either side, are shown still intact.

The arrangement of the step at the east end is different to that which exists to-day, and Prebendary Killigrew's pavement of marble lozenges is uniform throughout.

The Procession of the Knights of the Bath Passing out of the Abbey on June 26th, 1749 . . . *facing page* 190

This picture, the work of Antonio Canale, called Canaletto (1697–1768), was painted at the request of Dean Wilcocks, who placed it in the Deanery, where it has hung ever since. No less than four Installations of the Bath took place during his decanate.

The Procession is passing from the west door of the Abbey through St. Margaret's Churchyard to the Princes' Chamber. The concluding figure is that of Lord De la War representing the Great Master. He is immediately preceded by Dean Wilcocks, who is wearing what appears to be a girded alb and a scarf beneath his official mantle. The cassocks and long surplices of members of the choir standing on either side should also be noted.

This Installation took place not long after the completion of the two western towers of the Abbey, for which Dean Wilcocks was largely responsible and of which he was inordinately proud. This fact possibly explains the painting of the picture.

The Procession of the Knights of the Bath Passing Through the Abbey on June 1st 1812 . . *facing page* 193

Drawn by Frederick Nash. Engraved by C. R. Lewis.

This picture represents the Procession of the Knights of the Bath passing through the ambulatory to their Chapel prior to the ceremony of Installation.

The figures wearing white mantles are the Prebendaries of Westminster. They are followed by a group of Heralds and several Knights. The King's Almsmen are ascending the steps.

The Chapel of St. Edmund occupies the foreground of the picture. Its fine wooden screen collapsed with the weight of the spectators allowed to congregate upon it at the Funeral of the Duchess of Northumberland on December 18th, 1776. The dilapidated fragment on the right side of the picture is evidently intended to recall this disaster.

Engraved by Frederick Nash. Drawn by C. R. Lewis.

The Duke of York, who officiated as Great Master four times running, is in the act of ascending the steps to install the new Knights. He is followed by one of the Prebendaries, Dr. Ireland, subsequently Dean, for the age and infirmity of Dean Vincent prevented him from taking more than a small part in the ceremony.

The Royal Box over the altar concealing the tomb of Henry VII, and the vast gallery erected, partly for the musicians and partly for privileged spectators, testify to the crudity of the ideas then prevalent regarding worship and ceremonial.

Photograph by A. F. Brown.

Reproduced by permission of *The Times* newspaper.

On July 3rd, 1935, twenty-one Knights Grand Cross of the Bath were installed. Sir Eric Geddes, the senior Knight installed, is in the act of redeeming his sword from the Dean. His twenty colleagues, some of whom appear in the foreground, are holding their drawn swords by the blades with the hilts pointing towards the altar. The Canons of Westminster are standing on either side, while two of the Officers of the Order are supporting Sir Eric Geddes. Canons and Officers alike are arrayed in white mantles embroidered with the arms of the Order. The Great Master, the Dean, and the Knights Grand Cross are wearing crimson mantles.

Photograph by R. F. Fleming.

The altar and baldacchino consecrated on July 3rd, 1935, are as far as possible a replica of the work of Pietro Torrigiano. They were designed by the late Sir Walter Tapper, R.A. The frontal is Italian embroidery of the late seventeenth or early eighteenth century.

The great metal sconces on each side of the tomb of Henry VII and Elizabeth have once more been filled with candles after the lapse of several centuries.

# PART IV

# THE ROOD SCREEN, THE PULPITUM AND THE ALTARS OF THE NAVE

## 1. THE NAVE AND ITS ALTARS

THE western arm of the Abbey Church of Westminster covers no less than twelve bays, including the space between the two towers. A very considerable portion, however, upwards of one-third, was walled off to form the great inner chapel of the choir, terminating with the High Altar, the centre of the spiritual life of the convent.

Thus, a visitor entering by the west door would have found himself in a relatively small nave, the people's church, covering seven bays only and bounded on the east by the massive Rood Screen. The latter stood just at the point of junction between the lofty choir of Henry III and the low-browed Norman nave of Edward the Confessor, which did not entirely disappear until the early years of the sixteenth century.

The Rood Screen, which was probably a splendid work of art, extended across the nave from pillar to pillar and was prolonged across the aisles to the north and south walls. Like its companion in the Abbey Church of St. Albans, it was pierced by two doorways flanking a central altar, which both at Westminster and Canterbury, bore the dedication of the Holy Cross.

This nave altar was specially set apart for the laity, thus fulfilling an extremely practical purpose. In addition to the stream of pilgrims and other visitors eager to hear mass within the Abbey Church, there would also be a regular congregation drawn from local sources, consisting of servants and other persons associated with the life of the monastery, and the neighbouring citizens. At the same time, the monastic brethren maintained a firm hold upon

B

the nave and did not hesitate, when it suited them, to exclude the laity altogether.

The Rood Screen must have been possessed of considerable depth, half a bay at least, for at Westminster, as at Lichfield, its loft or platform contained an altar. The loft was surmounted by the great Crucifix flanked, according to tradition, by the figures of the Blessed Virgin and St. John the Evangelist, to which Henry III evidently attached great importance. An entry in the Close Rolls for the thirty-fifth year of his reign, discovered by Professor Lethaby, states that one Edward of Westminster was commanded to erect a large cross in the nave of the Abbey Church; and, at the same time, to purchase two cherubim to stand on either side.[1]

The altar on the loft bore the dedication of St. Paul and the Crucifix,[2] and pilgrims were accorded special facilities for performing their devotions here. They would ascend by means of a staircase on one side, and after kissing the feet of the Rood, would reach the floor by a similar staircase on the other side. In the Suppression Inventory of 1540 this altar with its immediate surroundings which included 'a pair of organs' was definitely styled the Rood Chapel.

Below, two other altars were attached to the Rood Screen on the north and south. They were dedicated respectively to the Blessed Virgin and to the Holy Trinity.

The northern altar and the space adjoining formed the Lady Chapel of the Romanesque Abbey, but after the erection by Henry III of an imposing new building dedicated to the Blessed Virgin at the east end of the church, this 'lady altar' in the nave was relegated to a secondary position. Hence it is described in the *Consuetudines* drawn

---

[1] Lethaby, *Westminster Abbey and the King's Craftsmen*, pp. 26 and 27.
[2] The position of this altar is not wholly free from doubt. The suggestion has been made that it stood somewhere in the north transept; but the former alternative seems the more likely.

up by Abbot Ware as 'the old altar of the Blessed Mary, Mother of God.'[1] Tradition has always associated it with the scene depicted on the screen in St. Edward's Chapel, where the Divine Child appeared to St. Edward the Confessor while assisting at mass.

On the south side stood the altar of the Holy Trinity with its enclosure, on which John Redying expended £20.

There is some reason for thinking that the nave also contained an altar dedicated to St. Helena, or perhaps that the central altar possessed the double dedication of the Holy Cross and St. Helena, for a painting or reredos was provided for the altar of St. Helena by Richard of Cirencester together with an image of Our Lady.[2]

At the west end the floor-space beneath the two towers was separated off from the remainder of the nave by stone screens. The reason for this treatment is not very clear. Possibly these enclosures were used as chapels; indeed, it has been suggested that the northern of the two may have formed the Chapel of St. Christopher.[3] Its two screens, on the east and south sides, survived for many generations; but they ultimately became the victims of an unkind fate and were compelled to give place to 'monumental usurpers'. The former must have perished when the monument of Sir Godfrey Kneller, subsequently removed to the south choir aisle, was set up here. The latter was standing so recently as 1808, in which year a drawing was made of it by John Carter. The erection of the huge monument of Captain Montague, since removed, was responsible for its destruction.

Both screens were excellent specimens of late perpendicular architecture. They were decorated with representa-

---

[1] *Consuetudines Sancti Petri Westmonasterii*, Henry Bradshaw Society, edited by E. M. Thompson, vol. ii, p. 46.

[2] Stanley, *Historical Memorials of Westminster Abbey*, 3rd edition, Appendix, p. 608.

[3] *Church Quarterly Review*, vol. lxiv, p. 40.

tions of Abbot Islip's rebus and were probably built during the closing years of his rule.[1]

NOTE

It should be stated that another opinion would place the altars dedicated to the Blessed Virgin and the Holy Trinity farther eastwards, in the space between the Rood Screen and the pulpitum, in the places now occupied by the monuments of Sir Isaac Newton and Earl Stanhope.[2]

## 2. THE DESTRUCTION OF THE ROOD SCREEN

Save for the stone screen which separates the space beneath the south-west tower on its eastern side from the nave, and a doorway on the north aisle, known locally as the Demon's Door, which gave access to the Sacristy, nothing remains to-day of these pre-Reformation arrangements. Of the Rood Screen not one solitary wrack has been left behind, though the late Mr. J. T. Micklethwaite, writing during the closing years of the nineteenth century, maintained that traces of the beam to which the great Crucifix must have been attached were still visible high up on the fifth pair of pillars from the crossing.

In many parish churches and in some cathedrals the rood screens or portions of them still survive, but it must be remembered that the Abbey, in addition to the assaults of fanaticism, has also suffered a restoration of the most drastic type. Commencing in the reign of William and Mary, under the direction of Sir Christopher Wren, it was not concluded for half a century. The exterior, save Henry VII's Chapel, was refaced from one end to the other. Scarcely one stone of the external casing of Henry III and his successors remains *in situ*. Again, many of the existing details of the interior date from this period. The gilding and other decorative work on the ribs of the vault are a case in point. It is probable that Wren and his suc-

[1] The southern enclosure now contains the Chapel of the Holy Cross (see below).   [2] F. Bond, *Westminster Abbey*, pp. 45 and 62.

cessor, Nicholas Hawksmoor, deliberately obliterated every trace of injury suffered by the interior of the building during the religious dissensions of the sixteenth and seventeenth centuries or as a result of the efflux of time. They made no attempt to replace any objects which had disappeared, but they took immense pains to remove every blot or scar. They were acting wisely from one point of view, but they managed to destroy any number of clues to the former history of the church, thus bequeathing to posterity a host of insoluble problems.

The elimination of Roods formed a prominent feature in the orgy of destruction which disgraced the reign of Edward VI. Early in 1548 there was published an Order in Council directing the removal of images, whether they had been abused or not. The traces of this evil policy may be seen to this day in the ruined sculptures so sadly conspicuous in church after church. It must have been at this time that the ruthless hand of the iconoclast fell with crushing weight upon the Abbey, one of the most prominent buildings in the country. The glorious Rood over the High Altar, and its companion surmounting the screen, would receive scant mercy from the gang of miscreants into whose hands the chief power in the realm had passed.

A certain number of these structures escaped this particular wave of devastation, but their doom was sealed; only a few more years of life remained to them. The omissions of the Edwardians were made good with drastic thoroughness by their Elizabethan successors. The Tudor Queen had not occupied the throne three years when another Order in Council was passed, insisting, in the most emphatic terms, upon the radical alteration of the upper portions of the rood lofts. The place marked for long generations by the Sacred Figure was henceforth to be graced by the erection of 'some convenient crest' along the beam.[1]

[1] *Hierurgia Anglicana*, vol. i, pp. 14–15.

No one could possibly accuse the Elizabethan episcopal bench of any lack of eagerness to enforce this injunction. Even Archbishop Parker, despite his reputed moderation, inserted an inquiry among his Visitation Articles as to 'whether the rood loft be pulled down according to the Order prescribed'; while later on Grindal, the northern Primate, commanded that 'the seller or loft be quite taken down unto the rood beam'.[1]

In no place were these vandalistic injunctions carried out more whole-heartedly than in the Church of Westminster.

## 3. THE PULPITUM AND ITS HISTORY DURING THE SIXTEENTH AND SEVENTEENTH CENTURIES

Like the great majority of churches of Benedictine foundation, the choir of the Abbey was demarcated off on its western side by a double barrier. The doorways on either side of the Altar of the Holy Cross led to an open space, covering not less than one bay, and bounded on the east by a massive structure, entitled the pulpitum, pierced by a single doorway in the centre, which gave immediate access to the choir, the returned stalls of which backed on to its eastern face.

Despite the eagerness of the Edwardian and Elizabethan vandals to consign the rich sculptures and groups of figures of the rood screens to the scrap-heap in deference to the prevailing fanaticism, a strong desire was manifested by both the Queen and the Archbishop to maintain inviolate the time-honoured distinction between nave and chancel. The Order in Council of October 10th, 1561, already quoted, was positive enough:

'Provided also that where in any parish church the said rood lofts be already transposed, so that there remain a comely

---

[1] *Hierurgia Anglicana*, vol. i, pp. 15–16.

partition between the chancel and the church, that no alteration be otherwise attempted in them, but be suffered in quiet.
And where no partition is standing there to be one appointed.'

This plain direction was followed up the following year
by the Archbishop, who in the course of his Visitation
Articles inquired with almost meticulous exactness, not
only whether the rood loft be pulled down, but also 'if the
partition between the chancel and the church be kept'.

Thus, the *screens*, or at least their lower portions, were
to remain, but the rood *lofts* were to be remodelled, while
the Rood itself, together with any attendant figures, was
to be consigned to total destruction.

These principles did not fail to secure a literal and loyal
obedience at the Abbey. The pulpitum, that is to say, the
eastern of the two barriers, was retained, although the
Rood Screen with its altars and its wealth of decorative art
succumbed to the fanatical zeal of the times. The former
has undergone extensive rebuilding and its western face
has been drastically modernized; but there is reason for
thinking that some portions of the medieval masonry still
remain embedded in more recent additions.[1] At any rate,
the principle urged by Parker has been consistently
maintained throughout.

The earliest pictorial representation of the pulpitum is
found in a large print showing the interior of the Abbey
looking westward from the presbytery in Sandford's *History
of the Coronation of James II*.[2] It does not add very much,
however, to our existing information, for it is impossible
to discover to what extent the permanent structure has
been hidden beneath the temporary fittings set up for the
Coronation. On the other hand, the old wooden doors are
distinctly portrayed, solid in their lower parts, but with
their upper panels pierced with fifteenth-century tracery.
They are enclosed in an arch and flanked by pilasters with

[1] Lethaby, *Westminster Abbey and the King's Craftsmen*, pp. 25 and 26.
[2] See vol. i, p. 126.

classical capitals. The latter with their decorations of fruit
and foliage have clearly been erected under Renaissance
influence, and probably date from the decanate of Dean
Neile in the early years of the seventeenth century. The
Abbey records show that that energetic administrator was
responsible for making important alterations in this part
of the Abbey in the year 1605:

'Item paid to Nicholas Sutton for foure dayes worke to help
John Wright carpenter to take down the ould Orgayne loft,
and to carry the tymber in to the storehouse, and to build up
the trymers when he sett them upon the stone wall by the
Queere, iiijs.'[1]
'Item for taking down the waynscott about the ould Orgayne
loft and for carrying the same unto the Storehouse ijsviid.'[2]

Sandford's print, then, depicts a state of things which
had been brought into existence by this early Stuart 'restoration' in which the original wooden doors had been
allowed to remain intact.

The next pictorial representation of the pulpitum is
found in Dart's *Westmonasterium*, published in 1723, a
work by no means remarkable for accuracy, but possessed
of considerable value by reason of its descriptions of objects which have disappeared since the early decades of the
eighteenth century. The picture dates from the end of the
reign of Queen Anne and is the work of T. Cole. It shows
the interior of the Abbey from the west end of the nave,
looking eastward. Not a trace exists of either Rood, Rood
Screen, or Rood Loft; but the pulpitum is fully in evidence, emphasizing the distinction between nave and choir
almost as thoroughly as of old. Its walls are absolutely
bare. There is not the faintest suggestion of an altar, while
the decoration which presumably graced the two empty
and somewhat grim-looking wall surfaces on either side has
completely disappeared. The arch over the opening, sup-
posing such to have existed, must have been destroyed

1 W.A.M. 41090.            2 W.A.M. 41071.

The Inside Prospect of the Church of St. Peter's Westminster.

AT THE END OF THE REIGN OF QUEEN ANNE

subsequently to the Coronation of James II. The wooden doors, too, have gone and their place has been taken by a pair of handsome gates 'grated with iron and gilt'.[1] They do not, however, altogether resemble the splendid specimens of eighteenth-century craftsmanship which delight our eyes to-day. Expert authorities attribute the latter to the beginning of the eighteenth century, but the evidence furnished by Cole's print seems rather to suggest that they were placed here a generation later.[2]

On either side of the entrance rise two lofty pilasters with pyramid-shaped pinnacles adorned with cherubs' heads and other devices, not unlike a pair of obelisks. They stood on plain stylobates on which were interposed two pillared pedestals, 'finely carved and gilt'. These pilasters are non-existent in any picture of later date. They must have been removed soon after the publication of Dart's history, when the pulpitum underwent further modification as a result of the erection of the new organ thereon in 1730.

This remarkable picture gives us a fairly good idea of the interior of the nave of the Abbey as it appeared during the seventeenth and early eighteenth centuries. Probably it differed but little from the state of things which prevailed during the Elizabethan period. It was reserved for the third decade of the eighteenth century to bring about the first important change witnessed since the upheaval of the Reformation.

[1] Dart, *Westmonasterium*, vol. i, p. 61.
[2] *Royal Commission on the Historical Monuments of London, Westminster Abbey*, vol. i, p. 53 *a*. During the last few years the gates have been beautifully gilded, and at the same time the tympanum, which one hundred years ago lost its decoration for some reason which can only be conjectured, has once more been filled with wrought-iron work.

### 4. THE ERECTION OF THE ORGAN ON THE PULPITUM AND OTHER EIGHTEENTH-CENTURY ALTERATIONS

On the eleventh day of October 1727 there took place the Coronation of George II. The historic organ on the north side of the choir associated with the names of Blow, Purcell, and Croft was either too old or too small to render efficient service in such a ceremony, and an instrument was specially built for the occasion by Christopher Schrider, son-in-law of the famous 'Father Smith'. It was subsequently presented to the Abbey by the King, and an order was given in 1728 to Nicholas Hawksmoor, who had succeeded Wren as Surveyor of Westminster Abbey, to furnish an estimate for a new screen for its accommodation.[1] The scheme was duly authorized by the Prime Minister, Sir Robert Walpole, and the work was started at once. A further document sets forth in some detail the work upon the screen carried out by a mason, Edward Stanton by name, during 1728, viz. 'pulling down two old stone pieces, taking up the paving and making models'.[2] Probably the pulpitum was rebuilt at least in part, and among other things the entrance to the choir was arched over, without which it would have been impossible to erect the organ in this new and more central position. The official opening took place on August 1st, 1730, according to an entry in the Precentor's Book, which records the name of the anthem sung on this occasion.

The appearance of this new instrument must have been most imposing, with its three towers and its two flats of gilded pipes. The character of the eastern portion of the case can only be conjectured as regards details; but in general appearance it doubtless resembled the handsome

[1] Westlake, *Westminster Abbey*, vol. i, p. 265.
[2] W.A.M. 34515, fol. 55*b*.

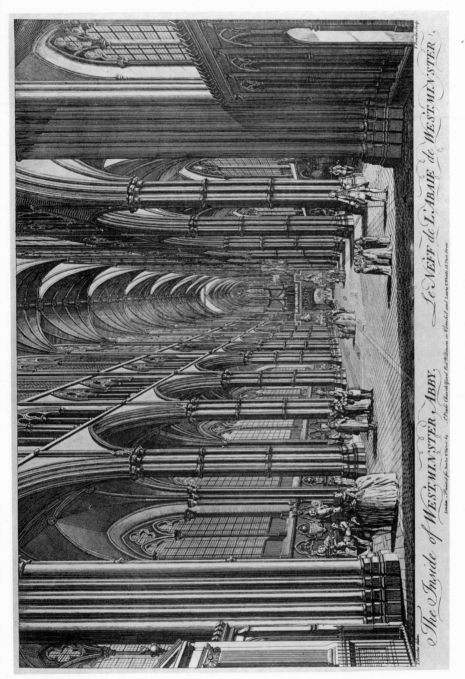

The Inside of WESTMINSTER ABBY.     Le Neff de L'Abaie de WESTMINSTER.

IN THE REIGN OF GEORGE II

Renaissance front which faced westwards down the nave. The change must have done not a little to brighten the bare and almost dreary appearance of the pulpitum as portrayed by Cole's print in Dart's *Westmonasterium*: indeed, the general effect must have been almost equal to that of the screens and superb organ cases which terminate the naves of York and Lincoln and the Antechapel of King's College, Cambridge. Unfortunately Schrider's case was destined to enjoy but a short span of life. Almost exactly one century later it was removed, for no apparent reason, and replaced by a modern organ case of 'imitation gothic' work devoid of merit.[1]

The two lofty obelisk-like structures disappeared. Obviously there was no room for them after the erection of the organ in the centre of the pulpitum. They were removed to a resting-place in the south-west tower immediately above the vault and hidden from view by the wooden flooring. Here they remained, forgotten and unknown, for several generations, until Sir Gilbert Scott in 1862 accidentally discovered them lying prostrate among a quantity of rubbish.[2] They have unfortunately been mutilated since Scott's day, but a portion of one of them may be seen in the nave, where it serves as a collection box. Another portion is preserved in the Norman undercroft.

One of the chief preoccupations of the eighteenth-century Chapter was the addition, ill-considered and almost haphazard, of a host of tablets and other mural monuments, good, bad, and indifferent, especially the latter. Every consideration of art and history fell into the background. The beautiful arcading of the walls was barbarously hacked away in order to secure adequate space for the commemoration of Georgian worthies. With such ideals uppermost in the minds of the official custodians of

[1] Chapter Book, Nov. 11, 1831, and Apr. 11, 1832.
[2] *R.I.B.A. Journal*, vol, xi, p, 116.

the Abbey, it was unlikely that the two great empty spaces on either side of the entrance to the choir, which met the eye every time they entered their church, would long remain untenanted. The temptation was too great to resist.

The southern space was the first to be thus embellished. The immense monument designed by Kent and executed by Rysbrack of the first Earl Stanhope was erected here in 1721. Six years later, the even more unsightly monument by the same artists which records the genius of Sir Isaac Newton took possession of the north side. The Dean and Chapter could scarcely have made a more unfortunate use of these two opportunities. Whatever may be the merits of the work of Kent and Rysbrack, the result is deplorable.

Of course the Chapter, like every one else, were the creatures of their age. They could hardly be expected to rise superior to the prevailing standards of taste, and it is only fair to say that they did not hastily fill up these two prominent spaces: indeed, it has been semi-officially recorded that this position, 'one of the most conspicuous in the Abbey, had been previously refused to the various noblemen who applied for it'.[1]

Rising above the summits of each of these two lofty structures was then erected a dripstone forming a somewhat clumsy canopy.

By this time the familiar gates of wrought iron must have been placed in the position which they still occupy, and a wonderfully beautiful addition they made with their charming scroll-work and acanthus enrichments. They do not receive one particle of the attention they deserve.

Thus, before our second George had sat on the throne of England many years, a complete transformation in the general appearance of the medieval pulpitum, so far as it still existed, had taken place. The original builders would have found a difficulty in recognizing it.

[1] *London Gazette*, Apr. 5, 1727.

29. Sir Isaac Newton.    ENTRANCE into the CHOIR.    30. Earl of Stanhope.

THE ENTRANCE TO THE CHOIR AT THE BEGINNING OF THE NINETEENTH CENTURY

## 5. THE PULPITUM IN THE NINETEENTH CENTURY

Still further changes took place in the pulpitum as a result of Henry Keene's reconstruction of the choir in 1775; but they did not affect the western face, which remained untouched for several generations. Not until the younger Wyatt had been succeeded by Edward Blore in the office of Surveyor in 1827 was any alteration attempted. With his arrival, however, another epoch of radical change was inaugurated.

One of his earliest undertakings was the embellishment on a grand scale of the pulpitum, or, as it now came to be termed, the screen. Blore's designs were accepted in 1828 by the Dean and Chapter,[1] and in the course of the next year or two they became an accomplished fact.

William Clark, one of the Abbey masons, giving evidence before the Select Committee on National Monuments and Works of Art some eleven or twelve years later, stated that he had helped to remove the whole of the screen[2] in favour of Blore's new structure. This must, however, have been an overstatement, for the interior, at any rate, of the screen to-day corresponds almost exactly with its condition at the end of the reign of George III, judging by the evidence afforded by at least one Abbey historian.[3] In all probability, then, it was only the western face which was thus consigned to destruction. A grand opportunity was offered to the votaries of the revived taste for Gothic architecture, and they seized it with both hands.

The screen consists to-day of an arcade formed by four buttresses decorated with diaper work similar to that which appears on the spandrels of the choir, and terminating in crocketted pinnacles. Not quite half-way up, the

---

[1] Chapter Book, Feb. 26, 1828.

[2] *Report of the Select Committee on National Monuments and Works of Art*, p. 72.

[3] J. P. Neale and E. W. Brayley, *History and Antiquities of the Abbey Church of St. Peter, Westminster*, vol. ii, p. 38.

buttresses are broken by brackets on which stand six regal figures, surmounted by rich canopies, grouped in pairs. They represent three of the royal builders of Westminster Abbey and their consorts, viz. Edward the Confessor and Edith, Henry III and Eleanor of Provence, and Edward I and Eleanor of Castile. They are poor pieces of work, and the screen gains nothing from their presence.

Between the buttresses rise three septifoil arches resting upon groups of clustered shafts with foliaged capitals and elaborately decorated spandrels. The structure is crowned by a parapet consisting of a series of quatrefoils.

The two outer arches rise immediately above the monuments of Newton and Stanhope, which are thus provided with canopies, though the incongruity is almost painful. The new work projects from what is presumably the masonry of the ancient pulpitum, in which the two tombs have been embedded to the extent of about three feet.

The architect has reserved the central compartment for more detailed treatment than its companions. A decorated gable rises immediately above the arch, extensively crocketted, and terminating in a large and ungraceful finial. Behind the gable are placed a pair of cusped arches contained in a larger one. The spandrel at the head contains a quantity of sculptured foliage and a large circle enclosing four triangular compartments filled with shamrocks. A flat arch stands behind the decoration and gives immediate access to the passage-way beneath the screen.

The general effect is mechanical and uninspired. To-day a judicious application of colour by a modern artist would mitigate the failings of Blore's insipid performance: but it is perhaps fortunate that the current fashion in his day did not beckon in that direction.

At the same time this elaborate overlay, dull and lifeless though it is and unworthy of its august surroundings, compares favourably with much of the imitation work in which the nineteenth century was so prolific. The interesting fact should be remembered that Blore was largely influenced by a building which had survived the vicissitudes of post-Reformation times and was still in existence not one hundred yards away. It perished in the fire which destroyed the Houses of Parliament a few years later. The destruction of the remains of the old Collegiate Church of St. Stephen, for three centuries the meeting-place of the House of Commons, has not been the least of the artistic tragedies endured by the metropolis.

The Dean and Chapter were not content with the modernizing of their screen. Without any apparent reason they now determined to destroy Schrider's organ case, and their Surveyor's design for a new structure was accepted.[1]  How they justified to themselves this piece of entirely unnecessary expenditure is a problem. Presumably, Schrider's dignified and imposing specimen of early eighteenth-century woodwork failed to commend itself to the ideas of the Gothic revivalists, now in the ascendant. No one seems to have uttered a word on its behalf. The command for its destruction went forth, and a few melancholy fragments in the triforium alone remain to tell the tale.

Blore's new organ case 'in the Gothic style' was no improvement upon its predecessor. Such pictorial evidence as has survived gives the impression that it was a feeble piece of work at the best.[2]

Before another twenty years had gone, this case had perished in its turn, without eliciting any expression of regret, and will be remembered only as a specimen of misguided squandering of money. Fortunately, the next set of changes were, regarded from certain points of view, deserving of high commendation.

The Dean and Chapter early in the reign of Queen Victoria committed themselves to the removal of Keene's

[1] Chapter Book, Mar. 1, 1831.          [2] See vol. i, p. 155.

eighteenth-century choir stalls, together with a number of other sweeping changes. Ultimately, they decided to include the organ in their great scheme of reorganization, which received final approval, after a good many delays, in the early part of 1845.[1]

In the general reconstruction the appearance of the screen underwent radical alteration. The organ was divided into two main portions, placed immediately beneath the arches of the north and south choir aisles. Each section was enclosed in a new case, of the 'imitation gothic' order, though not devoid of merit. The choir organ, as before, overhung the eastern arch.

History thus came to repeat itself. The Abbey witnessed a reversion to the state of things which had prevailed unbroken down to the reign of George II. Once more did the graceful lines of the apse become visible from the west end, as was obviously intended by its royal founders and builders. Every one was delighted, and from that time forward not one syllable of adverse criticism has been heard. Whatever changes the future may hold in store, it is inconceivable that anything will ever be done to destroy this wonderful vista, perhaps the greatest of the Abbey's many glories.

Unfortunately, Blore committed one grievous mistake. The twin organ cases, however effective their general appearance, proved thoroughly unsatisfactory from a musical point of view. The pipes were placed so low that the sound failed to travel adequately. Moreover, it so overwhelmed the organist seated at the console that the voices of the choir were almost inaudible in the organ loft.

Accordingly, at the time of the great rebuilding of the organ in the year 1884, inaugurated by Sir Frederick Bridge, it was wisely decided to elevate the two portions of the instrument, and the happiest results from an acoustical point of view were achieved. The organ remained,

[1] See vol. i, pp. 159 and 160.

THE INTERIOR OF THE ABBEY IN 1928

however, gaunt, bare, and forbidding-looking for a long
time. Funds were not available which would have permitted the rejuvenated instrument to be clad in the
becoming garb which it deserved. The Purcell Commemoration of 1894, however, was a godsend and produced sufficient money to provide the fine case designed
by the late Mr. J. L. Pearson for one of the two sides, while
its companion was erected out of the funds of the Dean
and Chapter a few years later. Pearson's cases are of the
most dignified character and represent a vast improvement
upon Blore's work half a century earlier. They have
added greatly to the beauty of the interior of the Abbey.[1]

None the less many people, probably the majority, will
unite in hoping that the last word has not yet been spoken,
and that the present appearance of this central portion of
Westminster Abbey may not be final.

While voices may still be raised to favour the destruction
of choir screens and their contents, new or old, saner
counsels now tend to prevail. The widening of the historical sense and the deeper reverence for the past, characteristic of the twentieth century, join forces readily with
that quickening of aesthetic judgement which detects the
artistic nemesis awaiting the arbitrary conversion of a
building functionally designed for two separate purposes
into a single unit imperfectly suited to either. It is realized
to-day that the ideals of the original founders and builders
of Westminster Abbey are deserving of a respect which
has not always been accorded to them in the past, and
should anyway command far greater weight than the
views of their descendants. None the less, the call for the
'vista' still persists in certain quarters. Are the opposing
points of view irreconcilable? Actually, the problem at
Westminster is not unlike that which confronted the
authorities at the Cathedral of Exeter during the middle

---

[1] These cases were temporarily removed while the organ was being rebuilt
for the Coronation. They have not yet been replaced. (1939).

of last century, which was there solved with considerable success whilst the work has been perfected more recently.

At Westminster the reduction of the screen to the extent of nearly fifty per cent. in depth would be the first step. The present arrangement by which it covers an entire bay is a wholly modern innovation, and dates only from the unhappy period when Dean Thomas and Henry Keene ran amok in the remodelling of their beautiful choir. A reversion to the original arrangement, which prevailed from the thirteenth century to the reign of George III, would give additional space which could be usefully employed. The positions of the six canonical stalls, three on either side, could then be altered so as to face north and south respectively, leaving the stalls of the Dean and the Sub-Dean 'returned', facing eastwards, in positions analogous to their stalls in Henry VII's Chapel. The monuments of Newton and Stanhope ought no longer to usurp the places of the two medieval altars, but should be transferred to a position hard by. It would then be possible to follow the Exeter precedent by piercing the two blind bays of the screen, now relieved of their tombs, and the revelation would be astonishing.

The ancient principle of a barrier between nave and choir would have been faithfully maintained; but a striking view of the Abbey from the west door to the high altar would be thrown open. On the one hand, worshippers would no longer be condemned, as at present, to sit in the transepts, out of sight of the officiant, and to partake in the services of the Church virtually round the corner, while on the other hand a great increase of seating accommodation would be secured for the ordinary services. It would be possible for the occupants of nave, choir, and lantern to offer their worship simultaneously and with a heightened sense of sharing in the Liturgy. Those in the nave, for instance, would no longer feel segregated during the rendering of the offices, since they would possess a full view of all that was taking place. The gain in the general sense of worship would be incalculable.

No one can claim that the present state of things is ideal. It has formed a target for criticism for many a long year, and small wonder. The change suggested above would of course fail to command universal assent; but it is not one of a novel character, for it was widely discussed in principle a century ago. Neither could it with any fairness be styled revolutionary, for no more than a return to the original conditions is sought. It would be no disrespect to the memories of Newton and Stanhope if their monuments were placed in somewhat different positions, while on the other hand historical landmarks would have been carefully respected and the time-honoured traditions of Anglican worship and ceremonial jealously maintained.

Last of all, it may fairly be asked whether the time is not overdue for the replacement of the Rood above the screen, and the restoration of the two altars of Old St. Mary and the Holy Trinity on lines similar to the recent restoration at Exeter. In days when visitors to the Abbey are numbered not by the hundred but by the thousand, it is no easy matter to preserve a devotional atmosphere in the building. The task is difficult enough even at the east end, which has the advantage of being pervaded by the solemnizing influence of the High Altar. In the nave, devoid as it is of any definitely Christian emblem save for the tiny chapel in the south-west corner, it is impossible. Considerations of space might make it difficult to re-establish the people's altar in its old position; but if the symbol of redemption could be prominently upheld in this part of the Abbey, a great step would have been taken towards the furtherance of increased devotion.

## 6. THE CHAPEL BENEATH THE SOUTH-WEST TOWER

The space beneath the south-west tower was enclosed by stone screens of considerable beauty, the work of the great builder Abbot, John of Islip. This secluded spot for many generations served as the head-quarters of the Consistory Court.

It is not generally realized that the area comprised in the two ancient parishes of St. Margaret and St. John Westminster formed, until comparatively recent times, a Peculiar, outside the Diocese of London, and subject to the direct jurisdiction of the Dean.

It was a picturesque and interesting survival of former days, and though it may not have made for efficiency, much less for uniformity, it is impossible not to regret its disappearance in the early years of the reign of Queen Victoria. The legislators of that uninspired epoch were largely devoid of historical sense or feeling. In their eyes picturesque anomalies, together with the charm and fragrance which they brought with them from distant times, were deserving of scant consideration, and the Westminster Peculiar was therefore reduced to the Abbey and its precincts.

The organization of this miniature diocese had included a certain amount of legal and semi-legal work. There were always wills to be proved and marriage licences to be issued, and a small court, in which the Archdeacon of Westminster, who was the responsible officer, could transact business, was an obvious necessity. This distant corner of the nave provided exactly what was wanted.

Traces of this phase in the history of the Abbey still exist. The south wall of this enclosure has been lined with a quantity of charming panelling, dating from the early years of the seventeenth century. It is divided into three

bays decorated with a quantity of strap-work and fleur-
de-lis ornamentation, and surmounted by a frieze with a
dentilled cornice of the most tasteful and attractive
character.

The northern screen, which seems to have been much
finer than that which remains on the eastern side, became
the victim of a vandalistic attack in a blind and unappre-
ciative age. The position seemed ideal to our Georgian
predecessors for the commemoration of Captain Cornwall,
who died a death of splendid heroism at the Battle of
Toulon in 1743. It was the first time that a deed of naval
prowess received the signal honour of a monument erected
by the authority of Parliament. Down therefore came the
magnificent old Gothic structure of Abbot Islip and in its
place there uprose a colossal and revoltingly ugly monument, almost the worst of the many disfigurements of the
nave. 'In its place is heaped up a prodigious mass of stones,
worked into forms at once sharing the sculptural taste of
the present day, and the architectural system of improving
upon the ancient architecture of the kingdom.'[1]

Not many years before the perpetration of the Cornwall
enormity another monument, scarcely less incongruous,
had completely walled up the eastern screen. With the aid
of an inscription from the pen of Alexander Pope it commemorated the brief and not wholly admirable career of
James Craggs, Secretary of State in the reign of George I.

Not long after the erection of the Cornwall monument
a vault was constructed beneath the floor in which rest the
bodies of Dean Wilcocks and other members of his family,
including his delightful son Joseph, 'the blessed heretic',
as he was felicitously termed by Pope Clement XIII, his
personal friend. During his long rule over the Church of
Westminster the two western towers had been at last completed, a result largely due to this excellent Dean's energy.
He took enormous interest in their upbuilding, and it was

[1] *Gentleman's Magazine*, 1799, p. 665.

in the highest degree fitting that he should lie here, be-neath what may not unfairly be styled his own work.[1]

At a later date the Consistory Court, to which the Early Morning Service was transferred from Henry VII's Chapel, received a most inconvenient addition in the ancient but sadly dilapidated font. Expelled from its traditional position in the western aisle of the north tran-sept by the erection of the vast mountain of masonry, designed by Nollekens and known as 'The Monument of the Three Captains', it had been flung contemptuously into the space beneath the north-west tower. It now sought a refuge, as it were, in a corresponding position beneath the south-west tower.

With the nineteenth century, additional monuments began to crowd up the space. The Baptistery, for such was the name by which the Consistory Court now came to be known, was invaded, first of all by an ungainly seated figure of William Wordsworth by S. G. Kimber. The selection of this position was due to 'the sentiment of a kinsman',[2] though it seems strange that the monument did not find a place in Poets' Corner near that of another member of the 'Lake School', Robert Southey.

As time went on, John Keble and Matthew Arnold came to be commemorated in the same place, while a stained glass window, presented by a citizen of the United States, recalls the memory of two writers of sacred poetry, both of whom passed their boyhood at Westminster School, George Herbert and William Cowper. Dean

---

[1] One hundred years ago there was placed on the east wall of this chapel an 'Order of Chapter' dated Feb. 27, 1755, authorizing the Dean to have 'a Vault made by the College Workmen in such part of the Church as his Lordship shall think fit, to contain the bodies of five or six persons, and to be for the use of him and his family, and that a Grant thereof do pass under the Common Seal in the like manner as was granted to Dean Neale and to Dean Atterbury'. For some unknown reason this inscription has disappeared.

[2] The Rev. Christopher Wordsworth, a nephew of the poet, was at the time Canon of Westminster (1844 to 1869) (Stanley, *Historical Memorials of West-minster Abbey*, p. 282).

Stanley's dream of making this angle of the nave 'the nucleus of a new Poets' Corner of future years'[1] seemed to be on the eve of fulfilment, in fact he actually bestowed upon it, in characteristic fashion, the picturesque title 'Little Poets' Corner'.

Meanwhile, an important change had already been carried out in 1850. The immense memorial of James Craggs was removed from its original position beneath the eastern arch to the back of the still larger Cornwall monument. In some respects this change was a great improvement, for it revealed the interesting perpendicular screen beneath the eastern arch, which was now repaired and refixed. The latter consists of two bays each containing cinquefoiled lights in a four-centred head with moulded and buttressed mullions and an embattled cornice. At some date unknown, the upper parts were cut through in order to form lights, the structure having originally been of a solid character.

Traces remain, too, on the inner side of the traceries of some extremely interesting wall-paintings attributed to the early seventeenth century. They have been brought to light, thanks to the efforts of Professor Tristram, within recent years. The actual reason for the addition of this decoration to the stonework is not very clear.

This was not the only change for the better. The immense Cornwall monument, originally the loftiest in the whole Abbey, obstructed so much of the light proceeding from the window in the south wall of the chapel as to create an impression of deep gloom at the west end of the nave, and matters were made still worse by the insertion of the dark coloured glass of the Herbert and Cowper Memorial Window.

It was accordingly decided to mete out somewhat drastic treatment to the monument. About ten feet were lopped off the summit of the great obelisk, one foot from

[1] Ibid., p. 302.

each side, and one foot and a half from the sides of the pedestal, thus securing a direct entrance from the nave into the enclosure.

The second or baptistery period in the history of this little enclosure came to an end during the decanate of Dean Stanley. It was a welcome change, for it must have been difficult to administer the Sacrament of Holy Baptism with adequate dignity in these extremely restricted surroundings. Only a mere handful of persons could possibly have taken part. At the same time a new pavement was laid down, consisting of Hopton Wood stone, care being taken to preserve the slab in the centre of the chapel which marks the last resting-place of the Wilcocks family.

For some time after the removal of the font this corner fulfilled no particular purpose in the general life of the Abbey, save for the utilizing of its walls as a receptacle for additional memorials, about the majority of which the less said the better.

After the Great War it was felt desirable to place in the church some permanent commemoration of those members of the Abbey staff who had given their lives for God, King, and Country, and the idea gradually took shape of converting this corner into a chapel hard by the grave of the Unknown Warrior and the Padre's Flag, in which such memorials could be erected. It was obvious, too, that a chapel in this spot, set apart for worship, would add a much-needed element of devotion and repose to a part of the Abbey hitherto given over almost entirely to hosts of visitors and sightseers.

Accordingly, this interesting little place entered upon the fourth phase in its story on Armistice Day 1925, when it was solemnly set apart by the Rev. W. H. Carnegie, Sub-Dean of Westminster, to serve as a chapel, in which those who had given their lives during the Great War should be held in constant remembrance. The Holy

THE ALTAR IN THE CHAPEL OF THE HOLY CROSS

Communion was celebrated on that morning in the new chapel, and the latter was at the same time dedicated to the Holy Cross, thus recalling the nave altar of pre-Reformation times.

The chapel was only partially equipped at first. It was the work of several years to raise the funds essential for supplying it with adequate furniture. The wherewithal was provided by (1) offerings from the members all over the world of the Mothers' Union, many of them in pennies; (2) a large sum of money collected by the splendid energy of Mrs. Julian Bennett, Mayoress of the City of Westminster from 1929 to 1931; and (3) an offering by a generous donor who insisted on remaining anonymous and who, sad to relate, died three months before the completion of the chapel. These gifts enabled a considerable scheme of reconstruction to be carried out which cleared the ground for further ornaments and furnishings.

The Cornwall monument was taken down and re-erected in the cloister. The nave gained enormously by its disappearance, but a heavy price had to be paid. It involved the ruin of the unspoilt entrance to the great cloister, which had escaped the addition of any tablet or monument all through the centuries. The monument of William Wordsworth was transferred to a far more appropriate position in Poets' Corner; while the elevation of that of Craggs to the sill of the window formed an equally great improvement.

Mr. J. N. Comper, to whom the work was entrusted, elected to abandon the precedent set by the stone screens of Abbot Islip, and the chapel is now entered through an elaborate screen of wrought iron weighing nearly five tons, richly decorated with bronze arabesques mercurially gilt. In the centre is enshrined the bronze trophy consisting of the shield and sword presented by the historic City of Verdun to the Lord Mayor of London. At the back of the trophy is a figure of St. Michael slaying the

E

seven-headed dragon. Above, on the cornice of the topmost tier of balusters are a plain cross and several candelabra supported by dolphins. The latter were selected to represent the Greek word ἰχθύς or fish, the letters of which spell the equivalent of Jesus Christ, Son of God, the Saviour.

Beneath the rose silk tester of the altar is a band of tabernacle work of English alabaster, decorated in burnished gold and colour, forming a canopy for the remarkably beautiful figures of the Rood, the Blessed Virgin, and St. John. In the construction of the altar itself the artist has departed from general medieval practice by providing a frontal of bronze gilt, containing a central pietà in low relief within a wreath of laurel which branches into acanthus and surrounds four cherubs holding certain instruments of the Passion, viz. the Cross, the Pillar, the Lance and Sponge, and the Crown of Thorns. This central subject is flanked by figures of two British mothers, both commonly represented with the Cross, namely St. Helena, mother of the Emperor Constantine, holding the True Cross which she 'invented' or discovered and St. Margaret, niece of St. Edward the Confessor, holding the 'Black Rood' of Scotland.

A fine Oriental carpet covers the floor immediately in front of the altar, while on the western wall has been erected a tablet commemorating the Empire's million dead, presented by the Imperial War Graves Commission. It is an exact replica of the tablets placed by the Commission in numerous French and Belgian churches. The inscription on the panel was composed by Rudyard Kipling. Over all hang a number of Colours representing the British Empire. The gift of the Imperial War Graves Commission, they were dedicated on November 10th, 1928.

The modelling of the various figures is the work of Mr. Bertram Pegram, the work being carried out by Mr. F. W. Knight. The frontal and hanging shown in the illustration were also designed by Mr. Comper.

Almost adjoining the Chapel of St. Cross is a wooden balcony projecting from the south wall of the nave. It was built by Abbot Islip in front of his private chapel. Documentary evidence being non-existent, the precise purpose of this gallery or balcony is not very clear, but it is at least conceivable that the Abbot had in mind the great Palm Sunday Procession, when a portion of the choir, stationed in an elevated position at the west end of the church, would sing the *Gloria, Laus et Honor tibi sit.* 'Certain children standing upon a high place right against the people, sing with a loud voice a certain hymn in praise of our Saviour Jesus Christ, which begins *Gloria Laus.* At the end of every verse the children cast down certain cakes or breads with flowers.'[1]

The front of the gallery consists of twelve closed panels, cinque-foiled ogee and traceried heads, and moulded mullions. Above was a range of open lights, which have unfortunately disappeared, though the mortices for the mullions still remain. Above is a panelled ceiling.

The Abbot's Pew is a charming specimen of early sixteenth-century woodwork; but it is obvious that the loss of the mullions and the consequent disappearance of the window-like effect have deprived it of no small amount of beauty.

[1] Becon, *Early Works*, p. 114.

# PART V

## THE CHAPEL OF SAINT EDWARD THE CONFESSOR

SO soon as we set foot in this wonderful place, we feel that we are treading upon holy ground. The glowing words of Flete, the monastic historian of Westminster Abbey, were fully justified even in the fifteenth century, and during subsequent generations they have become ever fuller of meaning. This far-famed chapel is surely the most sacred spot in the whole British Empire.

'Ex primitiva foundatione locus iste est regiae consecrationis, regum sepultura, repositoriumque regalium insignium; caput Angliae merito diademaque regni ab antiquo nominatur.'[1]

Such are Flete's words, but they are not the conclusion of the matter. What about the royal Saint himself? The last sovereign of the old Saxon house of Cerdic occupied a unique position in the heart of the English people. For many generations no saint in the Kalendar was more popular than St. Edward the Confessor. The arms assigned to him by the medieval heralds, viz. the cross and martlets upon a blue ground, were long regarded with peculiar veneration as a national emblem.[2] Not until two or more centuries had come and gone were they finally replaced by the red cross of St. George upon the white ground.

With the burial of this strange man in the church on which he had lavished his affection and his wealth, in whom the Anglo-Saxon and the Norman strands of race were woven together, the British Empire was born.

---

[1] John Flete, *History of Westminster Abbey*, edited by J. Armitage Robinson, p. 63.
[2] E. E. Dorling, *The Heraldry of the Church*, p. 132.

## 1. THE FIRST AND SECOND BURIAL-PLACES OF SAINT EDWARD THE CONFESSOR

The King drew his last breath on the fifth day of January in the fateful year 1066. According to Ordericus Vitalis, our principal authority, an interval counted by hours only elapsed between his death and his burial. He was laid to rest in the spot marked out by every consideration of sentiment and affection, in front of the High Altar of the Abbey Church.

From the very beginning a peculiar sanctity has surrounded the good King's resting-place. At the first opportunity after his great victory, William the Conqueror repaired to the grave to which, after duly performing his devotions, he presented two rich palls. Before the year was out, on Christmas Day, there took place the Coronation of the new sovereign, an event of the first importance, the influence of which has made itself felt continuously throughout our history. The precedent then set has been rigidly followed. One sovereign after another, two only excepted, has been conducted to this sacred place to receive the solemn unction and be invested with the crown of the realm at the hands of the Primate of All England.

The grave of King Edward, according to Sulcardus, the earliest of the Abbey historians, was of quite a simple description; but a change took place before the new reign had reached its close. It has been enshrined by Anglo-Saxon affection in a picturesque and touching legend.

St. Wulfstan, a stout old Saxon prelate, faced with the high-handed demand of Lanfranc that he should forthwith resign the See of Worcester, to which post he had been appointed by the Confessor, declined to surrender the symbol of his office into any other hands. 'They accuse thee of error in having made me a Bishop', he exclaimed, 'and me of presumption for having assented. I therefore resign my pastoral staff—not to those who demand back what they did not give—but to thee who didst give it me, I resign the charge of those whom thou didst entrust to my care.' Laying the crozier on the grave he proceeded, 'Receive my lord the King and give it to whomsoever thou mayest choose'. The crozier remained standing erect upon the tomb as if it formed part of the marble and turned neither to the right hand nor the left. Wulfstan alone possessed the power of removing it, for when at the request of the King and the Archbishop he laid hold of the crozier once more, it yielded to his hand, as if it had been stuck in clay!

The Conqueror, deeply impressed, determined forthwith to seek the aid of the craftsman in precious metals. The dignity of his predecessor's tomb must be augmented without delay, and the humble resting-place gradually developed into a sepulchre richly decorated with gold and silver.

As the years went on, the halo of sanctity surrounding the name of King Edward increased more and more. One thing, however, was still lacking, and it was a matter of first-rate importance. The canonization of the beloved King had long been ardently desired alike by Church and nation, but for some unexplained reason the request was at first met by Pope Innocent II with a blunt refusal.

In 1159, however, a new Abbot, Laurentius by name, was placed in command of the monastery, a man of strong personality. Determined to secure this inestimable privilege for his convent, he took the opportunity, when preaching in the Abbey before the King and the nobility, to make an earnest appeal to all present no longer to permit such a 'precious treasure' to remain concealed in its obscure resting-place. King, nobles, and monks were fired with enthusiasm. One and all they begged the Abbot no longer to hide 'so glorious a light from the world'.

SCENES FROM THE CAMBRIDGE LIFE OF ST. EDWARD THE CONFESSOR

(1) The opening of St. Edward's Grave

(2) The First Translation of St. Edward

Events developed in a highly propitious manner. Circumstances had changed. The money, of which no small amount was required, was now readily forthcoming. In the chair of St. Peter there sat Alexander III, a personal friend of the new Abbot. The influence of the throne was exerted to the full, and at length the long-delayed canonization became an accomplished fact. The name of King Edward was enrolled in the Kalendar of the Saints, and a bull was issued to the Abbot of Westminster directing that 'the body of the glorious King should be honoured here on earth as he himself was glorified in heaven'. The removal of the body of the new saint to a sumptuous and costly shrine followed almost as a matter of course.

The thirteenth day of October in the year 1163 witnessed the first of the Translations of St. Edward the Confessor. The sacred character of the occasion was emphasized by the fact that it took place at midnight. The body which, according to the historian, had undergone no sort of corruption, despite the passage of wellnigh a century, was enclosed in a chest of wainscot oak and transferred to its new and more splendid resting-place, which included, so it is supposed, a rich feretory. The ring said to have been bestowed upon Edward by St. John the Evangelist was removed from the royal finger and set apart as a relic. The vestments in which the King had been arrayed were found to be as fresh and undecayed as the body itself, and the Abbot had no hesitation in giving the vandalistic order for their conversion into three copes.

This great ceremony was performed in the presence of the King and Becket, now become Archbishop. The latter took the opportunity of presenting to the Shrine a great image of the Blessed Virgin, 'beautifully framed, made of ivory and much esteemed by him'.[1]

---

[1] John Flete, *History of Westminster Abbey*, edited by J. Armitage Robinson, p. 94.

From that time forward, the thirteenth day of the month of October has taken its place among the great feasts of the Westminster Kalendar.

Nothing more is heard of the Shrine of St. Edward during the reign of Henry II and those of his two unsatisfactory sons. It remained for our artist King, Henry III, with boundless generosity, to exalt the fame of his Saxon predecessor to an unprecedented height. The personalities of the two monarchs, so strangely alike in character and in some ways so extremely unattractive, are henceforth inseparably united and linked with the story of the great Abbey over the upgrowth of which they both watched with an undying love.

## 2. THE BUILDING OF SAINT EDWARD'S SHRINE

The boy king Henry III had barely reached manhood's years when he began to give substantial evidence of his affection for the proud church standing at the very doors of his palace.

Upwards of a century and a half had come and gone since Edward the Confessor had passed away. The dying King had realized, even more clearly than those standing about his bedside, the grievous trials and sorrows in which his Saxon subjects were soon to find themselves immersed. Several generations were destined to come and go before the recollection of that terrible time faded from the minds of men.

It is conceivable, then, that Henry III cherished the hope of developing among his island population a higher sense of national unity. He gloried in his descent from King Alfred. His veneration for the Confessor, after whom he named his first born, knew no bounds. Young as he was, with, in all probability, a lengthy reign lying ahead of him, it would have been natural for him to set before himself the attainment of this great ideal. The expression in some concrete form of a common devotion to the memory of the last king of the old dynasty could scarcely fail to draw closer the Saxon and the Norman peoples, as yet but imperfectly blended together. Edward the Confessor, Saxon by birth, but Norman by upbringing, was a figure which made appeal to both of the races over which the young King had been called to rule.

Be this as it may, Henry III at an early age came to be inspired by a truly magnificent conception. The Confessor should once more be translated, and this time to a building which should attain in every detail, so far as money and technical skill could ensure, the zenith of artistic excellence. The actual resting-place of the pious founder of Westminster Abbey must surpass in glory anything which the genius of mortal man had as yet achieved. It must be so overwhelmingly splendid that the eye of the most casual of visitors should be drawn away even from the beauty of the soaring arches and pillars of the church itself and be compelled to focus itself upon the sacred shrine with its blazing wealth of decoration at the east end.

The year 1230 stands out prominently in the story. It deserves to be marked with a white stone, for it was then that Henry III first gave outward evidence of his tremendous scheme by erecting a lady chapel at the east end of the church, a building of the early pointed type characteristic of the thirteenth century.

Six years later came the King's marriage, and Henry determined to signalize the event in a special manner. He directed that an image should be placed upon the twelfth-century Shrine of St. Edward fashioned after the likeness of a certain queen.

With the year 1241 we reach another important landmark. According to Matthew Paris, Henry now proceeded to entrust a body of highly skilled craftsmen with the responsible task of constructing, in a manner regardless of expense, a new and splendid shrine for the reception of the Confessor's remains.

'The King employed chosen goldsmiths of London to construct the shrine of purest gold and precious materials, and the workmanship surpassed the materials.'[1]

The historian's statement is confirmed by the following entry in the Liberate Roll of 26 Hen. III. It is quoted by W. Burges in his valuable monograph on the Confessor's Shrine.

'Deliver of our treasure, to our beloved clerk, Edward the son of Otho, £258. 9s. 1½d. for the acquittance of the works (operations) done by our order at Westminster from the day of the Holy Trinity in the 25th year of our reign to the Feast of SS. Simon and Jude next following. Deliver also the same, 10 marks for a certain wooden shrine for the work (opus) of St. Edward made by our order: and to the same £6. 10s. 0d. for marble bought for the same shrine by our order.'[2]

This extract is of great importance. It alludes in the clearest and most definite manner to two distinct things: first, the wooden foundation of a new feretory, to which plates of precious metal were ultimately to be attached, and secondly, the marble which was to be employed in the new basement or substructure on which the feretory with its precious contents would rest. So far as the substructure was concerned, this interesting scheme failed ultimately to materialize, but in the meantime steps were taken to push forward the work with the utmost dispatch. In the following year, 1242, orders were given that Edward, 'the King's beloved clerk', should be supplied with all the money necessary for the building of the Shrine, for the liveries of the goldsmiths at work thereon and for the marble.[3] In 1244 an image of the Blessed Virgin together

[1] Matthew Paris, *Hist. Angliae*, p. 287.
[2] Scott, *Gleanings from Westminster Abbey*, p. 132.
[3] Lethaby, *Westminster Abbey and the King's Craftsmen*, p. 73.

with an emerald and ruby were given by the Queen, while in the following year a royal command was issued to Edward to repair to Woodstock, in order that Henry might inspect a newly made figure of the Confessor.

Edward was the King's architect and man of business. His association with the new Shrine of the Confessor must have covered a great number of years, for in 1260 his name still appears in this connexion, though associated with those of the Prior and Sacrist of the monastery.

The eventful year 1245 at length arrived. The King had fairly embarked upon his gigantic undertaking, the rebuilding of the choir. It was obvious that this vast project would involve the complete rearrangement of the conditions under which the services of the Abbey Church had been rendered for nearly two hundred years. Very wisely, therefore, it was decided to allow the old Shrine to remain undisturbed till the last possible moment. Thus, the normal round of worship continued unbroken for a full seven years longer. Not until 1252, according to the Close Rolls of that year, were the orders issued (to Edward of Westminster, once more) to construct a temporary chapel, forty by twenty-five feet, 'in the new part of the workshop of the shrine', where the body of the Saint could be 'most commodiously placed',[1] for the time being.

Meanwhile, the stream of royal bounty displayed not the slightest sign of drying up, indeed Henry's zeal and devotion seemed actually to increase with the passage of time. Almost every year witnessed some notable addition to the treasures of the Shrine, culminating in 1253 with the drawing up of the royal will, in which there was bequeathed the immense sum of five hundred marks of silver to be expended, in the event of the King's demise, upon its completion.

By this time the walls of the new choir were steadily

[1] Scott, *Gleanings from Westminster Abbey*, p. 133.

rising from the ground. The King had intended from the
first that the last resting-place of the sainted Edward
should form the climax of a building, itself the very flower
of thirteenth-century architecture. To quote Wyke's
*Chronicle*: 'The King, grieved that the relics of Saint
Edward were poorly enshrined and lowly, resolved that so
great a luminary should not lie buried, but be placed high
as on a candle-stick, to enlighten the Church.'[1] Accordingly, the task was assigned to the royal workmen of
erecting here at the east end of the building a huge
mound of earth, quaintly designated by Dean Stanley,
'the last funeral tumulus in England'.[2] Tradition has not
hesitated to embellish history. For many generations it
was accepted as undoubted fact that several shiploads of
earth had been transported by the King's command from
the Holy Land, in order that the remains of Saint Edward
might, for the future, repose in a sanctity great beyond
words. The tradition is delightfully picturesque, and it is
impossible not to regret that a careful examination made
some years ago of the sacred mound revealed no trace of
any confirmatory evidence. A rough conglomerate of
ordinary building materials occupies the place formerly
supposed to consist of earth extracted from the sacred soil
of Palestine!

In the year 1258 there passed away Richard de Crokes-
ley, who had occupied the stall of Abbot for some twelve
years. The brethren elected in his stead one of their
number, by name Philip de Lewesham, who ruled over
the place hardly as many months. Even under the most
favourable circumstances it would scarcely have been
possible for Lewesham to confer much additional lustre
upon his position. His bodily proportions were framed
upon a scale so enormous as to render the customary visit
of courtesy to Rome on the part of every newly elected

[1] Wyke's *Chronicle*, vol. ii, p. 88.
[2] Stanley, *Historical Memorials of Westminster Abbey*, p. 112.

Abbot a sheer impossibility. This omission cost the convent dear. A heavy fine was imposed. No less than eight hundred marks changed hands and helped to swell the Papal coffers!

The new Abbot's unexpected death was a happy thing for all parties concerned, for the election of a successor brought to the front a man of outstanding personality. The choice of the convent fell upon Richard de Ware, one of the most remarkable figures in the medieval history of the Church of Westminster. He must have been the very antithesis of his corpulent predecessor.

Ware promptly set out for Rome, but he was sadly hampered by financial anxieties. He found himself compelled to borrow the sum of one thousand marks at exorbitant rates of interest in order to maintain himself. These difficulties were probably responsible for the prolongation of his stay in Italy for two years. The Abbot was, however, the last man to pass his days in idleness. He took good care that the great church, of which he was the official head, should in no way be a loser, and to this curious combination of circumstances we owe some of the most glorious treasures possessed by Westminster Abbey to-day.

The moment of Ware's election to the Abbot's stall was opportune to a degree. He entered upon his duties at a time when a general feeling of progress was in the air. The half-completed choir was already displaying promise of splendour unparalleled. It would have been strange if the new Abbot, thoroughly good man as he was, should have failed to catch the spirit of enthusiasm pervading the place. He soon found himself inspired with an eager desire to co-operate with the King, his master, in his wondrous undertaking.

During his stay in Italy, Ware became familiar with some magnificent specimens of the art of the craftsmen in marble and mosaic. Fired with ardent longing to promote the well-being of the House of the Lord far away on the banks of the Thames, his enrichment of that church with certain productions of Italian genius is fully intelligible.

And so, when he at length set forth upon his long homeward journey, half across Europe, he was accompanied, or perhaps followed, by 'certain workmen and rich porphyry stones whereof he made that singular, rare and curious Pavement before the high altar, and with these stones and workmen he did also frame the Shrine of Edward the Confessor'.[1] Among this group of highly skilled craftsmen appear the names of Odoricus, of whom we have already heard,[2] and Peter, the Roman citizen. Both men have left an abiding mark upon Westminster Abbey.

Posterity owes an incalculable debt to the splendid bounty of our third Henry. At the same time we should err greatly if we did not also recognize the single-hearted manner in which the King was supported by Richard de Ware, assuredly one of the most distinguished of the long line of Abbots and Deans who have presided over the fortunes of this great church. Had it not been for the zeal of this good man, the Abbey would lack to-day some of its greatest treasures.

The return of the Abbot, surrounded by his Italian friends, evidently brought about a general reconsideration of the designs originally drawn up for the Shrine of the Confessor. The native materials and workmanship, projected years before for the massive substructure, now lost their pride of place. It was impossible to deny the great importance of the unfamiliar ideas and methods introduced by the freshly arrived travellers. The gorgeous materials, too, brought by the Abbot and the members of

[1] John Flete, *History of Westminster Abbey*, edited by J. Armitage Robinson, p. 113. Weever, *Funeral Monuments*, p. 485.
[2] Vol. i, pp. 18–29.

his train added further support to these novel suggestions and must have filled the minds of the insular Englishmen with sheer amazement. A fresh impetus was given (though, indeed, such was hardly needed) to the great works then on foot, coupled with a change of direction as a result of Ware's long absence. Under such auspices, then, did the King and his friends embark upon the third decade in the story of the construction of St. Edward's Shrine.

The years went on and the glorious work continued steadily to increase in magnificence. The Patent Roll for 1257 contains a list of gold figures specially provided for its adornment. It is perfectly astonishing.[1]

'St. Edmund. Crown set with two large sapphires, a ruby and other precious stones, worth £86.

'King. Ruby on his breast, and other stones, £48.

'King. Holding in his right hand a flower, with sapphires and emeralds in the middle of the crown and the great garnet on the breast, and otherwise set with pearls and small stones, £56. 4s. 4d.

'King, with a garnet in his breast, and other stones, £25.

'King, with sapphires in his breast, and other stones, £59. 6s. 8d.

'Five golden angels, £30.

'Blessed Virgin and Child, set with rubies, emeralds and garnets, £200.

'King, holding shrine in hand set with precious stones, £103.

'King, holding in one hand a cameo with 2 heads, and in the other a sceptre set with rubies, prasinis and pearls, £100.

'St. Peter, holding in one hand a church, in the other the key, trampling on Nero, with a large sapphire in his breast, £100.

'A Majesty with an emerald in the breast, £200.

'There is also mentioned a great cameo in a golden case, with a golden chain, valued at £200, and another cameo, £28.'

The fact that one of these remarkable figures was intended to represent St. Edmund, King of East Anglia, gives some colour to the suggestion that its companions

---

[1] Scott, *Gleanings from Westminster Abbey*, p. 141.

were images of other English monarchs. The figure holding in its hands a model of the church could scarcely have
been other than that of Henry III himself, while the fact
that St. Peter was the official patron of Westminster Abbey
furnishes an obvious reason for his inclusion in the list.

Everything appeared to be moving in the happiest
manner when a sudden and terrible blow fell. It was the
year 1267. The heart of every single person in the convent must have been filled with consternation, while the
King must have been wholly beside himself with grief
and anxiety.

It could scarcely be claimed for Henry that the gifts of
government and administration occupied any prominent
position in his character. Troublous events, such as the
Barons' War, to give one instance only, were bound sooner
or later to react to a serious extent upon the royal finances.
Thus, a crisis of real magnitude, calculated grievously to
affect the fortunes of the Abbey, developed. The King
found himself in a desperate financial situation. He
scarcely knew where to turn for money, but at the same
time it was imperative that his manifold needs and neces-
sities should be met. There was no alternative. Finding
himself at a deadlock, he placed the jewelled treasures of
the unfinished shrine in pawn! They were valued at the
enormous figure of £2,555. 4s. 8d.[1]

Needless to say, Henry bound himself in a manner,
awful and solemn, to restore every item. Failure to carry
out this sacred engagement would involve the Royal
Chapel itself in the terrors of an interdict. A heavier
penalty for non-fulfilment of his obligations could hardly
have been devised. None the less, it must have been a sad
time for those many people to whom Westminster Abbey
had already become dear. They must have feared that the
completion of the golden shrine might even be postponed
to the Greek Kalends itself.

[1] Scott, *Gleanings from Westminster Abbey*, pp. 134, 135.

Happily, this dreary state of things proved to be of comparatively short duration. Fortune came once more to turn a smiling face upon the King. His financial difficulties, acute though they were at the moment, were somehow or other straightened out. He emerged from the dark cloud, and with the year 1269 he entered upon a new and brighter epoch. In all probability his closing years were by far the happiest of the old man's long and troublesome reign.

It is difficult, however, for us twentieth-century folk, when we celebrate St. Edward's Day, to conjure up before our mind's eye even a faint picture of the joy which must have filled the heart of the old King to overflowing on that autumn day in 1269. For eight and twenty long years had the Shrine been taking shape by slow degrees, and now it stood there in all its glory, something absolutely unique in the eyes of English people. All was now in readiness for the great event, so long and so ardently anticipated.

Troubles unspeakable had rolled over the King's head, many of them of his own making. Still, life and health had been preserved, and now a great privilege had fallen to his lot, a privilege accorded by divine providence to very few men indeed, the beholding with his own eyes of the tangible fruits of his labours. The sumptuous golden resting-place of the sainted Confessor which formed the outward and visible sign of Henry's devotion was now at last complete.

On the anniversary, then, of the first Translation of St. Edward's uncorrupted body, Henry summoned the nobility and burgesses to Westminster while every member of his family gathered round to share in his joy. The chest containing the sacred remains having been removed from its temporary resting-place, the King and his brother Richard, King of the Romans, carried it upon their shoulders; while his two tall sons, Edward and Edmund, the Earl of Warrenne and Lord Philip Basset, with as many nobles as could come near to touch it, supported

it with their hands while it was borne to its new home.[1]
On that great day the Sacred Mysteries were celebrated
for the first time, with great ceremony and exaltation of
heart, in the third church which rose upon the Isle of
Thorns.

But Henry was not yet satisfied. He appeared to be
drawn to this sacred spot as though by some invisible
magnet. He literally could not tear himself away. He
seemed totally unable to relinquish his labour of love and
admit that his glorious work was at long last complete. A
few years more of life still remained to him, and he continued to turn them to good account, now adding some
beautiful detail, now making some fresh offering to the
great mass of gold, silver, and precious stones which had
become to him the very apple of his eye. Nor again did he
confine himself to the actual structure of the Shrine. The
whole chapel came to bear witness in its gorgeous beauty
to the inexhaustible bounty of our artist king.

Over and above the long record of offerings already
described, Henry made a notable gift of four silver basins
for holding lamps. Two were suspended over the Shrine;
a third hung on the south side over the unmarked grave of
Matilda, Queen Consort of Henry I, and the fourth in a
corresponding position over that of the Confessor's own
spouse, Queen Edith.[2] The tradition which assigns the
burial-place of the latter of these two Queens Consort to
the Church of Westminster is very strong and obviously
harmonizes to the full with the general fitness of things. It is
only right, however, to state that this claim is not undis-
puted. The famous Abbey Church of Chaise-Dieu in
Languedoc proclaims its possession of her remains with
equal emphasis.

Another precious work of art which must have been

[1] Wyke's *Chronicle*, vol. ii, p. 88.
[2] *Consuetudines Monasterii Sancti Petri Westmonasterii*, edited by E. M.
Thompson (Henry Bradshaw Society), vol. ii, p. 45.

bestowed at the close of Henry III's career was the golden cup immortalized by Dante. It contained the heart of Henry, nephew of the King and son of Richard, King of the Romans and Earl of Cornwall, who was foully murdered in the Cathedral of Viterbo by the sons of Simon de Montfort. The mention of his heart forms the sole allusion to Westminster Abbey contained in the Divine Comedy.[1]

The story of the building of St. Edward's Shrine only came to an end when, after all those many years, the old King lay, quiet and still, upon his death-bed.

It has been calculated that Henry must have expended the vast amount of £80,000, calculated in terms of modern currency, upon the Shrine, let alone the huge cost of the magnificent choir which forms such an ideal casket. From first to last he had insisted upon the provision of the richest materials, and their intrinsic value was fully matched by the exquisite workmanship employed upon them. It occasions, therefore, but little surprise to learn that auditors were appointed by letters patent, almost as soon as the reign of Henry's son and successor had commenced, whose duty it was carefully to inquire into 'the great sums of money' expended since 1256 upon various objects in the Abbey, included among which was the Shrine of St. Edward the Confessor itself, as set forth in the accounts of the King's Craftsman, William of Gloucester, the goldsmith![2]

## 3. THE SHRINE OF SAINT EDWARD AND ITS TREASURES

The Shrine of St. Edward is to-day a pitiful wreck, the merest shadow of its pre-Reformation splendour. It is but cold comfort, too, to learn that it stands almost unique among the shrines of England, in that it has weathered the

[1] Dante, *Inferno*, xii. 115–20.
[2] Scott, *Gleanings from Westminster Abbey*, p. 113.

storms of the sixteenth century, albeit in a battered condition, while the great majority of its companions have disappeared from the face of the earth. What an awful orgy
of destruction is here indicated!

Still, St. Edward's Shrine will ever remain an object of
widespread renown. So large a portion has survived to
our own day intact, that to visualize the glorious structure,
as it must have appeared before the eyes of the people of
medieval England, is not by any means impossible.

The practice of erecting a shrine for housing the relics
of the saint to whom the prosperity of some particular
church was due, was a common practice during the Middle
Ages.[1] In churches of minor importance these shrines
were generally of small dimensions and were kept in all
sorts of places. Sufficiently small to be portable, they constantly figured in processions. Shrines of the first-class
order were, however, far more elaborate. Generally,
though not invariably, they were erected on a site, prominent and markedly sacred, between the High Altar and
the lady chapel. In this position they were of course
stationary and consisted of a richly ornamented covering
protecting the body, which was deposited in the upper
portion of a stone or marble basement, or perhaps actually
raised upon it.

These shrines of the first class usually consisted of four
distinct portions. At the west end stood the altar dedicated to the saint whose remains were here preserved. It
formed part of the solid basement or substructure. The
latter, frequently perforated with a number of niches,
supported the shrine proper or feretory, a wooden structure, ark-like in shape, its sides sumptuously adorned with
plates of gold and silver, and enriched with jewels and
enamels. To protect all this wealth of decoration from the
effects of the atmosphere, and perhaps also for reasons of a
more commercial character, there was suspended over the

[1] Rock, *Church of our Fathers*, vol. iii, cap. 10.

feretory, by means of chains let down from the vaulting, a wooden covering of great beauty entitled the 'cooperculum', which could be elevated by means of a counterpoise. This device was not normally put into operation without the offering of certain coins of the realm by pilgrim visitors desirous of beholding with their own eyes the great mass of treasure.[1]

It is a cruel tragedy that the besom of reforming zeal should have demolished with such unsparing hand all those splendid works of art which, bearing the designations of their respective saints, once graced our land. Of the Shrines of St. Cuthbert of Durham, of 'the holy blissful martyr' at Canterbury, of St. Swithun at Winchester, to give three illustrations only, not one solitary wrack has been left behind. Attempts have been made, not without success, to piece together some of the fragments of the Shrine of St. Werburga at Chester and that of England's protomartyr at St. Albans. One church alone, apart from that of Westminster, claims the high distinction of having successfully preserved the body of its saint in its original receptacle down to the present day, viz. that of St. White or Candida at Whitchurch Canonicorum in the county of Dorset.[2]

The churches of Westminster and Ely have experienced a more kindly fate (using the epithet in a relative sense) than the remainder of our great English Minsters. The two Shrines of St. Edward the Confessor and St. Etheldreda display a remarkable similarity in their general shape and outline. Moreover, they have managed to preserve for the delight of posterity the greater portion of their substructures. The Ely example is by far the less satisfactory of the two. Not only has it been forcibly removed from its original position, and deprived of the body of its royal Foundress; it has also suffered terribly at the

[1] Scott, *Gleanings from Westminster Abbey*, pp. 127, 128.
[2] *Archaeological Journal*, vol. lxiv, p. 119.

hands of the modern restorer. With execrable taste, a large piece of imitation work has been added to one side in order to fill the place of that which had previously perished. None the less, St. Awdry's Shrine still remains a work of remarkable beauty.[1]

On that great day in the year of grace twelve hundred and sixty-nine the coffer, plated with all manner of precious metals, in which the body of Saint Edward had been reverently placed, stood out with a prominence unknown to-day. All this glorious golden work glistening with jewels, rising behind and above the High Altar with its rich riddels and its low dorsal or reredos, formed a centrepiece, majestic beyond words, in full view of the occupants of choir and lantern. To quote another version of Wyke's *Chronicle*, 'the shrine of the most illustrious king, Edward the Confessor, was placed on high like a candle upon a candlestick so that all who enter into the House of the Lord may behold its light'.[2]

At the west end of the Shrine stood the altar of St. Edward. It probably did not differ greatly from its modern successor save for the riddels projecting at right angles on either side. Certain holes still exist to which the rods which bore these curtains were apparently attached. The reredos consists to-day of a thick vertical slab of stone projecting a few inches on either side beyond the arcaded portions of the shrine.[3] It is decorated with six diamond-shaped panels with interlaced borders, originally filled with lozenges of rich porphyry, two only of which survive. The reredos formerly rested, in all probability, upon the mensa itself, whereas to-day it is supported by two twisted columns, typically Italian in character and not a little reminiscent of similar shafts in the cloisters of the

[1] F. R. Chapman, *The Sacrist's Rolls of Ely*, vol. i, p. 98.
[2] Wyke's *Chronicle*, vol. ii, pp. 64 and 65.
[3] It is doubtful whether this is the original reredos. Probably it forms part of the Marian restoration of the Shrine.

Churches of St. John Lateran and St. Paul without the Walls at Rome.

On either side and wholly independent of the altar stood an isolated column, possibly one of those just mentioned. The pair bore golden images of St. Edward the Confessor in the act of displaying his ring, and his patron, St. John the Evangelist, attired in pilgrim's garb. These images formed one of the few links which connected Westminster Abbey with the unhappy Edward II.[1]

The huge tumba or substructure of the shrine, so fortunately preserved, is in shape a parallelogram, and is built up out of a number of marble slabs. It stands upon a plinth, one step above the floor-level, and is surmounted by an entablature. It is nine feet in height, five feet four and a half inches in breadth, and nine feet five inches in length. Three trefoil-headed niches deeply recessed and separated from each other by means of pilasters occupy the north and south sides, together with a similar niche at the east end. These niches served more than one purpose. A constant succession of pilgrims might have been seen kneeling therein during the daytime. At night sick persons would, from time to time, be left lying there under the care of the Keeper of the Shrine. The proximity of the uncorrupt body of the Confessor lying above in the feretory was naturally a great centre of attraction to those afflicted with diseases. It was a simple and easy method of touching for the King's Evil.

These niches or recesses are of considerable depth. They occupy almost the entire width of the Shrine, for the piece of masonry in the centre, dividing the northern from the southern rows, is a bare five or six inches in thickness. The transverse dividing slabs are of equal thickness, but other pieces have been added to their faces.

Each of these recesses terminates in a moulded trefoiled head cut out of slabs. To the jambs on either side

[1] Scott, *Gleanings from Westminster Abbey*, p. 139.

were attached a number of slender twisted shafts of
wonderful beauty. Seven of them have survived. Surrounding each recess was a border forming a rectangular
frame which Richard de Ware's Italian artists have sub-
jected to a remarkable variety of treatment; on the north
side a guilloche pattern, and on the south two bands with
circular interlacements placed at intervals. These two
interesting forms of decoration meet together in the centre
of the eastern recess in a somewhat clumsy and unsym-
metrical fashion. It seems strange that the gifted thirteenth-century craftsmen should not have succeeded in
devising a more satisfactory method of junction.

The backs of the recesses are decorated with blind
window tracery, closely resembling that in the windows of
the apsidal chapels. It consists of two lancets surmounted
by a circle into which a quantity of mosaic has been introduced. It was undoubtedly the idea of those who designed St. Edward's Shrine to convey an effect suggestive
of a stained glass window.

Above the recesses is a range of seven compartments,
originally panelled with lozenges of porphyry, placed
alternately upright and endwise, each with its own interlaced border of a guilloche pattern almost Oriental in
character.

At the time of its dedication, and for many generations,
the entire surface of the substructure formed a vast mass of
brilliant colouring. The lining or panelling consisted of a
marble inlay of richly coloured pieces of porphyry, cippo-
lino, and other valuable materials, surrounded by mosaics
in geometrical patterns, mostly on a gold ground, together with a quantity of tesserae of gilt glass. The glow
and sparkle of all this colour must have been amazing.
Almost every trace of the original brilliance has by now
vanished from the substructure, but a few square inches
covered with tesserae adorn one of the twisted columns at
the west end, while an imprint left here and there in the

cement enables us to gain some idea of the design of the patterns on the backs of the seven recesses. Their variety must have been marvellous, for there is no suggestion of any repetition.

The entablature was supported at the east end upon two detached spiral columns, both of which disappeared, probably during the troubles of the sixteenth century. One of them was, however, discovered by Sir Gilbert Scott, and has been replaced in its original position.

Above the niches ran a flat cornice displaying an inscription long since disappeared, inlaid in mosaic, on which was set forth the story of the building of the Shrine. A mutilated fragment at the east end alone survives to-day. Providentially, however, the wording of the inscription was recorded by the monk Richard Sporley, the fifteenth-century historian of Westminster.

Anno Milleno—Domini Cum Sexageno
Et Bis Centeno—Cum Completo Quasi Deno
Hoc Opus Est Factum, Quod Petrus Duxit in Actum
Romanus Civis:—Homo Causam Noscere Si Vis,
Rex Fuit Henricus—Sancti Presentis Amicus.[1]

The position of the inscription on the Shrine has formed a highly interesting problem. Careful measurements have been taken of the spacing of the various words. They prove incontestably that it must have commenced at the west end and been continued thence round the entire structure. Only by this means could adequate space have been secured. This fact proves that the retabulum must originally have stood at a lower level than the inscribed band, otherwise a portion of the lettering would have been concealed.[2]

The words of the inscription suggest that it was placed here as a memorial to Henry III after his death in 1272. According to Sporley, it consisted of gilt and coloured

[1] Richard Widmore, *History of the Church of St. Peter, Westminster*, p. 55.
[2] Society of Antiquaries, *Proceedings*, 2nd Series, vol. xv, p. 413.

stones, but a minute examination of such fragments as survive indicates that the letters were made of glass of a deep blue colour inlaid in a ground of gold mosaic. Only the matrices of the letters remain to-day.

The drastic restoration of St. Edward's Shrine carried out in the middle of the sixteenth century by Abbot John of Feckenham led to the complete concealment of the original inscription. It remained hidden beneath a quantity of plaster for the best part of two centuries. In April 1741, however, a portion of Feckenham's plaster covering either perished or was for some reason removed. Several words of the thirteenth-century inscription at once came to light. They were carefully examined by George Vertue, the famous engraver, who laid a Dissertation on St. Edward's Tomb before the Society of Antiquaries. He described 'the old mosaic inscription' as being 'almost defaced', 'the calcined glass yellow like gold and set in'.[1] Six words in all came to be revealed in this curious manner, viz. 'Petrus Duxit in Actum Romanus Civis.'

In a few months' time the early Georgian pilferers got to work. These precious remains from a distant past disappeared for ever, having been 'erased, picked out and taken away'.[2]

Immediately above the inscribed band stood the slab on which the shrine proper or feretory immediately rested. At the outset this slab was somewhat narrower and shorter than the inscribed band, and formed a kind of step above it. To-day its appearance is that of a narrow frieze immediately above the inscription, decorated with a pattern consisting of alternate circles and rectangles, all of them void so as to serve as matrices for mosaics.

Peter, the Roman citizen, to whom we owe both the substructure of St. Edward's Shrine and the tomb of Henry III, and likewise Odoricus, probably his father,

[1] Lethaby, *Westminster Abbey Re-examined*, p. 266.
[2] *Archaeologia*, vol. i, p. 32.

who was responsible for the equally wonderful pavement
of the presbytery, have placed the land of their temporary
sojourn under a debt which can never be over-estimated.
They must have stood unrivalled among the craftsmen of
their day. From Berwick-on-Tweed to Land's End this
amazing combination of marble, mosaic, and enamel,
Byzantine in character, though modified by Gothic influence, stands unique. To the work of these men of
genius our country can furnish no sort of parallel.

Another of the notable works of art attributed to Peter
is the tomb of Pope Clement IV, who died in 1268 at
Viterbo. It bears the signature *Petrus Oderisi*. The points
of resemblance between the English and Italian specimens
of this great master's work are most remarkable.

Professor Lethaby has made the interesting suggestion
that Peter and Odoricus belonged to 'some guild of
workers who prided themselves on seeking the inspiration
of ancient Rome and turning away from the art of the
Tedeschi of the Lombard School. Such a thought was the
germ of the whole Renaissance, which in essence was the
rebirth of national culture and the repudiation of Ger-
manism'. If the Professor's theory be correct, the position
in the history of art occupied by this work at the east
end of Westminster Abbey becomes possessed of twofold
importance.[1]

The third, and by far the most important, member of
the Shrine of St. Edward was the golden feretory, 'the
shining beacon of the whole church'. It is a tragedy of the
first order that at this point we find ourselves entering
upon the region of conjecture. So scanty is the material
available that we can only gain an incomplete and uncertain idea of its general appearance.

The documentary evidence consists of two highly interesting drawings in the Norman-French manuscript contained in the Cambridge University Library, usually

[1] Lethaby, *Westminster Abbey Re-examined*, pp. 227–31.

termed 'The Cambridge Life of St. Edward the Confessor'. This remarkable document, judging by internal
evidence, was addressed to Henry III's Queen Consort,
Eleanor of Provence, and must have been compiled some
time during the decade terminating in 1250. Quite possibly it was a present made by the King to his wife. It has
been edited in recent years by Dr. Montagu James, who is
of the opinion that it was compiled at St. Albans under the
superintendence of no less a personage than Matthew
Paris.[1]

The date of the manuscript is highly significant. It was
produced at a moment which may be designated the
parting of the ways. Much work still remained to be
carried out before the new Shrine could be regarded as
approaching completion. On the other hand, sentence of
death had undoubtedly been pronounced upon its twelfth-
century predecessor. It is more than probable that it had
already become a thing of the past at the time when
Matthew Paris was at work.

The pictures in the Cambridge Life of the Confessor
provide us with more than one alternative. Were these
pictures nothing more than the creation of an artist's
imagination, or was it the intention of the latter to perpetuate, as far as might be, the familiar outlines of the
twelfth-century Shrine? Or again, is it conceivable that
he simply intended to convey a general impression of the
new structure which was developing in size and beauty
with each year that passed?

Obviously the third choice would be far the most
satisfactory from our point of view, and there is a good deal
in its favour, for it is clear that the King's craftsmen had
already been engaged for a number of years upon the new
Shrine at the time when Matthew Paris started upon his
manuscript. Very probably the design for the feretory

[1] *La Estoire de Seint Edward Le Roi*, edited by M. R. James, pp. 12, 13,
and 17.

SCENES FROM THE CAMBRIDGE LIFE OF ST. EDWARD THE CONFESSOR
Cures at St. Edward's Shrine

had long been settled. Hence it is not unreasonable to assume that the artist had in mind the splendid new structure, which by slow degrees, and at the cost of infinite labour, was at that very moment being pieced together. To quote Professor Lethaby: 'the style is so advanced that it must resemble the new shrine, the design for which would have been known to Matthew Paris, who might quite conceivably have been consulted about it'.[1]

On the other hand, these illustrations convey little more than a general impression. Accuracy of detail was hardly to be expected. That they contain, however, more than one feature which came to be incorporated in the new structure, is an assumption not wholly unreasonable.

One of these illustrations displays the Shrine in rough outline. Substructure and feretory are alike indicated very distinctly, notably the latter, a highly elaborate structure of metal and enamel. On either side stand two detached columns, with foliaged capitals, surmounted by figures of St. Edward the Confessor wearing a dalmatic over a sleeved robe, crowned, the ring on his finger, and St. John the Evangelist attired as a pilgrim with hat on his back and a staff in his left hand. A number of people with open eyes are creeping through or kneeling in the various orifices of the substructure. Evidently they are the blind men led by a boy who are seen in the neighbouring picture to the left. The superstructure is divided into two stages, the upper consisting of a crocketed gable terminating in a finial. At its angles are ornaments like the heads of crosiers. Our Lord is depicted in the act of benediction in a vesica, and in two trefoiled arches slightly lower are two kneeling figures, one of them an angel. In the lower stage is the figure of King Edward seated beneath a trefoiled arch flanked by two bishops. At the side of the picture is a monk with face somewhat obliterated, singing *Te Deum laudamus*.

[1] Lethaby, *Westminster Abbey Re-examined*, p. 263.

The other picture is supposed to portray the Translation of 1163. The body of the saint is wrapped in an elaborate pall. Henry II and a bishop are bending over it, while two other bishops hold the feet. Its chief feature of interest consists in the side view of the feretory, which is divided into fields each containing quatrefoils with a nimbed figure within. The upper and lower bands are jewelled. The lid, which is coped and crested with large crockets at the ends, is upheld by two groups of men. On the side are four half-quatrefoils containing half-length figures. The base is covered with a cloth embroidered with lions passant.

We are indebted to Matthew Paris for yet another illustration of the Shrine, but as Professor Lethaby has remarked, it must be regarded as 'a symbol rather than an illustration'.[1]

It is difficult to appraise accurately the evidential value of these pictures, but a close agreement clearly exists between that which is entitled 'Cures at the Shrine' and the written evidence.

For nearly four centuries the place of the medieval feretory has been occupied by the wooden substitute placed here by Abbot John of Feckenham during the brief reign of Mary Tudor. It is at least possible that the existing ark-like structure may to some extent be suggestive of its predecessor. The Marian restoration of the Shrine took place barely twenty years after the iniquitous overthrow of Henry III's precious fabric. Many people would still be living who could recall its general appearance. Moreover, it is likely that Feckenham would use his best endeavours to reproduce in some degree its once familiar outlines in the humbler material of wainscot oak.

Judging, then, by such slender evidence as we possess, coupled with analogous examples, it seems justifiable to assume that the medieval feretory possessed a high-

[1] Lethaby, *Westminster Abbey and the King's Craftsmen*, p. 296.

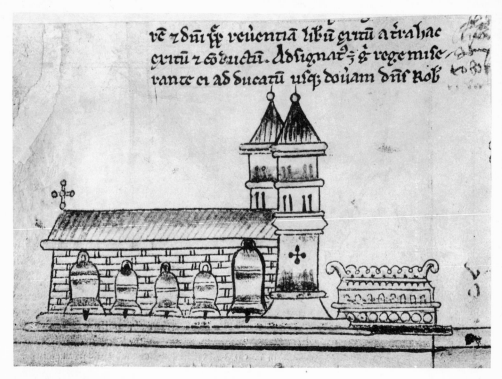

(1) THE CHURCH OF WESTMINSTER AND THE SHRINE OF ST. EDWARD

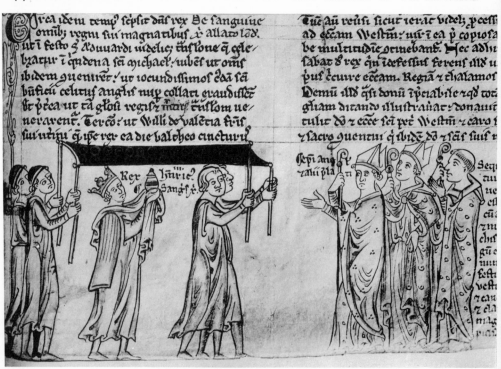

(2) THE PROCESSION OF THE HOLY BLOOD

pitched roof which gave it a shape not unlike an ark. It might be described as a large gable-ended coffin, cased entirely in sheet gold, covered with plates, arcades, and figures, all of gold set with precious stones, and a vast mass of jewels and enamels. To quote the words of one who assisted at the Translation of the year 1269, it resembled 'a basilica adorned with purest gold and precious stones'.[1]

The brilliant decoration of the feretory probably resembled in its general character the remarkable thirteenth-century Shrine of St. Taurin, the Apostle of eastern Normandy. This interesting survival, with its wealth of jewels and enamels, is religiously preserved in the sacristy of the parish church at Évreux which bears that dedication. At certain seasons, notably on the festival of the saint, which occurs in the month of August, the chasse is exposed for veneration in the chancel. A work of art resembling the Évreux example, but multiplied several times in size, must have been an amazing spectacle indeed.

It is impossible to visualize the appearance of the fourth and last member of St. Edward's Shrine. The inventory drawn up at the time of the Dissolution contains the following entry: 'In Seynt Edward's Chappell a fayre Godly shrine of Seignt Edward in marble in the myddes of the Chapell with a case to the same.' It can hardly be doubted that this 'case' or covering must have been in its own way no less beautiful than the actual Shrine. It is unthinkable that such men as Henry III and Richard de Ware would provide anything less than the very best, but of actual evidence not one particle exists.

Was the Shrine covered by a cooperculum hoisted up and down, as required, by pulleys fixed into the vaulting, or by a fixed tester or coopertorium of the type which still surmounts some of the royal tombs in St. Edward's Chapel? It is difficult to say.

In an inventory of the contents of this chapel compiled

[1] Lethaby, *Westminster Abbey and the King's Craftsmen*, p. 296.

by Dan Wyllyam Green, who was Keeper of the Shrine barely twenty years prior to the Dissolution, mention is made of a 'valaunce of blew velwett embroderyd with flouris of golde with the ymage of saynt Edwarde and Saynt John Euangelyste with another valaunce of blew damaske to hang the shryne and a creiste of tymber and of bron golde'.[1] Hangings of this description, it might be supposed, would hardly make for the easy working of a movable wooden cover or case. Again, a cooperculum would most certainly necessitate the provision of a number of chains (two at least) attached to and passing through the roof. The bosses of the groining display no trace of any such holes to-day, but it is, of course, conceivable that these holes, if such existed, were filled up during the great Wren restoration of the Abbey. Such problems are likely to remain insoluble.[2]

East of the Shrine stood the Altar of Relics, sometimes styled the Altar of the Holy Trinity. In the eyes of the pious Henry, this altar was an object of the highest importance. The King spared no pains to ensure that this central sanctuary should be equipped with objects of veneration wellnigh unique.

In 1247 he made announcement to his subjects of 'an inestimable benefit conferred by Heaven on the English nation'. It was a portion of the Precious Blood contained in a costly vase of pure crystal, the genuineness of which was attested by Robert, Patriarch of Jerusalem, and his Chapter.

Orders were accordingly issued to the magnates of the realm to meet the King at St. Paul's 'to hear some agreeable news'. The nature of the latter was not divulged till all had assembled, for the King's announcement must come as a surprise.

A procession was then formed, a picture of which has

---

[1] Westlake, *Westminster Abbey*, vol. ii, p. 505.
[2] Society of Antiquaries, *Proceedings*, 2nd Series, vol. xviii, p. 70.

been bequeathed to us by Matthew Paris. The King walked on foot, clad in a poor cloak of undyed wool, bearing the precious relic, and escorted from the City to Westminster by the Abbot and monks. He then proceeded to the Palace, where he passed through every room. At length he reached the Abbey and, after solemnly proceeding round the church, deposited the relic at the High Altar, where mass was sung by Walter de Suffield, Bishop of Norwich, who also preached the sermon.[1]

This notable offering was followed by another scarcely less precious in the eyes of medieval Englishmen, viz. a stone marked by the imprint of the Saviour's foot at His Ascension. Given to the King in the first instance by the Dominicans, he added it to the treasures which were now accumulating round the future shrine.

In later years other sacred objects found their way into St. Edward's Chapel, viz. a thorn which had once formed part of the Sacred Crown, an arm of St. Sylvester, and a tooth of St. Athanasius. Far transcending these precious objects, however, was the girdle of Our Lady. Tradition maintained that it had been worked by her own hands, subsequently becoming the property of St. Thomas. It passed into the hands of the Confessor, who presented it to his beloved Abbey.

As the years rolled on the enrichment of this national sanctuary with sacred objects came to be regarded by our sovereigns and other personages as a natural method of expressing their piety.

Edward I closely followed his father's example. According to Matthew of Westminster, his eldest son Alphonse in the year 1284 'offered up a certain ornament of gold' which had formerly belonged to Llewellyn Prince of Wales with other jewels also which were applied to the adornment of 'the blessed Edward'. 'Two years later the greatest of the Plantagenets' himself 'conveyed a considerable portion of

[1] Holinshed, Chronicles II, p. 415.

I

the Cross of Our Lord adorned with gold and silver and valuable stones which he had brought with him from Wales'. This gift was followed by a throne (doubtless King Edward's Chair) together with a sceptre and crown of gold.

Edward II signalized his Coronation by presenting a pound of gold fashioned in the likeness of the Confessor, and a mark of gold representing St. John the Evangelist. Neither was our third Edward behindhand. To his credit must be placed the offering of the skull, or a portion of the skull, of St. Benedict, the parent of this and many other monastic foundations.[1]

Westminster has never known a more devoted son than Richard II. Hence it was natural for that unfortunate monarch to follow the precedent set by his predecessors. To the ever-lengthening list of treasures he added a remarkable tablet of silver, on which was depicted in enamel the story of St. Edward and the pilgrim, given to him by the citizens of London.

It might be taken for granted that the Shrine would occupy a prominent position in the mind of that most bountiful of royal benefactors, our seventh Henry. In his last will and testament he bequeathed a figure of himself clad in full armour, 'wrought with plates of fyne gold', kneeling upon 'a table of silver and gilte' and 'holding betwixte his hands the croune which it pleased God to give us, with the Victorie of our Ennemye at our furst felde'.[2] He further directed that this image and crown should be placed 'in the mydds of the Creste of the Shryne of Saint Edward King in such a place as by us in our life, or by our executors after our decease shall be thought most convenient and honourable'—a curious arrangement which seems also to have existed in the abbey churches of St. Albans and Bury St. Edmunds.

---

[1] J. P. Neale and E. W. Brayley, *The History and Antiquities of the Abbey Church of St. Peter, Westminster*, vol. ii, p. 66.

[2] *The Will of Henry VII*, edited by Thomas Astle, pp. 35–6.

THE RELIC OF THE ASCENSION

We must return, however, to the Shrine as it appeared fresh from the loving hands of its Royal Founder. The scene of magnificence which met the eye in the year of Henry III's death must have been indescribable. Not the slightest barrier intercepted the gaze of worshippers in the choir. The whole shining mass of jewels and mosaics rose superbly behind the High Altar, and as it caught one ray of sunlight after another, it must have seemed to the on-looker an almost unearthly blaze of glory.

## 4. THE MOSAIC PAVEMENT

It is much to be regretted that the remarkable pavement of the Chapel of St. Edward is of necessity hidden from view. The friction caused by countless boots and shoes would soon reduce its beauty to a condition of irretriev-able ruin. Only the comparatively small portion therefore enclosed within the barriers which protect the Shrine and King Edward's Chair can be exposed with safety.

The pavement falls considerably short of the splendour displayed by the magnificent Opus Alexandrinum in the adjoining presbytery. It belongs to the same branch of decorative art, but it is of a simpler design, while its general details are altogether different. It suffers from its close proximity to one of the most amazing works of art north of the Alps. If it stood by itself it would elicit a general chorus of praise.

It forms a continuous pattern consisting mainly of dark stones cast into large single circles surrounded by smaller interlacing circles of mosaic, inserted into square slabs of bluish-coloured Purbeck marble. These circles are filled with numerous patterns containing stars, triangles, and other figures, and display an astonishing variety of design. Professor Lethaby has estimated that there are no less than two hundred different patterns.[1] Based for the most part

---

[1] Lethaby, *Westminster Abbey and the King's Craftsmen*, p. 327.

on hexagons, triangles within triangles, and other geometrical figures, and filled with thousands of tiny pieces,
the effect is almost Oriental. It would seem that the
marble slabs were laid down first of all. Subsequently,
and in all probability after the completion of the floor of
the presbytery, the vast mass of mosaic detail was inserted.

Everything suggests that the men who carried out the
work in the Confessor's Chapel had not attained the same
high level of craftsmanship as the band of geniuses to
whom we owe the pavement of the presbytery. The
circles have been applied in an extremely irregular
manner. No attempt has been made to respect the joint-
ing of the various slabs into which the patterns have been
inserted. The result was inevitable. This rather crude
irregularity of treatment, coupled with a great deal of
modern restoration, not always of a judicious character,
has produced a somewhat peculiar patchwork effect.

The late William Burges has put forward an interesting
theory to the effect that a body of English craftsmen came
to be fired by the desire to emulate the splendid work
carried out in front of the High Altar by the Italian craftsmen brought from Rome by Richard de Ware; and
further that their efforts met with only a qualified success,
for these inexperienced native artificers were unequal to
the task of producing anything calculated to vie with the
work of Odoricus and Peter the Roman citizen.[1]

This picturesque theory is unlikely to emerge from the
region of speculation. Professor Lethaby in one of his
later works cast doubt upon it, and pointed out that
mosaic work precisely similar in character may be seen
to this day in the Church of Santa Prassede in Rome,
bearing, moreover, the date 1238.[2]

Another theory, too, has been advanced to the effect
that there were utilized for the floor of the chapel only

[1] Scott, *Gleanings from Westminster Abbey*, p. 103.
[2] Lethaby, *Westminster Abbey Re-examined*, p. 225.

THE SHRINE AND THE PAVEMENT OF ST. EDWARD'S CHAPEL

such odds and ends of marble and mosaic as remained available after the skilled artificers had completed their task in front of the High Altar. The theory is incapable either of proof or disproof.

The pavement came to be broken in course of time and its symmetry marred by the insertion of four tomb slabs. Its historical associations were thereby enriched; but it lost in artistic effect to a more than corresponding extent. In the north-west corner is a mutilated but once splendid brass, covering the remains of Richard II's Chancellor, John of Waltham, Bishop of Salisbury. It was an evil day when that unfortunate monarch was led to inter his friend and favourite *inter reges, multis murmurantibus*.[1] The King's error was not forgotten, for this preposterous breach with tradition was in a later year brought up against him. In the eyes of his opponents this intrusion was not the least of his high crimes and misdemeanours.

On the south side lies the unfortunate Thomas of Woodstock, Duke of Gloucester, whose detestable murder at Calais, at the instance of his nephew, was another outrage for which the unhappy Richard had to pay dearly. Originally the slab bore a splendid brass. The indentation alone remains to tell the tale.

At the east end the remains of a cross set in glass mosaic can be detected, together with some slight remains of an inscription. It marks the graves of Margaret and John, children of William de Valence, a member of the great French family into which Henry III married. These children died in the years 1270 and 1277 respectively. It has been suggested that the two slabs form part of the original design for the floor of the chapel. The suggestion is not impossible.

The laying down of the pavement must have been proceeding much about the same time as that in front of the High Altar. The Pipe Roll for 1267–8 proves that

[1] Stanley, *Historical Memorials of Westminster Abbey*, p. 178.

payments were being made towards the stipends of certain of the *cementariorum pavetorum* who were then working before the feretory of St. Edward.[1]

Tombs and burial-places lie outside the scope of this volume, hence a bare mention must suffice of these four interments.  On the other hand, an indentation in the pavement to the north of the shrine, rarely exposed to public view, recalls a pathetic incident which took place here in the middle of the fifteenth century and upon which it is impossible to refrain from lingering a moment.

The chief figure in the story is the unhappy Henry VI. To his weak intellect the choice of a sepulchre in which his body should be laid to rest represented a problem well-nigh insoluble.  Over and over again would he wander across to the Abbey from the Palace hard by and, after praying for half an hour before the Confessor's Shrine, he would ponder over the problem in a moody silence, broken only by his rejection of the suggestions proffered, one by one, by the Abbot.  At long last he selected a spot between the Shrine and the tomb of Henry III.  The master mason was therefore summoned and with a 'pykkes' or 'instrument of iron' he marked out the site, eight by four and a half feet.  The place destined for the reception of a King's body remains unoccupied, but the lines scratched on the marble pavement by John of Thirske, on the day when Henry made his choice more than four and a half centuries ago, can still be detected.[2]

## 5. THE CHANGES MADE IN THE FIFTEENTH CENTURY

Little or no alteration took place in either Shrine or Chapel beyond the offering of additional treasures, for several generations.  It was far otherwise with the fifteenth

[1] Lethaby, *Westminster Abbey Re-examined*, pp. 224–5.
[2] *Church Times*, May 28, 1920, p. 529.

century, for that epoch was marked by two changes of real magnitude.

The first affected the general aspect of things to a comparatively slight extent. Still, it was a sufficiently radical performance. An even stronger expression would be justified, for it involved the complete demolition and subsequent rebuilding of the Shrine.

When Henry V, most popular of sovereigns, was cut off in the full prime of vigorous manhood, bequeathing his throne to a helpless infant, the whole land gave itself over to grief and consternation. His splendid exploits, military and political, at the expense of unhappy France, had made an ineffaceable impression upon the public mind. It was inconceivable that for their beloved King any place of sepulchre should be provided other than the chapel where four of his Plantagenet predecessors and their consorts had already been laid. In the eyes of the English people a building which already enshrined so many precious associations was the only possible resting-place for the conqueror of France.

It was easy to lay down a general principle; but its practical application was another matter altogether. Court and convent alike found themselves confronted by a puzzling problem.

The circle of royal tombs which by degrees came to mount guard over the body of the Confessor had been completed with the erection of the great sarcophagus of Richard II and Anne of Bohemia. No space remained either to the north or the south sufficient to accommodate another tomb, much less such a structure as public opinion demanded for the body of Harry of Monmouth. At the east end alone remained an unoccupied place, and even here the matter was beset with difficulty by reason of the Altar of Relics and the various caskets in which the treasures were enshrined. The erection of a tomb on this spot was clearly inadvisable, if not actually impossible.

The problem was considerable; but it was speedily solved and apparently without arousing scruples in any quarter. It was quickly decided to embark at all hazards upon a course of action so radical that in our time it would arouse a chorus of deep indignation from John o' Groats to Land's End.

The responsible authorities decided then, at the cost of the symmetry of the general surroundings and an obvious loss of dignity, to remove the Altar of Relics and its appurtenances from its time-honoured position at the east end to the north side of the Shrine. It was a drastic proceeding and it might well have given pause, when it was discovered that the space secured by this not wholly admirable manœuvre was quite inadequate for the grandiose scheme projected. They unhesitatingly pushed forward, however, with an audacity but little removed from irreverence, and ultimately decided upon a still more revolutionary change. By rebuilding the Shrine a few feet farther to the west, the needful space could be secured for the remains of the popular sovereign whose loss the country was bewailing. The problem must at all costs be overcome, even though it involved laying hands upon the costly and complicated work of Henry III.

These iniquitous proceedings fill us to-day with amazement and even scepticism; but there is not the slightest particle of doubt. The evidence is more than convincing. The stark fact is proclaimed before our eyes by the condition of the pavement at the east end of the chapel, a gaunt, bare space, wholly devoid of the beautiful marble and mosaic work of Henry III. Is it conceivable that one single piece of this historic area would have been left undecorated by the thirteenth-century artists in this strange fashion? Surely not. Those craftsmen would never have dreamt for one moment of leaving that ugly, incongruous patch; indeed, it did not even exist, for in their day it was covered by the substructure of the Shrine.

When the position of the latter was altered, however, this portion of the floor was laid bare and the defect has never been made good.

The Chantry Chapel, the work of John of Thirske, which as the years rolled on, by degrees filled up the space behind St. Edward's Shrine, was a glorious addition to the Abbey, and will always enjoy a premier place among its treasures. On the other hand, the removal and rebuilding of a work of art, covered with such an immense quantity of elaborate detail as the Shrine, was a task so risky that people might well have quailed before it. It seems strange, too, that the sacred character of the Confessor's resting-place did not automatically impose a veto upon all such happenings. None the less, history reveals no trace of hesitancy in essaying the task, and the deed was done. St. Edward's Shrine was removed from its original position immediately beneath the central boss of the apse, and set up two feet farther to the west. What an immense amount hinged upon those four and twenty inches![1]

Such were the doings of our fifteenth-century forebears in the green tree. It now remains to tell the further tale of what they did in the dry.

The rebuilding of the Shrine was a performance sweeping enough in all conscience, but it was the merest trifle compared to that which followed a generation later. The former must have been a work of immense labour, demanding meticulous care and accuracy, but the task seems to have been carried out with absolute conscientiousness down to the tiniest details. The second of these great fifteenth-century changes transcended its predecessor in every possible way. It represented a veritable revolution. It struck a blow at the very root of the great central conception which underlay the scheme, so carefully and lovingly thought out by Henry III.

It had been the darling object of that pious monarch to

[1] Lethaby, *Westminster Abbey Re-examined*, p. 266.

exalt the memory of the last representative of the old Saxon house of Cerdic in every possible way. The tradition of St. Edward the Confessor must be preserved inviolate in the minds of men. His golden feretory must be elevated far above the floor of the chapel. It must stand out before the eyes of every man, woman, or child who found their way within the Abbey walls, as the most outstanding object in the church. To the very end of his days must each pilgrim carry with him the indelible recollection of this wondrous picture. The resting-place of the great national saint must remain an ever-present reality.

Unfortunately, the fifteenth century was characterized by a falling away from original ideals. In some ways that century was scarcely more reverent in its dealings with the past than its roundly abused successor, the nineteenth. Respect for the customs and traditions of a former generation, for the memory of the artist King, disappeared altogether. Not the slightest qualm seems to have arisen in the minds of these Yorkist Englishmen. That it was their bounden duty religiously to abstain from any rough handling of a venerable tradition never apparently occurred to them for one moment. The command therefore went forth, and the whole scheme of things at the east end of the Abbey was rudely destroyed. It was a tragedy of the first order, one of the earliest, though not the last, which the Church of Westminster has been condemned to endure.

A mighty wall of demarcation, then, was erected, extending right across the apse immediately behind the high altar, from pillar to pillar. The Shrine, save perhaps for a few inches at the top, ceased to be visible from the body of the church, while the surrounding company of royal tombs was ruthlessly invaded, three of their number being shut off from its immediate neighbourhood. The 'shining beacon' which for two centuries had served 'to enlighten the whole church' was henceforth enclosed within a space so narrow that its light was invisible to all save a privileged few.

No one can deny the claim of this new enclosing wall to beauty of the highest order. It is a magnificent specimen of the later Gothic art. On the other hand, it was the offspring of an ideal which stood in direct antithesis to that which two hundred years before had inspired King Henry III. It was an act of unhistorical and unprincipled vandalism. Whatever may be the intrinsic beauty of this fine specimen of perpendicular architecture, it merits a criticism scarcely less forcible and sweeping than that which is directed against some of those nineteenth-century enormities which are the bane of every art lover to-day. Extenuating circumstances may perchance be adduced, but they carry us only a short distance. Whatever may have been the precise motives of those who were at the head of affairs, the adverse judgement of posterity upon their actions, viewed as a whole, cannot surely be one whit too strong.

## 6. THE STONE SCREEN

The screen belongs to that group of works of art which is so magnificently represented in the Cathedrals of Winchester, St. Albans, and Southwark, in Christ Church Priory, Hampshire, and in All Souls College, Oxford. It differs from them in that it consists of one stage only. The great Rood with its attendant figures, already described, would have rendered the addition of a second stage impossible.

The screen dates from the reign of Edward IV. The work at the back of King Sebert's tomb hard by, carried out probably at the same time, is adorned with the *rose-en-soleil*, a badge of the Yorkist monarch.

It is thirty-seven feet in length and fourteen feet two inches in height and is pierced at the north and south ends by two openings known respectively as the King's Door and the Queen's Door, each of which is surmounted by a two-centred arch and a three-centred rear arch. The latter is set in a square frame divided by means of a wide hollow into two orders. Traces remain of elaborate foliage decoration in the architrave at the head of each doorway. Between the doorways is a wide recessed seat with a double range of panelled niches separated by small triplicated columns from which spread the groinings of a remarkable canopy. The latter consists of five semi-octagonal tabernacles with foliated pendants and ribbed vaulting of great elaboration, all of them differing in design and terminating in pinnacles. The doorways are flanked on either side by large niches, each of which contains an octagonal pedestal, panelled, foliated, and crested, together with a canopy displaying tabernacle work similar to that above the seat.

The details of these canopies bear a close resemblance to the beautiful work surmounting the entrance to the Chapel of St. John the Baptist in the north ambulatory, the gift of Edward IV's Consort, Elizabeth Wydville. This similarity furnishes an additional argument in favour of a Yorkist date for the erection of the screen.

The structure terminates in a deep frieze. The upper portion with its foliated decoration suggestive of strawberry leaves is cruelly decayed; but beneath, in a large hollow moulding and practically perfect, are a series of fourteen carved groups arranged in loops. They represent events, both historical and legendary, connected with the life of St. Edward. They are separated from each other by means of large trefoiled ornaments, on some of which appear blank shields, surrounded by rays.

These groups of figures have in the opinion of Dr. M. R. James been copied from a manuscript Life of the Confessor in the possession of Trinity College, Cambridge.[1] 'Both in selection and in composition the pictures in the manu-

[1] B. 10.2.

(*a*) The Nobles swearing allegiance to Queen Emma

(*b*) The Coronation of King Edward

(*c*) The Divine Child appearing to King Edward

SCULPTURED GROUPS ON THE STONE SCREEN IN THE CHAPEL OF
ST. EDWARD THE CONFESSOR

script are so closely related to the sculptures that the latter might well be supposed to have been adapted from them.'[1] They are as follows:

(1) *The Oath of Fidelity.* The prelates and nobles of England with uplifted hands swear their allegiance to the unborn babe of Emma, the second wife of Ethelred the Unready.

(2) *The Birth of Edward the Confessor*, at Islip, near Oxford, which land he subsequently granted to the Abbey. The connexion between the two places still survives for the patronage of the living is in the hands of the Dean and Chapter. Queen Emma is seen reclining in a State bed; while two attendants stand near, one of whom is holding the infant.

(3) *The Coronation of Edward the Confessor on Easter Day, 1043.* The new King is seated upon a chair of state supported by two prelates, one of whom wearing a mitre is in the act of crowning him.

(4) *The Devil and the Danegeld.* King Edward is depicted in a state of alarm at the sight of the Devil dancing upon the barrels, in which was stored the hated Danegeld. So horrified was the King that he restored the money to its owners and remitted the tax for the remainder of his reign. This sculpture is incomplete, the figure of the Devil having been destroyed.

(5) *King Edward and the Thief.* King Edward while in bed beholds a thief about to carry away a quantity of treasure out of a coffer which the Chamberlain, Hugolin, had negligently left open. He warns him to be off in case he should be caught and subsequently refuses to allow the Chamberlain to pursue the thief.

(6) *The Miraculous Appearance of Our Lord in human form to King Edward during Mass.* On the left is the King kneeling at a faldstool. On the right is the celebrant, whose head has disappeared. The chalice is seen on the altar, behind which is a reredos. The event is traditionally associated with the altar of the Holy Trinity in the nave.

(7) *King Edward's Vision of the Drowning of the King of Denmark.* A knight is struggling in the water, having fallen out of a boat in which he was rowing towards a ship filled with spearmen.

(8) *The Quarrel between Harold and Tosti, the two sons of Earl Godwin, at King Edward's table.* The King prophesies to his

[1] Lethaby, *Westminster Abbey and the King's Craftsmen*, p. 21.

wife and his father-in-law the terrible dissensions leading to an evil end of the quarrelling brothers. On the table is a covered cup together with several articles of food.

(9) *King Edward's Vision of the Seven Sleepers of Ephesus.* A legend states that seven Ephesian Christians took refuge in a cave during the Decian persecution. There they fell asleep, and many generations afterwards were found still slumbering. One day, after partaking of the Blessed Sacrament, the King had a vision in which he saw the sleepers turn from their right to their left sides and learnt that they would remain in this position seventy years, during which time the Normans would reign over England. In order to test the truth of this vision, three mounted messengers, a bishop, a monk, and a soldier, visited the cave as depicted on the frieze, and found the sleepers in the position stated by the King.

(10) *King Edward and the Pilgrim.* The King, who has just been present at the consecration of a church dedicated to St. John the Evangelist, meets a pilgrim. Having already emptied his purse he takes the ring from off his finger and gives it to the pilgrim, who has asked an alms for the love of St. John, one of the King's favourite saints.

(11) *The Restoration of Sight to the Blind.* The King is washing his hands in the background. An attendant, believing the water to have acquired miraculous properties, washes the faces of four blind men at the door of the palace, makes the sign of the cross, and their sight is restored.

(12) *St. John the Evangelist and the Two Pilgrims.* Two Ludlow pilgrims in Palestine, having lost their way, meet a venerable man who conducts them to Jerusalem. Next day the old man stated himself to be St. John the Evangelist, and gave them the King's ring with instructions to return it to him, at the same time announcing his approaching death.

(13) *The Meeting of King Edward and the Two Pilgrims.* The pilgrims return to England as quickly as possible and deliver the ring and the message to the King at one of the royal residences, Havering-atte-Bower in Essex.

(14) Subject doubtful, possibly connected with the conse-cration of the original Abbey.

The screen has suffered terribly during the centuries which have passed since its erection. The inevitable work-ing of time could not fail to make inroads upon such a vast

(*a*) King Edward giving his ring to a beggar

(*b*) St. John giving the ring to two Ludlow pilgrims

(*c*) The pilgrims returning the ring to King Edward

SCULPTURED GROUPS ON THE STONE SCREEN IN THE CHAPEL OF
ST. EDWARD THE CONFESSOR

mass of delicate detail, to say nothing of the vandalistic exploits of reformers and restorers. Again, the effect of the cold, damp atmosphere of the unwarmed Abbey upon the surface of the stone was in former years disastrous. By the middle of the nineteenth century the screen was approaching a state of ruin. Portions of it could almost have been blown away by one blast from a pair of bellows.

Fortunately, modern science came to the rescue before the situation was wholly irretrievable. A solution of shellac was applied in 1857 under the superintendence of Sir Gilbert Scott. Thanks to the induration thus brought about, the process of decay was arrested, and has proceeded no further. 'All was transfixed and consolidated by the most gentle application of the solution.'[1]

Later on the heating apparatus was installed and an amazing change for the better was at once produced. The condensation of dew which had continued unchecked for centuries and with such disastrous results forthwith ceased. No change has ever wrought more beneficially in the conservation of the many treasures of the Abbey.

At the outset the screen was richly decorated with colour. Blue and vermilion were the hues mainly employed for the background, and for the interstices of the delicate network traceries of the soffits of the canopies. In the early years of the nineteenth century, when the great history of Neale and Brayley was being compiled, traces were still visible here and there of a certain amount of gilding on raised patterns.[2]

We must be thankful that despite the loss of the western face, that on the east retains its authentic character and is still able to convey to twentieth-century folk some faint suggestion of its medieval splendour.

---

[1] *R.I.B.A. Proceedings*, vol. vi, p. 114.
[2] J. P. Neale and E. W. Brayley, *The History and Antiquities of the Abbey Church of St. Peter, Westminster*, vol. i, p. 59.

## 7. THE CHAPEL OF SAINT EDWARD ON THE EVE OF THE DISSOLUTION OF THE MONASTERY

During the heyday of its renown the Shrine of St. Edward must have been a principal centre of religious devotion in our land. On the annual feast of the Saint's Translation it was the custom for the chief citizens of London to pay an official visit, while processions were made to the sacred spot by all the religious communities. The various members of the Royal Family were frequent visitors. At the three great festivals of Christmas, Easter, and Whitsun, the general public were wont to flock hither in immense numbers. On occasions of national festival and rejoicing, such as the great victory of Agincourt, the leaders of the nation were wont to make their offerings at the Confessor's Shrine as an official act of gratitude to Almighty God.[1]

The beauty of both Chapel and Shrine filled the mind of every visitor with amazement. A party of Bohemian travellers, for instance, who visited the Abbey in the middle of the fifteenth century, were dumbfounded by the sight of the golden feretory studded with masses of gems, and the collection of relics, 'so numerous that two scribes writing for two weeks could hardly make a catalogue of them.'[2] Trevisano, an Italian traveller, who found his way to our shores in 1497, declared that 'neither St. Martin of Tours' (one of the most famous of all the medieval centres of pilgrimage), 'nor anything else which I have ever beheld, could be put into any comparison with it'.[3]

A document in the Abbey Muniment Room, unearthed by the Rev. H. F. Westlake, gives an extremely clear idea

[1] J. P. Neale and E. W. Brayley, *The History and Antiquities of the Abbey Church of St. Peter Westminster*, vol. ii, p. 67.
[2] Stanley, *Historical Memorials of Westminster Abbey*, 3rd edition, Appendix IV.
[3] Lethaby, *Westminster Abbey and the King's Craftsmen*, pp. 9–10.

of the furnishings and the general appearance of St. Edward's Chapel in early Tudor days. The document in question is entitled an Inventory drawn up by one 'Dan Wyllyam Grene, late keeper of Saynt Edwardys Shrine, and of the Relycs of Saynt Peter's Church of Westminster'. It appears that Grene vacated his post during the eleventh year of the reign of Henry VIII and, in accordance with custom, handed this written summary of the treasures in his keeping to his successor, Henry Wynchester.[1]

In addition to this valuable document we possess the lengthy inventory drawn up some twenty years later at the tragic moment of the Suppression, which throws still further light upon this fascinating subject.[2]

The two documents, although divided from each other by only twenty years of time, are not wholly identical. Changes of a minor description would doubtless always be taking place in so great a church. It must be remembered, too, that an onslaught was made upon the Shrine nearly four years before the final collapse of the convent. It is more than probable, therefore, that a good many of the furnishings disappeared during the outrage of 1536, and hence would find no place in the Suppression Inventory of 1540.

The earlier of the two documents states that the great centre piece of the chapel, 'the fair goodly shrine of St. Edward in marble', possessed certain special hangings, the nature and character of which are loosely indicated. The descriptions given by Dan Wyllyam Grene of these 'valaunces' which were suspended on either side could hardly be briefer; but they plainly indicate magnificence, e.g. a valaunce of 'blue velvet embroidered with flowers of gold with the image of St. Edward and St. John Evangelist';

---

[1] Westlake, *Westminster Abbey*, vol. ii, pp. 504, 505.
[2] *Transactions of the London and Middlesex Archaeological Society*, Old Series, vol. iv, pp. 313–64.

'blue damask with ostrich feathers', and 'crimson baw-dekyn embroidered with blue garters and flowers of gold'. Mention is made also of a cloth of immense historical interest, being 'the gift of St. Edward which hung about the Shrine'. Above, probably at the west end, was suspended 'a crest of timber and bron gold', the gift of Dan Thomas Lyons.

For some unexplained reason two of the seven Royal Tombs surrounding the Shrine, those of 'King Edward with the Long Shanks' and Richard II, seem to have been accorded special treatment in the matter of hangings. The latter, for instance, possessed 'a canvas cloth stained black with a White Heart'. No allusion is made to any hangings for the remaining five tombs.

Careful arrangements were made for the regular exhibition of the Relics. Four stools standing on Turkey carpets were provided on which they were placed on official occasions. They were protected from irreverent handling by a chain of iron; and a cloth was also provided 'stained with the Twelve Apostles to hang about them'.

The altar at the west end of the Shrine was surrounded by riddels or curtains, eight sets in all, which were changed almost as frequently as the frontals, with the colours of which they harmonized. The beauty and magnificence of many, perhaps all, of these fabrics can hardly be doubted, judging by such descriptions as 'blue with branches of white and birds of gold', 'red bawdekyn diaper with leaves of gold', and 'red, the ground with branches and honeysuckles of green velvet and flowers of gold'.

Carpets, of which several are mentioned, were spread in front of the altar, which was flanked by the two twisted columns supporting the images of St. John the Evangelist and St. Edward the Confessor. During the season of Lent these figures were covered with white cloths.

Numerous sets of vestments for the officiating priest;

several candlesticks, including a pair of standards of latten; cushions of cloth of gold and other rich materials; a silver-gilt chalice weighing fourteen ounces, and a variety of other ornaments, indicate that the Chapel of St. Edward had been furnished down to the last details in a manner sumptuous beyond words.

Lamps and candles, too, would be twinkling in all directions, conveying an indescribable sense of mystery. The words of Professor Lethaby can surely be no exaggeration. 'The splendour and associations of the place, the royalty, relics, and rites, the still effigies of the dead, the polished surfaces of marble shafts and mosaic floor reflecting the lights, must have made a strange, hypnotizing impression on the minds of those admitted to "experience it".'[1]

Alas, of all this magnificence the mutilated substructure of the Shrine and the Royal Tombs alone remain!

## 8. THE DESTRUCTION OF THE SHRINE

Dan Wyllyam Grene completed his inventory and handed over the contents of St. Edward's Chapel to his successor in 1520. In less than twenty years the awful tempest of the sixteenth century broke. It lasted for the next twenty-five years and more. By the time the last act in the shameful drama had been concluded the Church of Westminster had been reduced almost to a bare shell. Of its medieval wealth and glory only the merest shadow remained.

It was in July 1536 that the first blow fell. A general order was issued by Thomas Cromwell in which the removal of all shrines, relics, and images was straitly enjoined. The command could hardly have been couched in more stringent terms. It dealt a blow at the very heart of medieval Westminster. Whatever greatness of destiny the future might hold in store for the Abbey, a child could

[1] Lethaby, *Westminster Abbey Re-examined*, p. 282.

hardly fail to realize that with the disappearance of the Shrine of St. Edward and the hallowed remains preserved therein, the whole life and worship of the place, as understood by the men of that day, was bound to be completely revolutionized.

Sweeping though the command was, Abbot Benson and his colleagues lost no time in rendering their compliance. Possibly they were actuated by motives of policy, under the belief that a ready obedience might, perchance, secure the convent against future depredations. It was a vain hope.

The golden feretory was seized and presumably melted down in order to meet the demands of the rapacious King, while the body of the saint was reinterred, either in the floor of the chapel or in some other part of the church.

What was the fate of the huge tumba or substructure? The subject has given rise to no small amount of speculation. It is one of the many problems connected with Westminster Abbey still awaiting solution.

It was the original opinion of Sir Gilbert Scott that 'the marble substructure was only taken down far enough to allow of the removal of the body, as its parts have been displaced in refixing as far down as that but no further'.[1]

Towards the close of his long tenure of the office of Surveyor, however, Scott completely went back upon this statement: 'The fact has been ascertained', he wrote, 'that the whole of the Shrine (basis) had been taken down and rebuilt, and that even the steps had been reset and misplaced, the marks worn by the pilgrims' knees—still very distinguishable—being quite out of their proper places.'[2] Scott vouchsafed no reasons for this change of front, but his theory has not lacked support. His penultimate successor in the post of Surveyor, the late Mr. J. T. Micklethwaite, a noted archaeologist, also main-

[1] Scott, *Gleanings from Westminster Abbey*, p. 59.
[2] Scott, *Personal and Professional Recollections*, p. 153.

tained that the Shrine had undergone complete demolition, that it was laid low even to the ground, and that the
body of the Confessor was reinterred in a grave dug on
this site.[1]

On the other hand, Professor Lethaby in more recent
years has made the extremely apposite comment that the
immense expenditure of time and money required to
effect the total demolition of the substructure was calculated to make the authorities think once, twice, and three
times over before they embarked upon such a prodigious
undertaking.[2] The cupidity of Henry VIII and the so-
called churchmen who surrounded him, if not wholly
appeased, was doubtless highly gratified by the seizure of
the costly feretory. The cultus of St. Edward the Confessor had been abruptly terminated. His body had been
reinterred in some relatively obscure position. How much,
if anything, then, would be gained by laying violent hands
upon the tumba? It was not calculated to add much to the
contents of their pockets. With the disappearance of the
golden ark and the body, the Shrine had become evacu-
ated of almost all meaning. Why not, then, let well alone?

The subject is intensely interesting; but it is unlikely
that it will ever be cleared up.

The immediate fate of the altar at the west end of the
Shrine is also uncertain. Such evidence as we possess
indicates that it continued to be used for the celebration
of mass for several years longer, down to the Dissolution
at least, and probably until the Edwardian period of the
Reformation had commenced. The list of vestments and
other ornaments which, according to the Suppression Inventory of 1540, were set apart for use in St. Edward's
Chapel, clearly points in this direction.

It would have been a brief respite, however, a few years
at the most, before the hammer of destruction descended

---

[1] Society of Antiquaries, *Proceedings*, 2nd Series, vol. xv, p. 413.
[2] Lethaby, *Westminster Abbey Re-examined*, p. 266.

and the altar came to be involved in the same cruel fate as the feretory. During the greater part of the dreary Edwardian days the appearance of the chapel must have suggested the very abomination of desolation.

For generation after generation had St. Edward's Shrine stood there unimpaired. Changes had been made from time to time, but only with the object of enhancing its beauty. Not until the sixteenth century was that beauty reduced by one iota. The tragic overthrow of the Shrine must have brought sadness to many a heart, while the artistic loss inflicted upon the nation at large was incalculable.

## 9. THE MARIAN RESTORATION OF THE SHRINE

Mary Tudor ascended the throne on the sixth day of July 1553. She lost no time in directing her attention to the Abbey, where she must have found abundant scope for her energy. The conditions prevailing within its precincts were ill calculated to give satisfaction either to her or any one else.

The Collegiate Church brought into being by her father had scarcely emerged from the experimental stage and so far had done little to justify itself. At its head was Richard Cox, a Protestant of the most unpleasant type. He had succeeded Richard Benson, the erstwhile Abbot, who had in 1540 undergone a metamorphosis into a Dean.

The thirteen years covered by the rule of these men, the two first to occupy the great position of Dean of Westminster, had been a time of utter degradation. Immense portions of the conventual buildings had been ruthlessly destroyed, while the Abbey Church itself had been despoiled of the greater portion of its treasures. It was not to be expected that Mary would tolerate such a scandalous state of things a day longer than she could help.

Vigorous steps were quickly taken. Cox, by reason of

MAVSOLEVM Sive FERETRVM S⁰. EDVARDI CONFESSORIS REGIS ANGLIÆ.

Marmor Porphyrico & Serpentino, Opereque insuper musivo eleantissime ornatum uti hodie in Ecclesia Westmonasteriensi conspicitur.
Sumptibus Societatis Antiquariæ Londinensis. MDCCLXXIV.

J. Talman. delineavit.                                                                      G. Vertue. Sculp.

OMNIBVS INSIGNIS:  VIRTVTVM : LAVDIBVS:  HEROS: SANCTVS EDWAR  DVS 48

# THE SHRINE OF ST. EDWARD THE CONFESSOR

his complicity with Lady Jane Grey's party, immediately
fell beneath the Queen's ban. He was deprived of his stall.
Shaking the dust of this country off his feet, he found a con-
genial resting-place in one of those centres of continental
Protestantism which had given themselves over to the
whole-hearted furtherance of the Reformation.

Nine of the Prebendaries of reforming tendencies,
among them Grindal, a future Primate, and Nowell, subsequently Dean of St. Paul's, were deprived a few months
later. The other three conformed, for which act they were
rewarded in a later age by the addition of the word 'turn-
coat' to their names in the Chapter Book! The way was
now clear for a sweeping reversion to the former régime,
an object upon which Mary had set her heart.

Unfortunately, the Queen was ill-advised in the carrying out of her policy, notably in the selection of the chief
agent. Hugh Weston, whom she now summoned to suc-
ceed Cox in the Dean's stall, was a man of execrable
character. He soon manifested his utter unfitness to
govern the Collegiate body, and in a short time succeeded
in creating trouble in every direction.

All this, belongs, however, to another story. We are
here only concerned with the Confessor's Chapel, which
before long began to exhibit outward and visible signs of
change. The commencement of the year 1555 was
marked by the re-establishment of the altar, which event
took place, very appropriately, on the anniversary of the
Confessor's death. 'Item, the v day of Januarie was Sent
Edwardes Day, and there was sett up the scrynne at West-
mynster, and the aulter with dyvers juelles that the quene
sent thether.'[1]

An auspicious opening of the New Year perhaps, but it
was not altogether devoid of sadness. Mary's gift of
'dyvers juelles' indicates the plunder and ruin which had

---

[1] *Chronicle of the Grey Friars of London,* quoted in Scott, *Gleanings from
Westminster Abbey,* p. 140.

taken place. To regain the splendour of former times was a far distant and almost impossible ideal. Queen and Chapter alike were situated in sadly straitened circumstances. The gathering up of such few fragments as remained represented the full extent of their capacity.

Such was the first step in the restoration of St. Edward's Chapel to some measure of its original comeliness. Another two years and more then passed away, during which a far-reaching scheme took shape in the mind of the Queen, viz. the restoration and re-endowment of the historic monastery at Westminster. The Collegiate Church had fallen into such evil odour that strong action was demanded. Weston had proved an utterly incompetent head, and scandal had become busy with his name. At length, towards the close of the year 1556, Mary felt herself in a position to act. Her father's Collegiate Church was dissolved after its brief and unedifying career of sixteen years. Weston was got rid of by the offer (or bribe) of further preferment, a method of dealing with failures which has been of immense convenience to the powers that be in all generations. The Deanery of Windsor was placed in his unworthy hands, though he only retained it a short time. His evil life compelled Cardinal Pole to take summary proceedings.

The places of the twelve Prebendaries who disappeared after the last Chapter Meeting, on September 25th, 1556, were now filled by a small body of fourteen Benedictine monks who had been recruited not without difficulty.

At the head of the re-established monastery the Queen placed her own Confessor, John Howman of Feckenham, Dean of St. Paul's, one of the few attractive characters in a depressing epoch. A learned scholar, an admirable preacher, a man of genuinely tolerant disposition, he earned respect wherever he went. He had few, if any, enemies, a fact which speaks volumes in those exacerbated times.

Feckenham entered upon the duties of Abbot on the Eve of St. Clement (November 22nd) 1556, and was consecrated a few days later. He little realized that his public career would reach an untimely end in less than three years. But his memory will remain ever green at the Abbey. Had it not been for his zeal and enthusiasm, it is unlikely that posterity would ever have gazed upon St. Edward's Shrine, the restoration of which was dear above all things to his heart.

The Abbot lost no time in getting to work. At the end of three months all was in train for the third Translation of St. Edward, the altar and shrine having been replaced, as we have seen, two years before.

Despite the Lenten season, the ceremony took place on March 20th, 1557. Judging by Machyn's account, it must have been an event of signal pomp and splendour.

'The xx day of Marche was taken up at Westminster against with a honderyd lights, Kyng Edward the Confessor in the sem plase where ys shryne was, and ytt shalle be sett up agayne as fast as my Lord Abbot can have ytt done, for ytt was a godly shyte to have seen yt, how reverently he was cared from the plasses that he was taken up wher he was led when that the abbay was spoiled and robyd; and so he was cared and goodly syngyng and sensyng as has bene sene and masse song.'[1]

It must have been a great occasion for Feckenham and his handful of monks; but it was one of the last happy days they were destined to enjoy.

By this time the restoration of St. Edward's Shrine must have been on the high road to completion. A month later a visit was paid to the Abbot by the Duke of Muscovy, who, after dinner, was specially conducted to the east end of the church 'to se sant Edward shryne new set up'.[2]

Feckenham's work of restoration was characterized by

[1] Diary of Henry Machyn, Mar. 21, 1557. Quoted in Scott, *Gleanings from Westminster Abbey*, p. 140.
[2] Diary of Henry Machyn, Apr. 21, 1557.

one important departure. The golden feretory in which the Saint's remains had been housed for so many years having disappeared, it was decided to utilize the substructure itself as a burial place and reinter the Saint's coffin therein. Accordingly, a cavity was hollowed out of the solid masonry, seven feet nine inches in length, two feet ten inches in width, and three and a half feet in depth.[1] It must have been an arduous undertaking. Here then, just over twenty years after the monstrous sacrilege of July 1536, were the remains of St. Edward laid to rest and surrounded once more by some measure of the dignity which they had enjoyed ever since the beginning of the year 1066.

At the same time considerable alterations were made by Feckenham in the entablature or upper portion of the substructure, necessitated, doubtless, by this important change in the position of the coffin.

Originally the marble substructure had been surmounted by a flat cornice, along the outer face of which ran the inscription. A slab somewhat narrower and shorter lay upon it, forming a kind of step upon which coffin and feretory immediately rested. The slab was now lengthened and widened, to serve as a frieze, while about it Feckenham erected a new moulded cornice projecting several inches over the substructure. The cornice does not contain the slightest trace of ancient work. Had such been available, the Abbot would almost certainly have utilized it.

These developments brought, not unnaturally, certain consequences in their train. Among other things, they reacted most unfortunately upon the interesting Latin inscription in letters of blue glass mosaic placed here by the thirteenth-century builders of the Shrine. It received scant mercy at the hands of the Abbot, who did not hesitate to cover it with plaster! It is possible that Feckenham, who was obviously actuated throughout by the best of

[1] Society of Antiquaries, *Proceedings*, 1915–16, p. 76.

motives, could not help himself. He may have found the letters of the inscription damaged beyond repair. It is only fair to give him the benefit of the doubt. None the less his action was regrettable.

The Abbot cannot, however, escape the severe condemnation of posterity for his outrageous substitution of an entirely new inscription. The historical reference to 'Peter the Roman Citizen' was abandoned: and, likewise, the delightful termination, 'Reader, if thou wouldst know how it was, it was because Henry was the saint's friend'. Apparently the original founder of the Shrine counted for little or nothing in the Abbot's eyes, for the new inscription, presumably the composition of Feckenham himself, is devoid of any allusion to Henry III and is confined to a simple eulogy of the Confessor terminating with Feckenham's own monogram. The lettering consists of gilt capitals on a dark ground. It commences on the south side and runs as follows:

'Omnibus Insignis: Virtutum Laudibus: Heros: Sanctus, Edvardus, Confessor, Rex Venerandus: Quinto Die Jan. Moriens 1065. Super Aethera: Scandit, Sursum Corda. I. F.'

Time has dealt hardly with Feckenham's inscription. It was scarcely to be expected that a material so fragile as plaster would remain intact for an indefinite period. A considerable portion has disappeared, but the missing words have providentially been preserved by Widmore.[1] Very probably they were still intact when he wrote his history in the middle of the eighteenth century. At any rate, his authority cannot possibly be challenged.[2]

During the troublous times of destruction the substructure of the Shrine had suffered unspeakable injury. The whole of the costly and elaborate mosaic work with which its sides were lined in the thirteenth century must have perished. Perhaps it had been wantonly picked off. The

---

[1] See p. 49.
[2] Widmore, *History of the Church of St. Peter, Westminster*, p. 75.

temptation to relic hunters, all and sundry, to help themselves to pieces of the desecrated and rifled tomb would obviously be considerable. Years of neglect, following on the rough handling of 1536, would more than account for all this damage.

To replace this precious material was a task beyond the power of the plucky Abbot, hampered as he was in every direction. He did the best he could, but it was an unsatisfactory makeshift. He filled the empty spaces from which the mosaic had disappeared with patches of plaster, gilded and painted over with a pattern suggestive of mosaic work.

Feckenham next directed his attention to the upper and most important member of the Shrine. The golden ark was a thing of the past. To replace that great mass of jewelled magnificence was a sheer impossibility. Queen and Abbot would gladly have denied themselves to the last farthing if by so doing they could have restored the former glory, but they were only too well aware that it was the day of small things, and that with their limited resources such an idea was but an idle dream. Still, something had to be done. To leave the remains of St. Edward lying in the midst of the great tumba without any semblance of protection was clearly impossible.

Such then was the origin of the existing wooden top, which stands immediately over the coffin. It is a compromise, no doubt, due to the difficulties of the times; but a compromise by no means devoid of merit. Its authors would never have claimed that it could bear comparison for one moment with its amazing predecessor; but, before it came to suffer injury, it must have presented an extremely dignified appearance. Probably the work of foreign craftsmen, it is possessed of great interest as being one of the earliest woodwork examples in this country of Italian Renaissance design.[1]

[1] Society of Antiquaries, *Proceedings*, 2nd Series, vol. xv, p. 413.

This wooden feretory mainly consists of wainscot oak. It is divided into two stories of unequal dimensions, each possessing its own entablature. On either side of the lower story are six semicircular arches with panels, separated from each other by pilasters of the Ionic Order. At the east end are three similar arches, and at the west a wider arch flanked by coupled pilasters. The upper story consists of four arches on either side and two at each end, separated by coupled pilasters of the Corinthian Order. The whole structure was originally surmounted by a gabled roof. The pilasters were decorated with panels encrusted with small squares and lozenges of glass mosaic. In the spandrels were larger panels of glass backed with paint so as to suggest green porphyry. This inlay of glass, variously coloured, was intended no doubt to suggest in some faint measure the brilliant enrichments of the original Shrine.

After the lapse of more than three and a half centuries this wooden top lacks neither beauty nor historical interest. At the outset it must have been a delightful piece of work, its outlines being perhaps reminiscent of its more splendid predecessor.

Since that time the feretory has suffered deplorable maltreatment. The gabled roof has wholly disappeared, likewise a considerable portion of the entablatures of both stories. None the less, it testifies abundantly to the enthusiasm of the pious Abbot.

The altar at the west end of the Shrine, as already stated, had been restored to use two years earlier, but it is probable that the great slab which to-day forms the retable was set up by Feckenham. Like everything else, it has suffered severely, for the lozenges of porphyry which formed its principal decoration have for the most part disappeared. It has generally been supposed that this slab formed the original reredos of St. Edward's Altar, though for some unexplained reason Feckenham thought fit to raise it, thus making a slight alteration in its position. To-day it is partly supported by two twisted columns, whereas in former times it must have rested directly upon the mensa.

There is an interesting tradition, however, that the retable was brought by Feckenham from the neighbouring Chapel of St. Edmund and that it never belonged to the original structure of the Shrine at all. The tradition is incapable either of proof or of disproof; but it may quite likely be correct.[1]

When Feckenham entered upon his duties as Abbot, he found himself confronted by an utterly chaotic state of affairs. In his work of restoration, it is fully conceivable that he was compelled to avail himself of the first materials which came to his hand without giving overmuch heed to the function they originally fulfilled. There is a certain suggestion of haste, moreover, in his work. Very possibly he realized that he was fighting against time, and he therefore set himself to utilize his brief opportunity to the full. Thus in barely twenty-two months he repaired the frieze, built the new cornice, applied an elaborate treatment of plaster work to the substructure, filled up a quantity of empty matrices, painted the new inscription and the imitation mosaic panels, and finally crowned his work with the wooden feretory.

A hasty and clumsy performance perhaps, but it would be ungracious to criticize it. Had it not been for the energy of Feckenham, the Shrine of St. Edward the Confessor would have remained neglected indefinitely, perhaps for ever. The fact that the last king of the old Saxon line has been lying here undisturbed, ever since the reign of Mary Tudor, has undoubtedly proved the salvation of a mutilated but still beautiful work of art. The latter, no longer the centre of a cult of widespread renown, passed into the category of royal tombs; and as such, secured for

[1] Westlake, *The Story of Westminster Abbey*, p. 171.

itself such slight modicum of respect and immunity from interference, as subsequent generations thought fit to accord to the resting-places of the Plantagenets, by which it was surrounded.

The body of St. Candida, like that of St. Edward the Confessor, is believed still to rest in its original Shrine at Whitchurch Canonicorum, but save for this solitary and not very prominent exception, the Abbey stands in this respect unique among the Churches of England,[1] an achievement due in the main to one man alone.

In the long roll of founders and benefactors of the Church of Westminster, a place in the very first rank must surely be assigned to the name of John of Feckenham, whose zeal for the honour of God's house stands without a rival.

## 10. THE SHRINE IN POST-REFORMATION TIMES

The melancholy reign of Mary Tudor came to an end on the seventeenth day of November 1558, and the nation breathed a sigh of relief. It fell to the lot of Feckenham to lay the poor, broken-hearted woman in her last resting-place, and to preach a funeral sermon on the words 'I praised the dead more than the living'. Filled with melancholy anticipations for the future, it also included an eloquent eulogy upon the 'innocent and unspotted Queen'.[2]

It must have been a sad time for the Abbot. He of all people was alive to the good qualities possessed by the tragic figure which had just passed away. It must have seemed to him that the heavens and the earth were shaking. He knew only too well that much which he himself held dear was threatened to its foundations.

For the moment, however, things continued at the Abbey much as usual. Elizabeth was crowned on January 15th, 1559, under the old rite, save that a portion was

---

[1] *Archaeological Journal*, vol. lxiv, p. 119.
[2] Fuller's *Church History*, A.D. 1558.

rendered in English. Feckenham took the prominent
part in the ceremonial assigned by custom to the Abbot of
Westminster, but it must have been a strange occasion.
Cardinal Pole was dead, and a large proportion of the
dioceses were devoid of their chief pastors. An outbreak
of the plague had just taken place and the episcopal bench
had suffered severely. Heath, the northern Primate, declined to attend, and his lead was followed by all the sur-
viving bishops save one, Oglethorpe of Carlisle. No other
Coronation either before or since has ever witnessed the
strange spectacle of an episcopate reduced to a state of
attenuation bordering upon zero.

Parliament met ten days later, and Feckenham, as
Abbot of Westminster, took his seat in the Upper House
with the rest of the Peers Spiritual. Never since that date
has the House of Lords numbered a mitred Abbot among
its members. He made a brilliant speech on behalf of the
old order, but the tide was running strongly against him.[1]
The tokens of impending change were only too obvious.
Under such auspices did the year 1559 open, the saddest,
in all probability, that he had ever known.

Meanwhile, rumour was busy with the Abbot's name.
It was confidently asserted that the new Queen had designed him to be Pole's successor at Lambeth, a desire
which was fully intelligible. Her personal feelings were
strongly conservative, and she could hardly have made a
wiser choice among the ecclesiastics of the right. Feckenham was universally respected, both for his ability, and
his moderation. Moreover, personal ties of no common
order existed between the Queen and himself. There is
reason for thinking that she owed her life to his influence
during those dark days when, a prisoner in the Tower, she
lay at her sister's mercy. Again, had he not quite recently
stood beside her at the great moment of her Sacring, when
practically the whole of the Anglican episcopate had

[1] Strype's *Annals*, vol. ii, p. 438, App. IX.

absented themselves? But the tempting offer, if ever made, only met with a firm refusal. The Abbot remained adamant.[1]

Deprivation speedily and almost necessarily ensued, for the monastery officially came to an end on July 10th, 1559. The miserable business was followed by long years of enforced idleness as a State prisoner, a heavy trial for this active-minded man, marked at times by needless rigour. No one could ever have said his *Nunc dimittis* with a gladder heart than did John of Feckenham a quarter of a century later in Wisbech Castle.

The little company of Benedictines having been dispersed, the Queen decided to follow her father's example and re-establish the Collegiate Church; but it was a lengthy proceeding. For eleven months after the overthrow of the monastery and the deprivation of Feckenham the Abbey remained without any staff at all. Not until May 12th, 1560, was the charter of foundation signed by the Queen; and then upwards of a month elapsed before the Archbishop of Canterbury and other Commissioners were authorized to place the Dean, William Bill, in possession of the new Royal College of St. Peter in Westminster.

On June 30th, 1560, the twelve new Prebendaries were installed, and before long the hand of one of these ecclesiastics, John Hardyman, fell heavily upon the Abbey.[2]

It must have been at this dismal moment that St. Edward's Chapel once more suffered desecration. The actual Shrine escaped, it is true, but the altar, together with Mary's pathetic gift of 'dyvers juelles', disappeared for ever. No specific evidence exists as to the date of its destruction; but it is obvious that a chapel of such prominence and importance was unlikely to escape the iconoclastic attentions of so ruthless a miscreant as Hardyman.

[1] Fuller's *Church History*, vol. ix, pp. 6, 8, 38.
[2] Vol. i, p. 56. It is exasperating to think that, although John Hardyman received well merited punishment, his offences were condoned the following year by the offer of a stall at Chester!

Since that date the Shrine has experienced no small measure of neglect and a certain amount of damage; but broadly speaking, its general appearance, save for the addition of the modern altar and its furniture, must be very much the same to-day as it was in 1559.

Despite the loss of the altar, various old traditions associated with this chapel continued to survive. From time immemorial it had been customary at the conclusion of the great solemnity of the Coronation to deposit at the Altar of St. Edward certain pieces of the Regalia, together with the cope, the dalmatic, the stole, and the alb with which the Sovereign is invested during the rite. No attempt was made to alter, much less abolish, this time-honoured ceremonial. A wooden table was erected for the occasion at the west end of the Shrine, designated in the rubrics of one Coronation Order after another, St. Edward's Altar. Here, or possibly at the High Altar, at the well-ordered Coronation of Charles I, Laud (now become Bishop of St. David's, but still retaining his prebendal stall at the Abbey), 'hallowed the cream' for the unction in the early morning before the ceremony.

In subsequent generations a massive wooden table of seventeenth-century date seems to have occupied this time-honoured spot. According to Abbey tradition, it was utilized during the period of the Commonwealth, by being placed 'tablewise', in the middle of the choir, in place of the overthrown and desecrated High Altar. This fine piece of furniture now stands in the Jericho Parlour.

The feeling of veneration for this once famous object of pilgrimage never wholly died out. According to a curious statement made by Brayley, it was customary down to the time of the French Revolution to collect the sweepings of the floor all round the Shrine and then transmit these fragments of sacred dirt to Spain and Portugal![1]

[1] J. P. Neale and E. W. Brayley, *The History and Antiquities of the Abbey Church of St. Peter, Westminster*, vol. ii, p. 69 note.

On the other hand, it can hardly be claimed that the official guardians of the Shrine evinced any overwhelming zeal for the well-being of the precious treasure entrusted to their keeping. Irreparable damage was inflicted upon the feretory by the workmen during the preparations for James II's Coronation; indeed, the negligence of the Dean and Chapter of that day, who seem to have allowed all and sundry to clamber over the Shrine at will, fills our twentieth-century minds with combined amazement and resentment. The destruction of part of the inscription[1] during the reign of George II is another illustration of their neglect.

A kind of blindness seemed to have settled down upon the public mind where the glories of pre-Reformation art were concerned, and the opinion expressed by John Ralph may be taken as fairly characteristic of the times.

'The enclosure behind the altar commonly known by the name of St. Edward's Chapel has nothing remarkable in it, but certain Gothique antiquities, which are made sacred by tradition only and serve to excite a stupid admiration in the vulgar.'[2]

It is wellnigh heart-breaking to read some of the early nineteenth-century descriptions of this noble Shrine, 'once the glory of England, but now neglected, defaced and much abused':[3] or again, 'a few hardly perceptible traces of its former splendour exist. Only two of its spiral pillars remain, the western and a capital at the east. The wooden Ionic top is much broken and covered with dust. The mosaic is picked away in almost every part within reach.'[4] This miserable state of things is fully confirmed by another contemporaneous statement to the effect that 'its recesses once resplendent with images now hold but broken gallipots and drawing boards of the artist'.[5]

[1] Lethaby, *Westminster Abbey and the King's Craftsmen*, pp. 321-2.
[2] John Ralph, *Critical Review of Public Buildings, in London and Westminster*, p. 86.    [3] Malcolm, *Londinium Redivivum*, p. 94.
[4] Allen, *History of London*, vol. v, p. 59.
[5] *Handbook to Westminster Abbey*, p. 63.

Mercifully, the nineteenth century which opened so inauspiciously was destined to witness the termination of long generations of neglect. A new era was about to open, which, whatever its shortcomings, would be characterized by a sounder knowledge, and a more reverential attitude towards this wonderful monument of the past, than had been known since the days of John of Feckenham.

## 11. THE BURGLARY

In the year 1683 there appeared one of the early guide books of Westminster Abbey entitled *Monumenta West-monasteriana*.

This somewhat inaccurate volume was written by a certain Henry Keepe *alias* Young. The known facts of his life are neither numerous nor important. He was a member of the Inner Temple. He was not unknown as an author, and he took the opportunity of James II's accession to announce his perversion to the Roman faith.

Keepe states that while engaged in collecting materials for his work he managed one day to climb on to St. Edward's Shrine, 'by the help of a ladder', and seized the opportunity to examine the royal coffin. 'I have seen a large chest or coffin,' he wrote, 'made of sound, firm and strong wood, bound about with strong bands of Iron, lying about the midst of the inside of this Shrine, where I suppose, the body of the pious King may still be conserved.'[1]

Two years after the publication of Keepe's guide book there took place, on April 23rd, 1685, the Coronation of James II. Not for the first, nor yet for the last time did the interior of the great church suffer rough treatment at the hands of the workmen engaged upon the preparations for this great event. On this occasion the Shrine of St. Edward, in particular, fell a victim to the culpable carelessness

[1] Keepe, *Monumenta Westmonasteriana*, p. 138.

of these gentry. It was the custom at that time when arranging St. Edward's Chapel as a retiring chamber for the King and Queen, to cover it over with a roof, which fact probably accounts for much of the damage suffered by the Royal Tombs.[1] At the nineteenth-century Coronations and at the Golden Jubilee Service of 1887 this irreverence reached its zenith, when the entire east end was converted into a gallery occupied by musicians or spectators, or both.

It would seem that during the preparations for James II's Coronation a heavy plank or pole fell directly upon the fragile woodwork of Abbot Feckenham's substitute for the golden feretory. The ridge of its gabled roof was smashed in, and an irreparable disaster was the result. Nor was this all. The coffin containing the Confessor's remains, a few feet beneath the roof, shared in the injury, and to a serious extent, for a breach of some dimensions was made in its upper surface.

It did not require any vast amount of intelligence to realize that with the ridge of the feretory once broken in, a first-rate view could easily be obtained of the interior of Feckenham's woodwork by any one who cared to take the trouble to follow Keepe's example and clamber on to the top of the substructure. It is possible, too, that the top may have been temporarily removed, which would simplify matters still further. Such evidently was the view taken by one of the Lay-Vicars, Charles Taylor by name, a somewhat inquisitive person, who appears to have possessed an antiquarian turn of mind even in those days of limited historical interest.

'During the eighteen years I have belonged to the choir of the church,' he wrote, 'it was a common tradition among us that therein was deposited the body or remains of the holy King Edward the Confessor.'[2]

[1] *Gentleman's Magazine*, 1817, p. 33.
[2] This and certain other quotations in this chapter are taken from Taylor's pamphlet alluded to on p. 96.

Fired, then, by his antiquarian enthusiasm Taylor, a few weeks after the Coronation, viz. on 'St. Barnaby's Day between eleven and twelve o'clock', embarked upon a tour of discovery together with two friends. His examination was exhaustive to a degree. He soon discovered the existence of a hole in the coffin 'about six inches long and four inches broad'. He then had the barefaced audacity to insert his hand, which at once came into contact with a quantity of bones. Undeterred by this gruesome experience, he continued to poke about and, to quote his own words, 'turning the bones which I felt there drew from underneath the shoulder bones a Crucifix richly adorned and enamelled, and a Gold Chain of twenty-four inches long the which I immediately showed to my friends, they being as much surprised and as much admired the same as myself.'

The discovery was not, however, without its embarrassments, as Taylor realized:

'I was afraid to take them away with me till such time as I had acquainted the Dean as the governor and chief Director of our Church; and thereupon I put them into the coffin again with a full resolution to inform him.'

The Dean could nowhere be found, and so,

'fearing that this holy treasure might be taken thence by some other persons, and so concealed by converting it to their own use, I went (about two or three hours after) to one of the Quire, who immediately accompanied me back to the monument, and from whence I again drew the aforesaid Crucifix and chain, who beheld them with admiration. . . .

'At the time, when I took them out of the coffin, the aforesaid cross and chain, I drew the Head to the hole, and view'd it, being very sound and firm, with the upper and nether jaws whole and full of teeth, with a list of gold above an inch broad in the nature of a Coronet, surrounding the Temples; there was also in the coffin white linnen, and gold colour'd flower'd silk, that looked indifferent fresh, but the least stress put thereto shewed it was well nigh perish't. There were all his Bones, and much dust likewise, all which I left as I found taking only thence along with me the Crucifix and the Gold Chain.'

Three weeks and five days passed by. It would seem that the thief was somewhat appalled by these happenings as well he might be. Accordingly, he retained the rifled treasures in his possession, on the advice of his friend, and apparently kept his own counsel, presumably for fear of possible consequences.

At length he plucked up his courage. The matter was submitted to his former chief, John Dolben, recently promoted to the Archbishopric of York, under whom Taylor had served at the Abbey for a great number of years. The northern Primate brought the latter into touch first with Archbishop Sancroft, who inspected the treasures and 'look'd upon 'em as great pieces of antiquity', and then with Sir William Dugdale. By degrees these events reached the ears of the King.

An interview followed on July 6th, and Taylor found himself conducted to the royal presence by Dean Sprat; 'and being no sooner introduced into his Majesty's closet (where I had the honour to Kiss his Royal hand) but upon my knees I delivered them with my own hands to him, which his most Sacred Majesty was pleased to accept with much satisfaction.'

Taylor then retired, leaving the treasures 'safe as being now in his Royal possession'.[1]

The conduct of James II left a good deal to be desired, though he did at least take effectual steps to ensure the future safety of the Confessor's remains. A 'new strong wooden coffin' in which to enclose the old, broken one was provided by the royal command, each plank being 'of an extraordinary strength and goodness, two inches thick and cramped together with large iron wedges, where it now remains as a testimony of his pious care, that no abuse might be offered to the sacred ashes therein reposited'.

---

[1] By what was regarded as a happy coincidence the relics were discovered on the day of Monmouth's landing and given to the King on the day of his victory at Sedgemoor.

The bill for these various pieces of work has been discovered in the Accounts of the Paymaster of Works and Buildings.

'Paid to Matthew Bankes for a large coffin by him made to enclose the body of Saint Edward the Confessor and setting it up in the place in the year 1685—6L. 2s. 8d. And to William Backe, Locksmith for large hinges and rivetts and 2 crossebars for the said coffin £2. 17. 7.'[1]

Thus any repetition of Taylor's exploits was rendered wholly impossible.

The King's 'pious care' did not, however, extend to the treasures so monstrously abstracted from the coffin. He evinced not the smallest hesitation about retaining the crucifix and chain in his own possession!

Here the matter ended for the time being; indeed, it might quite easily have been forgotten altogether, had not Taylor, with no small amount of nerve, ventured to record his burglarious proceeding about two years later in a short but sensational pamphlet. The latter appeared on February 6th, 1687, signed by 'Charles Taylour, Gent.' and is entitled 'A true and perfect narrative of the strange and unexpected finding the crucifix and gold chain of that pious prince, St Edward the King and Confessor, which was found after 620 years interment and presented to his most sacred majesty King James II'.

Taylor's literary efforts do not appear to have attracted the amount of attention which would naturally be expected. Perhaps this was hardly wonderful. Great events were going forward at that time in both Church and State. England was in the throes of a constitutional crisis, and the minds of all were concentrated upon subjects of the gravest possible character.

Later on, the rumour spread abroad that the pamphlet had been published under a pseudonym, and that the signature 'Charles Taylour' was but a disguise for the 'ingenious

[1] J. Timbs, *Curiosities of London*, p. 129.

Mr Keepe'. This statement has been repeated by almost all the Abbey historians, as well as by the *Dictionary of National Biography*. It is, however, a complete mistake. The Abbey records fully confirm Taylor's statement that he had been for many years a member of the choir. Keepe played more than one part in the course of his career; but at no time was he ever officially associated either with the choir or any other department of the Abbey. Thus we are clearly concerned with two different individuals.

Taylor's extremely discreditable story was received with considerable scepticism both at the time and subsequently. Thirty years later the well-known antiquary, John Talman, received the permission of the Dean and Chapter to make an examination of the coffin. He went, or thought he went, into the subject exhaustively. The results of his investigations were drawn up in a Report, presented to the Society of Antiquaries in 1722, in which he unhesitatingly rejected the story from beginning to end, basing his opinion upon 'the appearance of the coffin which appears to have been nowhere broken or new cased as Taylor represented'.

None of the later historians made any attempt to controvert Talman's opinion. Gough evidently had his doubts,[1] and in the great work of Neale and Brayley the writers have adopted an attitude of non-committal, not untinged with disbelief.[2]

None the less, Taylor's account of his sacrilegious exploits was absolutely true from beginning to end. Evidence was all the time in existence, though still unpublished, of such weight as to confirm it up to the hilt. Had this irrefutable testimony been brought to the light of day at that time, the opinions of Talman and others would have been completely demolished.

[1] Gough, *Sepulchral Monuments of Great Britain*, vol. ii, pp. 6–8.
[2] J. P. Neale and E. W. Brayley, *The History and Antiquities of the Abbey Church of St. Peter Westminster*, vol. ii, p. 71 note.

In the famous *Diary*, the first edition of which was not published till 1818, John Evelyn has recorded a conversation as having taken place in the Deanery at Winchester between himself and James II not long after the burglary, viz. on September 16th, 1685, during a royal visit to that city. The King spoke of 'the golden crosse and chaine taken out of the coffin of St. Edward the Confessor at Westminster by one of the singing men, who, as the scaffolds were taken down after his Maty's coronation, espying a hole in this tomb and something glisten, put his hand in and brought it to the Deane and he to the King'.[1]

Over and above this extremely weighty testimony, for Evelyn's name speaks for itself, further evidence was in existence of a still more powerful character, hidden away for a good century and a half in a succession of private libraries. It is a wonder that it managed to escape the wastepaper basket.

This second piece of evidence brings us into touch with that excellent man Symon Patrick, not the least eminent of the the later Caroline Divines. His authority is unquestionable.

Patrick was appointed to a prebendal stall at the Abbey in the year 1672. He at once took possession of 'a house (No. 1) new built in the little cloisters of Westminster Abbey'. To this peaceful abode he became devotedly attached. 'Here we enjoyed many happy days, and my wife thought it the sweetest part of our lives which we spent here.'[2] Like many other prominent ecclesiastics of that epoch, Patrick was a pluralist, combining his Westminster preferment with the Rectory of St. Paul, Covent Garden, and later with the Deanery of Peterborough. His connexion with the Abbey, for which his affection never waned, covered seventeen years. At the expiration of this time he was consecrated to the Bishopric of

---

[1] Evelyn's *Diary*, vol. ii, p. 177.
[2] Patrick, *Works*, vol. ix, p. 467.

in writing all this, that I have
pass'd by some things with out notice
which I now call to remembrance, &
shall here tho' out of the order of
time set them down as things
memorable.

When the workmen were making
Scaffolds in the Church of Westminster
for the Coronation of K. James, they
chanc'd to bore a hole into the
tomb of Edw: the Confessor. So that
they cou'd see the shroud wherein
his body was wrapt: which was a mixt
colour'd silk, very fresh. By this
they got a great deal of mony
from people who hearing of it
came to see it; & made the hole
wider & wider till they cou'd put
their head into the tomb. Which
one of the Virgers hearing of, went
& forbad them to suffer this, or threat:
=ned to have them turn'd out of their
work by Sr Chris: Wren. This made
them forbear to admit people to

A PAGE FROM THE DIARY OF SIMON PATRICK AND A
PORTION OF ST. EDWARD'S SHROUD

Chichester, whence he was shortly translated to Ely, dying there on May 31st, 1707.

Patrick must have been a man of extraordinary diligence. He has left behind him the record of a faithful parish priest, an exemplary bishop, an effective preacher, and a copious writer of theology, especially on its devotional side. Added to this, his life as one of the leading London clergy brought him into close touch with public affairs, notably in the stirring days immediately preceding the Revolution. Such was his renown for sagacity and moderation that Archbishop Sancroft was glad to avail himself of his counsel during the crisis produced by the issue of the Declaration of Indulgence. Patrick possessed antiquarian gifts, too, of no mean order. Having been asked to prepare for publication the monumental *History of the Church of Peterborough*, a manuscript compiled by Simon Gunton, one of the Prebendaries, he not only carried out this request, but finding Gunton's history erroneous in many respects, he 'made many additions to it, as large as the book itself, and corrected many mistakes in it'.[1]

In spite of these manifold preoccupations Patrick found time to write an *Autobiography* of some length, dealing more especially with that portion of his career which preceded his elevation to the episcopate.

A year before his death the old man took up his pen anew, in order to recall certain 'things memorable' which he had failed to record in their proper chronological sequence, when writing the first draft.

The *Autobiography* is a work of the most entertaining character, as fresh and readable as if it had been written yesterday. Incidentally it throws a good deal of light upon church life in the metropolis during the thirty years which followed the Restoration.

Strange to say, this interesting document remained

[1] Patrick, *Works*, vol. ix, p. 484.

unknown for several generations. Some time after Patrick's death it passed into the hands of the Ven. Samuel Knight, D.D., Archdeacon of Berks., the biographer of Colet and Erasmus, and one of the founders of the Society of Antiquaries. Knight started to write a life of the Bishop using the *Autobiography* as the groundwork. He died leaving his task unfinished, and it was not until 1839, one hundred and thirty-two years after Patrick's death, that the manuscript was at last given to the world in a small octavo volume. A second edition appeared nineteen years later, furnished with a quantity of valuable notes by the Rev. Alexander Taylor, Fellow of The Queen's College, Oxford.

Among the 'things memorable' which the old bishop made this special effort to record, on the eve of his departure from the world, were certain events which occurred in the year 1685, including the subject of this chapter. It would be a pity to relate it in any words save those of Patrick himself.

'When the workmen were making scaffolds in the church of Westminster for the coronation of King James, they chanced to bore a hole into the tomb of Edward the Confessor: so that they could see the shroud wherein his body was wrapped; which was a mixed coloured silk, very fresh. By this they got a great deal of money from people who hearing of it came to see it; and made the hole wider and wider, till they could put their hand into the tomb. Which one of the vergers hearing of, went and forbade them to suffer this, or threatened to have them turned out of their work by Sir Christopher Wren. This made them forbear to admit people to come into the chapel. But one Taylor, being a singing man in the church, prevailed with them one day to let him in with some friends of his to see the tomb; and he thrust his hand so far as to pull out the shroud, and together with it a crucifix hanging on a gold chain, weighing about ten guineas. This he brought to the chanter[1] of the church, who went immediately to search if he could find anything more, but could not, only several of his bones, and

---

[1] The Rev. Stephen Crespion, also Sub-Dean of the Chapel Royal and subsequently Prebendary of Bristol. The expression 'Chanter' signifies the Precentor.

particularly a thigh bone, which was very large. Then he carried the crucifix to the dean, the bishop of Rochester, who went with Taylor to the king, representing to him how honest he was in not concealing this treasure. His majesty was highly pleased with it, and pulled a crucifix out of his pocket, and showed it to them, telling them it was his late brother's. He immediately ordered Taylor fifty pounds which was paid him out of the privy purse. And he spake to Sir Christopher Wren to make up the coffin strongly again, which was only of elm, hooped with iron, very coarse and cloutery.'

The two accounts of the burglary by Patrick and Taylor do not agree in every detail. The former did not record this portion of his recollections until after the lapse of twenty-one busy years, while the latter was perhaps not disinclined to add a certain amount of embroidery when transmitting his own story to paper. Hence it is not difficult to account for such minor discrepancies as exist.

Patrick's evidence must be accepted, however, without hesitation. The testimony of a member of the Westminster Chapter actually on the spot would carry immense weight under any circumstances. Coupled with the high character and the known integrity of such a man as Patrick, himself an antiquary of no mean ability, it becomes absolutely conclusive, especially when supported by Evelyn's testimony.

In the second edition of the *Autobiography* the editor has added a further piece of most remarkable information. He states that he found a fragment of material rather less than an inch square pinned to the Bishop's manuscript. It appeared to be a woven fabric of black and yellow silk and had evidently formed part of the Confessor's shroud. The fact of the burglary is surely proved up to the hilt.

The story is possessed of immense interest, but none of the parties concerned cut very creditable figures. It was an age when Deans and Chapters possessed the laxest notions of their responsibilities as the official custodians of our great churches. The irreparable damage sustained by the mosaic pavement in front of the High Altar, twenty-five years later, forms a signal illustration of the lack of care characteristic of the times. Artistic and historical knowledge, so far as the wonders of pre-Reformation days were concerned, was at a low ebb in the England of the Restoration and the Revolution. The vast majority of people had little conception of its value.

On the other hand, the deplorable lack of reverence displayed by every one from the King downwards fills us with amazement. There can surely be no other word for such abominable proceedings than that of sacrilege. Whatever allowances may be made for Taylor, the conduct of James II when he helped himself to the contents of his predecessor's tomb was reprehensible to a degree. Neither, again, was the excellent Patrick beyond criticism. Good and upright man though he was, the telltale piece of the Confessor's shroud shows that he, too, played a part, although possibly a small one, in the rifling and plundering of the last resting-place of the revered founder of Westminster Abbey.

It would be interesting to know how much, if any, of the Confessor's shroud survived these weird and untoward happenings. Of the many people who must have investigated the coffin before their activities were checked, some, at least, did not leave the Abbey empty-handed. Ralph Thoresby, the Leeds antiquary, writing twenty-nine years later, states that he spent part of a summer Sunday in visiting a Mr. Wootton of Bloomsbury, a brother antiquary, who showed him several curiosities and gave him some, 'particularly a small shred of the silk shroud of King Edward the Confessor cut off when the coffin was accidentally broke (by fall of a pole) at the Coronation of King James the Second'.[1] Evidently the worthy Prebendary was not by any means the only pilferer!

[1] *Diary of Ralph Thoresby*, vol. ii, pp. 218 and 219.

What, in conclusion, can history tell us about the Crucifix and Chain?

Taylor has given a minute description of both ornaments in his pamphlet, from which the late Mr. F. J. Micklethwaite drew the conclusion that they were Byzantine work of the eleventh century.

'The chain was full twenty-four inches long, all of pure gold, the links oblong and curiously wrought; the upper part whereof (to lie in the nape of the neck) was joyned together by a locket composed of a large round nob of massy gold, and in circumference as big as a milled shilling, and half-an-inch thick; round this went a wier, and on the wier about half-a-dozen little beads hanging loose and running too and again on the same, all of pure gold and finely wrought. On each side of this locket were set two large square red stones (supposed to be rubies); from each side of this locket fixed to two rings of gold the chain descends, and meeting below passes through a square piece of gold of a convenient bigness for the same purpose. This gold, wrought into several angles, was painted with divers colours resembling so many gems or precious stones, and to which the crucifix was joined, yet to be taken off (by the help of a screw) at pleasure. For the form of the cross it comes nighest to that of an Humette Flory among the heralds, or rather the Botony, yet the pieces here are not of equal length, the direct or perpendicular beam being nigh one-fourth part larger than the traverse, as being four inches to the extremities, whilst the other scarce exceeds three; yet all of them neatly turned at the ends, and the botons enamelled with figures thereon. The cross itself is of the same gold with the chain; but then it exceeds it by its rich enamel, having on one side the picture of our Saviour Jesus Christ in His Passion wrought thereon, and an eye from above casting a kind of beam upon Him; whilst on the reverse of the same cross is pictured a Benedictine monk in his habit, and on each side these capital Roman letters:—

On the right limb, thus:—    And on the left, thus:—

|  |  |  |  |  |
|---|---|---|---|---|
|  | (A) |  |  | P |
| Z | A | X | A | P |
|  | A |  |  | H |

This cross is hollow and to be opened by two little screws towards the top, wherein it is presumed some relic might have been conserved.'[1]

The ultimate fate of these treasures, of which James II had become the possessor in this scandalous fashion, is wrapped in a mystery from which it is never likely to emerge.

It has been stated that the King lost them and made no secret of the fact. One of those who attended him on his flight, and subsequently wrote a letter entitled 'Particulars regarding the escape of James II', states that the latter 'pleasantly entertained them' by discoursing on various subjects, including a cross which he had lost. 'He told us how much it was to be prized for it was St. Edward the Confessor's and had a piece of the true real cross in it on which our Saviour suffered.'[2]

Thoresby in the passage already quoted remarked that 'a gold chain and crucifix (taken out of the said coffin at the same time)' were found on the person of the King and stolen 'when he was rifled at his abdication'.

It has also been stated that it figured at an auction about the year 1820. The very beautiful ornament then put up for sale is, however, a cross and not a crucifix, and cannot possibly be identical with that which Taylor handled. Evidently archaeology was not a strong point with the organizers of the auction, for in the same sale catalogue there appeared something designated the 'crozier' of Edward the Confessor!

As a matter of fact, every one of the above theories or statements is incorrect. The Crucifix and Chain are almost certainly in existence to-day, although their whereabouts cannot be determined. In a rare book published in 1871, entitled *Les Derniers Stuarts* by the Marquise Campan de Cavelli, there is quoted the Will of

[1] Society of Antiquaries, *Proceedings*, 2nd Series, vol. ix, pp. 228–9.
[2] *Brittanic Magazine*, vol. v, 1797.

THE COFFIN OF ST. EDWARD THE CONFESSOR

Marie Beatrice d'Este, widow of James II, better known as Mary of Modena. It is dated August 10th, 1702, and it contains directions to the effect that certain things were to be handed over to James III, among them 'une boîte contenant une croix et une chaîne trouvées dans le tombeau de Saint Edouard in 1685'.[1] Thus these precious treasures were never lost at all, but were duly placed in the hands of Marie Beatrice his wife by the exiled King.

## NOTE

The manuscript of Patrick's *Autobiography* remained for several generations in the possession of the Knight family. At the time of its first publication in 1837 it belonged to Mrs. Knight of Milton Hall, Cambridge. At a later date it became the property of the Cambridge University Library, where it may be viewed to-day. The curious fragment of the Confessor's shroud has been fastened to one of the pages, by a stout pin, probably by the Bishop himself.

## 12. THE SHRINE IN THE NINETEENTH CENTURY

The body of St. Edward the Confessor has lain in peace ever since the events recorded in the last chapter. No attempt has been made to alter the position of the coffin, much less examine its contents. It lies in the large cavity hollowed out of the massive substructure. The chest itself is smaller than the cavity, being seven and a half feet in length, two feet in breadth, and one foot eleven inches in depth. It is enclosed by five clamps with hinged joints each of them three inches in width, together with similar bands placed likewise at the head and foot. It is further protected from interference by two stout iron bars across the top, built into the sides of the solid masonry of the Shrine and set in beds of lead. These are probably

---

[1] I owe this interesting piece of information to my friend Mr. Laurence Tanner, M.V.O., Keeper of the Muniments at Westminster Abbey.

intended to serve as tie rods. It would be impossible to lift the coffin out of its present resting-place without inflicting serious injury upon the substructure itself.

Thus the coffin of St. Edward has succeeded in escaping even the historical zeal of Dean Stanley, whose interest in the details of the burial-places of departed royalties amounted wellnigh to an obsession!

The substructure, on the other hand, received some important additions or, it would be more correct to say, replacements during the surveyorship of Sir Gilbert Scott, whose interesting account of St. Edward's Shrine deserves to be more widely known.

The thirteenth-century builders of the Shrine erected at each corner a remarkable twisted column of extremely curious design as well as two others supporting the images of St. John the Evangelist and St. Edward. The two latter were re-erected during the Marian restoration by Fecken-ham, though not in their original positions. No attempt was made, however, to replace their companions. Pre-sumably the Abbot supposed them to have perished. Events proved that he was wrong, at least in part.

Lying derelict on the floor of the triforium, Henry Poole, the master-mason, found in 1856 some six or seven fragments which he was able to prove must at one time have formed part of one of the missing columns. With the most painstaking care and no small amount of ingenuity, he managed to piece them together. The result was a re-created column which was now inserted between the old base and the capital (the latter having survived all through these centuries) at the south-east angle of the Shrine. Scott, when this great find was submitted to him, found it necessary to add a small piece of new work in order to effect a proper junction; but with this slight exception the whole column is of thirteenth-century date. It forms a most welcome addition to the interest and beauty of the Shrine.[1]

[1] *Royal Institute of British Architects, Proceedings,* vol. vi, p. 114.

A few years later, in 1868, the Surveyor made a most extraordinary discovery. Imbedded in a blocked-up window in the ancient dormitory, now forming part of Westminster School, he found a piece of beautifully moulded Purbeck marble. How, why, and when it found its way here remains a mystery.[1]

He realized that it must at one time have formed part of the original entablature surrounding the substructure of the Shrine. Careful measurements subsequently proved that it had belonged to the west end of the southern portion, that it was in fact 'a piece of the return of the cornice by its western end over the reredos'.

Scott and other people were, naturally, eager to replace this precious find in its original position; but the subject was beset with more than one difficulty. It was obviously out of the question to remove Feckenham's cornice in order to replace this piece of the entablature. There appeared to be only one way by which their object could be achieved, namely, by pulling down the entire west end of the Shrine which had stood there untouched, save for the removal of the altar, ever since the reign of Mary Tudor. It was a drastic proceeding, to use no stronger words; but Scott was the last man to shrink from radical measures, even when ancient work was in question. Overwhelming evidence as to this side of his mentality is displayed by our cathedrals to-day, though in this particular case a good deal can be claimed in his favour.

Accordingly he set to work. The removal of the huge retabulum formed the first step in the process. This task accomplished, it was then found possible to excavate the pair of twisted columns upon which the retabulum had rested for three centuries, and which were partly embedded in the floor of the chapel. Scott found that these two columns, though larger in diameter, agreed in height with their companion at the east end of the Shrine, rescued

---

[1] Stanley, *Historical Memorials of Westminster Abbey*, p. 112 note.

by him a few years previously.[1] It would seem then that
he found no less than four feet of pillar buried beneath the
surface of the ground on either side. Probably they are
the two columns which stood separately and which for
generations were surmounted by the figures of the two
Saints given by Edward II.

More interesting still, it was discovered that these
pillars contained a mass of rich decoration upon their
lower portions consisting of a quantity of mosaic tesserae
which must have lain hidden away beneath the floor for
many generations.

Scott's investigations revealed the further fact that
during the Marian restoration the retabulum had been
lifted three inches above its original level, thus covering
the whole of the western portion of the frieze or band on
which the thirteenth-century inscription had been set
forth. The reasons for this extraordinary and unnecessary
alteration are obscure. Feckenham's restoration of the
Shrine was a clumsy, botched-up affair at the best. The
alteration of the position of the retabulum, the concealment of the original inscription and the substitution of
another, the employment of the two Italian columns for a
function wholly different to that which they had fulfilled
for centuries, and the burial of these fine pieces of mosaic
work several feet beneath the floor, form a lengthy
catalogue of artistic misdemeanours, all of which now
stood fully revealed to view.

What policy, then, did Scott decide to adopt in the face
of this confused state of things? It is clear that he was
wholly precluded from replacing all this great mass of
material in precisely the same position as that in which
he found it. The discovery of the fragment of the pre-
Reformation entablature had made a radical alteration
in the situation. Naturally, he was extremely anxious that
the latter should once more form part of the structure of

---

[1] Scott, *Gleanings from Westminster Abbey*, pp. 59–60.

the Shrine which it had graced in former days; but it was not an easy matter. Only by altering the position of the retabulum and lowering it three inches to the original level was it possible to reinsert this treasure.

Accordingly, Scott lowered the retabulum, filling the space left empty above it with a piece of plain stone, while he inserted the newly discovered fragment at the south-east corner of the Shrine, whence it jutted out some nine inches beyond the angle. Judging by various pictures, the effect of this very considerable projection must have been extremely ungainly, but there is good reason for thinking that a similar arrangement had existed in medieval times.[1] Careful measurements show that without the extra space afforded by such projections at the west end of the Shrine, it would have been impossible to include the original inscription in its entirety.

Scott's work, however, did not remain *in situ* for many years. The queer-looking projection failed to commend itself to one of his successors in the office of Surveyor. It would, perhaps, have been a different matter if it had not stood alone. It was therefore removed from the position in which Scott had replaced it, and to-day it forms not the least interesting of the treasures contained in the Museum.

For the policy he adopted in dealing with the piece of the architrave and the retabulum Scott could clearly plead strong historical justification. The clumsy work of Feckenham was amended and things were brought back to their original condition. It was far otherwise with the two twisted columns. Divorced from their proper function, and converted into pedestals for the support of the retabulum with a considerable portion of their beauty hidden underground, they presented a really tragic spectacle; but Scott unfortunately failed to utilize his fine opportunity of rectifying this misarrangement.

[1] Lethaby, *Westminster Abbey and the King's Craftsmen*, pp. 325–6; id., *Westminster Abbey Re-examined*, p. 229.

Had there been any idea in the minds of the Dean and Chapter of re-erecting the Altar of St. Edward, Scott would possibly have cleared up the muddle and rested the retabulum upon the mensa, thus reverting to the original arrangement. In this case it would have been a simple matter to restore the two twisted columns to their original positions on the flanks of the altar. The middle of the nineteenth century was not, however, an age in which a proposal for the re-erection of St. Edward's Altar was likely to find much favour. Another forty years were destined to pass away before any such scheme could be regarded as a practical possibility.

Scott therefore replaced things as he found them, but with a distinct change for the worse. The lowering of the retabulum compelled him to bury the two twisted columns supporting it in the floor to the extent of an additional three inches. On the other hand, he had not the heart to cover up again the brilliant colours of the beautiful mosaic tesserae, for it is the lower not the upper portion of the shaft which they adorn. Accordingly, he turned the columns upside down, and they remain in that position to-day with their bases uppermost! It was a clumsy piece of work fully on a par with Feckenham's praiseworthy but bungling efforts three centuries before.

The time has surely come for making good Scott's lost opportunity. It would be a perfectly easy matter to excavate the two twisted columns once more, and replace them in their original positions, leaving the retabulum to be supported on the mensa of the modern altar. The full beauty of the twin columns would then be visible; and in days to come they might even be crowned with the figures of St. John the Evangelist and St. Edward the Confessor, as of old.

## 13. THE REFURNISHING OF THE SHRINE AND CHAPEL AT THE CORONATION OF EDWARD VII

Queen Victoria died early in the year 1901, and before long preparations commenced for the Coronation of her son. It was a serious and complicated matter. Sixty-three years had come and gone since the last of these imposing events. Only a handful of aged persons, one or two members of the choir, for instance, were still alive in 1902 who had been present within the Abbey on that glorious June day in 1838. Personal experience simply did not exist.

It was well known that the Coronations of Queen Victoria and her uncle William IV had been characterized by slovenliness unspeakable, and it was determined to take no risks. Anything even remotely suggestive of such brilliant muddling was unthinkable. Moreover, the public mind had undergone a complete change of out-look. Things accepted without question in 1838 could not fail to meet with stern condemnation in 1902. Nearly seventy years had come and gone since the commence-ment of the Oxford Movement, and in the interval a great deal had been learnt. The attainment of a lofty standard of worship and ceremonial at the solemn sacring of Edward VII was felt on all sides to be imperative.

It was obvious that the Chapel and Altar of St. Edward could not fail to be affected by these loftier ideals. Thus the use of the customary makeshift table was promptly negatived. The Dean and Chapter decided to replace the permanent altar after nearly three hundred and fifty years of neglect, and the matter was entrusted to their Surveyor, Mr. J. T. Micklethwaite.

This reversion to the arrangements of pre-Reformation times was welcome to a degree; but it cannot be said that the method adopted by Micklethwaite was altogether successful. A footpace of black Irish marble was constructed at the west end of the Shrine, and on this were erected a pair of stout legs, of the clumsiest description, on which the new mensa was supported. Hideous in itself, the design was utterly out of keeping with its surroundings. If the altar were not always covered with hangings, in accordance with the English tradition, its ugliness would be unbearable.

Above, on the cornice of the Shrine, he placed a small rood, together with the attendant figures of the Blessed Virgin and St. John the Evangelist made of carved and gilded wood. It was at the best only a moderately interesting piece of work, though the subsequent application of colour by Mr. Clement Skilbeck has produced a marked improvement. Over Feckenham's wooden feretory was thrown a pall of stamped crimson velvet, intended, doubtless, to represent a medieval cooperculum. The latter terminated at the western extremity with a shield bearing the Confessor's Arms wrought in enamel. These changes without doubt represented a great advance; but the general effect was not wholly satisfactory, owing to the crude colour of the pall and the coarsely designed lettering of the gold embroidery over its lower border.

A festal frontal and dorsal of the same material as the pall, but with the design richly outlined in gold thread, a frontlet embroidered with various national devices, and a plain frontal, together with a pair of metal candlesticks of a very ordinary character, formed the altar furniture. No one could accuse the authorities of being actuated by any very grandiose ideas.

The Westminster Chapter, from the time of its establishment in Elizabethan days down to the middle of the nineteenth century, thanks to the system of wholesale pluralities, almost invariably contained at least one member who had received episcopal orders. Since the reduction of the twelve Prebendaries to six Canons in the early forties of the last century this has rarely been the case; but it happened that at the beginning of the year 1902 the Right Rev. J. E. C. Welldon had been appointed to a canonry on his resignation of the Bishopric of Calcutta, in succession to the Rev. Charles Gore, consecrated to the Bishopric of Worcester. On the eventful ninth day of August in the year 1902 it fell, then, to the lot of the new junior Canon to consecrate the new altar and to 'hallow the cream' thereat, during a short break made during the Procession of the Regalia, the first of the great ceremonies which precede the rite of sacring.

The Holy Communion was celebrated at the new altar for the first time a few weeks later, on the Feast of the Translation of St. Edward, and again on Holy Innocents' Day, the Feast of the Dedication. This practice has been maintained ever since, St. Peter's Day, the Feast of the Patron Saint, being added subsequently by Dean Ryle, and the Death Day of St. Edward by the present dean. No celebration had taken place in this Chapel, so far as is known, since the beginning of the reign of Queen Elizabeth.

The various changes in St. Edward's Chapel were hailed with general enthusiasm. The dreary and woe-begone appearance of the place had at last come to an end. To the inexperienced eyes of early twentieth-century folk, the chapel now displayed a suggestion of almost medieval splendour. This impression, though not un-natural, was erroneous. As the years passed on, it came to be realized that the altar furniture and ornaments were sadly incomplete and scarcely worthy of their august surroundings. By degrees, however, numerous additions have been made, not a few of them of real magnificence, which help in some measure to recall the stateliness of pre-Reformation times; while the crudity of the crimson velvet pall has given place to a silken covering of great beauty, first used at the marriage of their Royal High-nesses the Duke and Duchess of Kent.

The altar has been further enriched by a pair of silver candlesticks for the *mensa* of Renaissance design, the gift of their Majesties King George VI and Queen Elizabeth on the occasion of their marriage on April 26th, 1923, also by a rich sequence of heraldic frontals designed by Mr. W. H. Randoll Blacking. A pair of standard candlesticks of silvered bronze were given in December 1923 by the Order of Crusaders.

## 14. THE SHRINE OF SAINT EDWARD DURING THE GREAT WAR

The second decade of the twentieth century witnessed perhaps the most extraordinary of all the many events connected with St. Edward's Shrine. With the second year of the Great War it became clear that the Abbey and its treasures stood in deadly jeopardy. Who knew but what a bomb falling out of the skies would reduce some precious object, and perhaps the entire building, to utter ruin?

It was little that the Dean and Chapter could do to ensure the safety of their church from danger; but they neglected no possible precautions. Feckenham's wooden superstructure was removed *in toto* after which twelve hundred sandbags were piled above and around the substructure. This protection would have done little to mitigate the results of a direct blow, had such a disaster befallen the place; but they at least ensured the safety of the work of Peter the Roman Citizen, and the remains of the sainted Confessor, of which it formed the casket, from damage caused by flying splinters. Mercifully, this terrible possibility never materialized.

In the course of all these happenings the iron-bound coffin of St. Edward, securely wedged into the masonry by means of massive iron stanchions, was once again revealed, ere the thick barrier of sandbags hid it from view. Who would have believed that the removal of the super-

THE ALTAR AND SHRINE OF ST. EDWARD THE CONFESSOR ON CHRISTMAS DAY, 1933

structure would actually bring to light a relic of the later days of the Stuart dynasty? Such, however, was one of the minor results of the Great War!

Lying about in the cavity were discovered a number of small oddments, such as nails, lozenge-shaped pieces of glass, which evidently had once decorated the wooden top, a brass button, a halfpenny dated 1725, and, most remarkable of all, a folded letter[1] bearing the signature 'William West': addressed to his friend, Charles Hart, living at the Crown Inn, Bridgnorth.

William West was speedily identified. He served for a good many years on the Abbey staff as a guide or 'tomb shower'. He died on April 11th, 1714, and was buried in the Dark Cloister. Thus, the letter was at least as old as the end of the reign of Queen Anne, and perhaps a good deal older, for it was discovered that West was receiving a stipend of forty shillings as College Barber, with an additional stipend as Keeper of the Clock so far back as 1701. Perhaps he was one of the numerous people like Charles Taylor who took the opportunity of having a look round after the disaster to the superstructure in 1685?

The letter is as follows:

Dear frend,                                        February the 3rd
I make bould to trouble you w[th] These fue Lines to satisfy you I am In good health: Living in hopes to see you once: in London ... n: So That I should be very g .... d; your Frend William Cole[2] Cole remembers His Love to you being my Cheaf Compannyion at the tombs so That I here your in good health wich is the most of my satisfacktion desiring to here from you and *if* you can conveniantly to send a Cock for a token against sraftusday will drink your health and eat him for your sack no more at present But i rest your Loveing frend

                                        WILLIAM WEST
                                        for Charles Hart
Shrapshaire                             att the Crown Inn
  w[th] Caire                           In Bridgnorth[3]

[1] W.A.M. 57255.                    [2] Erased.
[3] Society of Antiquaries, *Proceedings*, 1915–16, pp. 76–7.

The carnovale with which West hoped to celebrate the approaching Shrove Tuesday ('sraftusday') must have been shorn of most of its glory by the non-delivery of his letter!

## 15. KING EDWARD'S CHAIR

'Looke ye there, gentlemen, there's a curiosity for ye! In that chair the Kings of England were crowned. You see also a stone underneath and that stone is Jacob's Pillow!' *'I could see no curiosity* either in the oak chair or the stone! could I, indeed, behold one of the Old Kings of England seated in this, or Jacob's head laid on the other, there might be something curious in the sight, but in the present case there was no more reason for my surprise than if I should pick a stone from their streets, and call it a curiosity, merely because one of the Kings happened to tread on it as he passed in a procession!'[1]

Many people in the eighteenth century would unhesitatingly have echoed Goldsmith's contemptuous allusion to this precious relic. There was Peter Kahn, for instance, a famous Swedish botanist who visited the Abbey in 1748. Into his utilitarian mind neither artistic appreciation nor yet historical sense could effect an entry, for he exclaimed, 'Many a poor old woman has a better and more handsomely made chair than this!'[2]

None the less, the Stone of Destiny and the Chair which encloses it are embedded in the heart of the English monarchy. They form 'a link which unites the throne of England to the tradition of Tara and Iona'.[3]

In the eyes of 'the greatest of the Plantagenets', the stone was a relic precious beyond words. To the active and vivid mind of Edward I it would be an achievement of the first order could he but remove this wondrous emblem of sovereignty from its time-honoured home in Scotland and provide it with a new home, like the golden coronet of the last native Prince of Wales, recently sus-

[1] Goldsmith, *Citizen of the World*, Letter xiii.
[2] Hutchings, *London Town Past and Present*, vol. i, p. 510.
[3] Stanley, *Historical Memorials of Westminster Abbey*, p. 83.

pended by his little son, Alfonso, in close proximity to the Confessor's Shrine.

Legend has surrounded this historic stone with a cloud of mystery. According to one tradition, by no means the least probable, it actually supported the head of the great St. Columba in his death throes. Within the walls of Scone, however, whither it was brought by King Kenneth II in A.D. 840 from the Castle of Dunstaffnage, it became possessed of an assured historical position. Here this shapeless piece of sandstone from the west coast of Scotland (for geology has little doubt as to its Scottish origin) had been jealously preserved for generations.

'Una petra magna super quam reges Scociae solebant coronari.'[1] Encased in a chair of wood it had come to serve as the 'Sedes Principalis' of the Kingdom of Scotland, upon which the monarchs of that realm were solemnly enthroned by the Earls of Fife.

Considerations such as these could only enhance the value of this glittering prize in the eyes of our first Edward. The sacred stone once securely lodged in his hands, a blow wellnigh mortal would surely have been launched against his hated rival in the north.

It was the year 1296. The King crossed the border in the spring. Edinburgh Castle fell in June, and was quickly despoiled of a great mass of treasure. Three coffers containing plate and jewelled vessels were seen before long on their way southwards with the further enrichment of Westminster as their objective. A few weeks later Edward pushed on into Perthshire. Early in August he gazed for the first time upon the Stone of Destiny, the Lia-Fail itself.

Its fate was sealed. The King, according to one account, first of all procured his own coronation thereon, in order to assert his headship and lordship over the Scots. He then transferred the Lia-Fail to his own possession.

[1] Wardrobe Account of Edward I : Lib. Quotidianus, quoted in Neale and Brayley, vol. ii, p. 127.

Somewhat later, though the actual date is uncertain, the journey from Scone southwards commenced. Very possibly the stone was conveyed by means of a pole slung between two horses.[1] The massive iron rings, so securely wedged into it that they appear to be wellnigh part of the stone itself, suggest the employment of this method of transport. Be this as it may, the shameless robbery was smoothly and satisfactorily perpetrated. Everything went 'according to plan', without one single hitch, and at no great distance of time the Lia-Fail safely reached the metropolis.[2]

As a result of King Edward's action, the British Empire that was to be became possessed of a treasure far surpassing in historical grandeur the sacred stones upon which were once inaugurated such potentates as the Kings of Sweden at Upsala or the Kings of Hungary at Presburg or Pesth. The famous building, the Königsstuhl, with its stalls of stone, at the junction of the Rhine and the Lahn, which might well have vied with Westminster as a sacred centre of kingship, was deprived of every particle of living significance when Napoleon, with a contemptuous gesture, dismissed the Holy Roman Empire out of existence. In England the passage of time has only emphasized the moving historical associations of the Lia-Fail. It remains the central symbol of a vigorous life, national, royal, imperial, which has never throbbed with greater vigour than it does to-day.

This much battered relic is a piece of coarsely grained sandstone, rectangular in shape ($26\frac{1}{2}$ inches in length, $16\frac{1}{2}$ inches in breadth, and 11 inches thick). About the middle of the back edge is a rough cutting in the form of a Latin cross, and on the top surface is a kind of groove or rectangular sinking. It has been suggested that this depression formerly contained the metal plaque placed here

[1] Lethaby, *Westminster Abbey Re-examined*, p. 258.
[2] *Archaeological Journal*, vol. xiii, pp. 249–55.

by King Kenneth, on which was inscribed in the form of a couplet the famous prophecy:

Ni fallat fatum, Scoti, quocunque locatum
Invenient lapidem, regnare tenentur ibidem.

which has been somewhat freely rendered into English as follows:

Unless the fixed decrees of fate give way
The Scots shall govern and the sceptre sway
Where'er this stone they find, and its dread sound obey.

It was Edward's original plan to enclose the Lia-Fail in a chair of metal-work, probably bronze, and a start seems to have been made by Adam, the 'King's workman'. He soon changed his mind and the final decision was given in favour of wood.[1] The King then sought the aid of Walter of Durham, the Painter, another of those men of supreme genius who have left their mark upon Westminster Abbey.

Full details of the story are furnished by the Wardrobe Accounts of the reign. The King first of all paid the sum of one hundred shillings for a chair of wood, fashioned after the design of its rejected predecessor of metal. Later on Master Walter received 13s. 4d. for the work of carving, painting, and gilding two small leopards of wood on either side of the chair. Finally he was paid £1. 19s. 7d. 'for making a step at the foot of the new chair in which the Scottish stone is placed near the altar, before the Shrine of St. Edward, and for the wages of the carpenters and of the painters, and for colours and gold employed, also for the making of a covering to cover the said chair'. The work is said to have been completed in March 1300.

King Edward's Chair is made of oak fastened together by means of pins. It has a high, plain back finished with a moulding, in the centre of which is an acute gable, with carved arm rests, the external surface of the sides being panelled. Beneath is a horizontal moulding and four panels with trefoiled heads.

[1] Lethaby, *Westminster and the King's Craftsmen*, p. 297.

Upon this oaken surface the artist laid a coat of gesso, subsequently gilded. The gold was first of all applied by means of the white of an egg, and then burnished. Finally, a pattern was pricked upon it with a blunt instrument. The amount of labour involved must have been enormous, for every line of the pattern had to be expressed in a succession of infinitely tiny dots.

The abominable treatment which the Chair has suffered during its long life of more than six centuries has reduced the various subjects of the rich gilt gesso decoration to a condition of almost complete invisibility. Still, William Burges was able to detect something of a design seventy years ago,[1] and the work of renovation carried out by Professor Tristram in recent times has not only revealed certain traces of decoration but has also (we may hope) permanently arrested any further advance in the process of deterioration and decay.

A large piece of panelled diapering of foliage and grotesques is distinctly visible on the inside face of the right arm. It is matched on the left arm by a design of birds and foliage. The four narrow outer panels of this arm are still to a great extent complete.

The back of the Chair contains a range of six panels with trefoiled heads, the space above being filled with panels both pointed and rounded. It was originally adorned by a pricked background on which was depicted the seated figure of a King with his feet resting upon a lion. The latter has undergone cruel maltreatment; but a paw of the lion and the sides of the throne are still just distinguishable.

The Lia-Fail is placed immediately beneath the seat, which is boxlike in shape, and rests upon a kind of middle frame supported by four crouching lions on a plinth. The back and sides of the latter were originally filled with open quatrefoils, which unfortunately have lost the shields they once enclosed. The front row has been entirely destroyed,

---

[1] Scott, *Gleanings from Westminster Abbey*, p. 125.

in fact only four quatrefoils survive out of the original total of ten.

The arms of the Chair were probably moulded at the outset; but they suffered such deterioration that at some unknown date it was found necessary to cover them with stuffed canvas padding, for which in recent times velvet has been substituted.

There is good reason for thinking that inlays of coloured glass upon a gilded or silvered ground, somewhat similar to those on the retabulum of the High Altar, played their part in the decoration, more especially in the tall pediment and the spandrels between the cusped heads of the panels. John Carter, who had the advantage of examining the Chair before the end of the eighteenth century, entertained no doubt at all upon the subject.[1] 'The spandrels were decorated with small sprays painted on a metal ground (gold or silver foil) and covered with glass, as may yet be seen in three or four places.'

The existing step together with the lions at the angles is modern work.

There never was a shadow of doubt as to the place destined by Edward I as the future home of the 'Scots Stone', and the stately throne of which it thenceforth formed a part. A note in the inventory for the last year of that monarch's reign would seem to be conclusive.

Mittebatur per preceptum regis usque abbathium de Westmonasterio ad assedendum ibidem juxta feretrum S^ti Edvardi in quadam cathedra lignea deaurata quam Rex fieri precepit ad perpetuam rei memoriam.

When Edward deposited the much-coveted prize within the walls of the Abbey he was eager to present this trophy of his conquest to the Chapel of the Confessor. Already had he manifested this same desire in the celebration of his triumph over Wales.

But in this, one of the greatest as it was one of the last of

[1] John Carter, *Antient Architecture of England*, vol. ii, plate VI.

R

all his manifold achievements, he went a step farther. Not only should the Benedictine Abbey of Westminster be transformed into an English Scone, the possessor of the regal seat *par excellence*, that same seat must also serve as a cathedra, a counterpart of the metropolitan throne of Canterbury, a sacred chair which, elevated upon the step provided by Walter the Painter and facing westwards, would be visible down the whole length of the choir. The King's aim and object has been summed up in the words of Walsingham, 'Jubens inde fieri celebrantium cathedram sacerdotum.' The King could hardly have manifested his affection and veneration for the Abbey in a more striking fashion.[1]

It was a magnificent conception. King Edward's Chair erected upon this platform, at the west of the Confessor's Chapel, upon a piece of floor-space still apparently indicated by the absence of any decoration and visible over a large part of the building, would forthwith become invested with a dignity second only to that of the sacred Shrine itself. It is deeply regrettable that the great King's scheme, overwhelming alike in its grandeur and in its simplicity, should have been subsequently emptied of its original impressiveness. So soon as the perpendicular screen had come into being, King Edward's Chair ceased of necessity to occupy its former central and commanding position. The fifteenth-century guardians of the Abbey never did a worse thing.

It is difficult to determine precisely what happened after the erection of this great wall of demarcation, for the evidence is almost nil. The Chair may have continued to stand in St. Edward's Chapel in the position which it occupies to-day. Or, on the other hand, it may have been removed into the presbytery, and placed immediately in front of the Sedilia facing northwards in a place analogous to that of another ceremonial chair[2] in the Cathedral of

---

[1] Stanley, *Historical Memorials of Westminster Abbey*, p. 54.
[2] Symon Gunton, *History of the Church of Peterborough*, plate IV.

Peterborough. Such is the explanation which has been suggested of a curious-looking piece of furniture in the great picture of the east end contained in the Islip Roll.[1] All this, however, is mere conjecture. The hard fact remains that a grievous injury was inflicted upon both Chair and Church and one which could never by any possibility be made good except by the removal of the screen.

And so we leave the mighty Edward in his triumph. Subsequent centuries have only served to emphasize its magnitude. His great ideal, the conversion of the Abbey Church of Westminster into an English Scone, has been realized to the very full. The work of the King has lived and continued to grow as generation has given place to generation. To the crowds who throng the great church from every part of the Empire, this battered old chair makes an appeal which touches the innermost fibres of our being.

The King's object was not, however, achieved in a moment. The rage and anguish felt by the Scottish nation can well be imagined, and elicit no small amount of sympathy from us even to-day. Efforts were made by them without ceasing to secure possession of their treasured relic once more, and thus rebuild the shattered foundations of their monarchy. They were very nearly successful. During the reign of Edward III, in the Treaty of Northampton in 1328, and again in 1363, was a definite undertaking given to replace the Lia-Fail in the hands of its original owners; but no! Although orders were given for the delivery of the stone through the sheriffs to Isabella, the Queen-mother, for its restoration to the Scots, the sheriffs refused to act.[2] 'The Stone of Scone on which the Kings of Scotland used at Scone to be placed on their inauguration, the people of London would by no means whatever allow to depart from themselves.'[3]

[1] Vol. i, p. 50.     [2] *Church Quarterly Review*, vol. lxvi, p. 352.
[3] *Chronicle of Lanercost*, p. 26.

By this strange succession of events, then, has it come about that the Lia-Fail forms to-day 'the one primeval monument which binds together the whole Empire'.[1]

The fact is practically assured that every sovereign from Edward II onwards with two exceptions has been solemnly consecrated upon this historic seat. It is true that no specific mention of the Royal Chair in connexion with any of the Coronations prior to that of Henry IV is extant; but it is incredible that a Stone of such unique and historic import should have failed to occupy a prominent position in the official ceremonial on the three previous occasions. The monarchs in question would have been slow-witted indeed, if they had thrown away so magnificent an opportunity of investing their sovereignty with the additional glamour which the Lia-Fail could not fail to contribute.

The Coronation of our fourth Henry on the great central festival of the Church of Westminster, the Feast of the Translation of St. Edward the Confessor, in 1399, was a critical moment in English history. A breach had been made in the direct line of succession of the House of Plantagenet, and the future course of events must have appeared in the eyes of the average beholder to be marked with uncertainty. Special precautions were necessary, which fact explains the emphasis laid upon the Scottish Stone. Again, a phial of sacred oil, said to have been bestowed by the Blessed Virgin upon St. Thomas of Canterbury during his exile in France, made its appearance for the first time at this Coronation, while the significance of the allusion in one of the official sermons to Jacob, and the success which attended that Patriarch's somewhat unworthy manœuvres, must have been sufficiently obvious. The authorities were evidently determined to surround the first Lancastrian monarch with every possible safeguard.

[1] Stanley, *Historical Memorials of Westminster Abbey*, p. 63.

Into the record of one Coronation only has an element of doubt crept in, and, though it must not be ignored, it does not amount to a great deal.

It was the Coronation of Mary Tudor. Bigoted to her finger-tips, that unattractive sovereign is said, according to one account, to have suspected that King Edward's Chair had suffered pollution with the enthronement of her Protestant half-brother thereon. Terrified lest the contagion, even after the lapse of six years, might conceivably be imparted to her own person, an appeal was made to the Papacy to save the situation.

Julius III lent a favourable ear to the request and forwarded a new chair to England, after he had duly sanctified it with the Papal benediction. It forms to-day one of the treasures of the Cathedral of Winchester, where it probably figured at Mary's marriage.

The actual part played by Queen Mary's Chair, as it is termed, in the Coronation ceremony is extremely doubtful.[1] King Edward's Chair is definitely mentioned in the official account; and it is inconceivable that public opinion, either in that or any other age, would have tolerated the substitution of a modern importation from abroad, in place of the time-honoured throne. It is far more probable that the latter was used in the traditional manner during the ceremonies of unction and coronation, and that the Queen occupied the new chair only during the introductory portion of the rite.[2]

The seventeenth century proved by far the most outstanding epoch in the history of King Edward's Chair since its construction by Walter the Painter. It is highly improbable that any future century will ever witness three events all of them of such high significance and importance.

The first was the Coronation of James I on July 25th, 1603. It was a dreary occasion. The Plague was raging

[1] *Gentleman's Magazine*, 1838, p. 612.  [2] Planché, *Regal Records*, p. 16.

throughout the metropolis, and the Royal Progress from the Tower to Westminster, by far the most popular feature of the customary ceremonial, was perforce abandoned. On the other hand, the prophecy associated with the Lia-Fail, and which, according to tradition, had at one time been actually inscribed upon its surface, received literal fulfilment after long centuries, when Archbishop Whitgift poured the consecrated oil upon the person of the Scottish King and placed the Crown of St. Edward upon his head. James Stuart sat there amid the acclamations of his new subjects, the first King of the 'Great Britain' that was to be. The link between the Scots and the historic Stone of Destiny had been forged anew, never to be broken again. From 1603 onwards, our land has never known any sovereign in whose veins the Scottish blood did not flow.

Fifty years later, King Edward's Chair, with a shameless disregard for tradition, was transported from the Abbey to Westminster Hall, where there was erected over it a 'prince-like canopy of state' and Oliver Cromwell took his place thereon as Lord Protector of the realm. The ceremony was entitled an 'Installation'; indeed, hardly any other title was possible. There was no semblance of either crown or sceptre, for the Regalia had been wantonly destroyed eight years before. To the majority of Englishmen, however, this strange and unprecedented occasion must have seemed very much like the establishment of a new dynasty, even though such words as 'king' and 'crown' were conspicuous by their absence. Such, too, was evidently the opinion of the powers that be, judging by their attempt to recall some slight portion of the ancient ceremonial. That the 'Chair of Scotland' should have figured with such prominence in Westminster Hall on that twenty-sixth day of June in the year 1657 speaks volumes for the commanding position which it had long enjoyed in the life of the English people. From one point of view, this Installation of the Lord Protector was one of the most momentous happenings ever known in the history of King Edward's Chair. That it was also an outrage of the first order is equally obvious.

The accession of the joint sovereigns William and Mary towards the close of the same century, was another unique and unprecedented event; but it only served to emphasize the immense importance attached to this venerable throne. It was as a regnant monarch, not as a queen-consort, that Mary II passed up the Abbey, walking not in front, but side by side with her royal spouse. The sacring of a queen consort differs in not a few respects from that of a regnant monarch, notably in the procedure employed at the anointing and the crowning. That Mary II should kneel at the supreme moment at the steps of the High Altar, like Anne of Denmark and Mary of Modena, was therefore unthinkable. Her sacring must not be allowed to differ in the slightest detail from those of the two Tudor sisters. There was no alternative then, save to provide a second royal chair, in which she could be seated, while, like her husband, she was anointed and invested with the full symbols of sovereignty by Henry Compton, Bishop of London.

Queen Mary's Chair is made of oak, and designed after the model of King Edward's Chair; but it is a poor and clumsy piece of work compared with its more ancient companion. The raised panels on the back and sides are wholly devoid of any decoration. It was also set a good deal lower, in order that the head of the young Queen might not appear on a higher level than that of her diminutive husband.

After the Coronation of the Joint-Sovereigns on April 11th, 1689, the new chair found a place, close to Walter of Durham's masterpiece, on the west side of the Confessor's Chapel. Here it remained for upwards of two centuries, with the result that wholly erroneous impressions

grew up round it. To the majority of persons it came
to be regarded as the official seat of the Queen-Consort.
That it claimed to be no more than a survival of a unique
event in the long history of the Coronation ceremony was
known to relatively few. Ultimately, its totally unhistorical and meaningless position, parallel and on a level
with the older throne, was realized and an important
change was inaugurated during the decanate of Dean
Armitage Robinson. King Edward's Chair, while retaining its time-honoured position, was elevated upon a
dais with great appropriateness, as being the living symbol
of British Kingship, while Queen Mary's Chair, a link
with the Revolution and of deep interest, was separated
from it and placed at the east end of the Chapel of King
Henry VII.[1]

Yet another event of outstanding importance, equally
unique with those which have gone before, has marked
the wonderful history of this old Chair. Once, and once
only, has it fallen to the lot of an English sovereign to be
seated officially therein on more than one occasion, and
this brings us to the great reign of Queen Victoria. On
June 28th, 1838, a young girl barely twenty years of age,
she had received, with the same ceremonial as her predecessors, the gifts of unction and coronation at the hands
of the aged Archbishop Howley. 'As she sate immovable
on the throne, when the crown touched her head, amidst
shout and trumpet and the roar of cannon there must have
been many who felt a hope that the loyalty which had
waxed cold in the preceding reigns would once more
revive in a more serious form than it had, perhaps, ever
worn before.'[2] When forty-nine years later, on June 20th,
1887, she for the second time occupied the historic seat in
front of the High Altar of the Abbey, and received the
blessing of Archbishop Benson, surrounded by the love

---

[1] Queen Mary's Chair has since been placed in the Norman Undercroft.
[2] Stanley, *Historical Memorials of Westminster Abbey*, p. 100.

and admiration of all, it was realized how abundantly that hope had been fulfilled.

Let the beloved and venerated occupant of the chair at that overwhelming moment tell the story in her own touching words:

'I sat *alone* (oh! without my beloved husband for whom this would have been such a proud day!) where I sat forty-nine years ago and received the homage of the Princes and Peers, but in the Old Coronation Chair of Edward I, with the old stone brought from Scotland, on which the old Kings of Scotland used to be crowned.'[1]

'My robes[2] were beautifully draped in the chair. The service was very well done and arranged. The Te Deum by my darling Albert sounded beautiful, and the anthem by Dr. Bridge was fine, especially the way in which the National Anthem and dear Albert's Chorale were worked in.'[3]

In conclusion, it is impossible to repress a feeling of deep indignation at the present condition of King Edward's Chair. In days like our own, when the historical sense is once more permitted to count for something in our national life, it would seem incredible, were it not for the

---

[1] It must be explained that the Sovereign occupies three chairs in succession at the Coronation, viz. (1) a Chair of State placed on the south side of the presbytery, during the first part of the service till the conclusion of the sermon; (2) King Edward's Chair, which stands facing the High Altar just above the steps leading to the presbytery, where the ceremonies of Unction, Investiture, and Coronation are performed by the Primate; (3) the Throne, standing farther to the west on the dais entitled the 'theatre' in the centre of the lantern, where takes place the Enthronization and the Homage of the Peers. At the great Jubilee service in 1887 King Edward's Chair alone was used. It stood beneath the lantern surrounded by the seats occupied by the members of the Royal Family.

[2] At the Coronation three sets of robes are worn by the Sovereign: (1) the Parliament Robe of Crimson velvet, till the moment when the Coronation ceremonies proper commence; (2) the Vestments which are successively assumed after the Sovereign has been placed in King Edward's Chair, viz. the Colobium Sindonis or Alb, the Armill or Stole, the Super-tunica or Tunicle, and the Imperial Mantle or Cope; (3) the Royal Robe of Purple Velvet which is assumed in Saint Edward's Chapel at the conclusion of the service immediately before the final procession. At the Jubilee service of 1887 these robes were spread over King Edward's Chair.

[3] *Letters of Queen Victoria*, edited by G. E. Buckle, 3rd Series, vol. i, p. 324.

evidence before our very eyes, that this priceless inherit-
ance could ever have been reduced to such a tragic condition.  Goldsmith's gibe, with which this chapter opens,
supplies a more than sufficient explanation.

In the days of Addison, and for long years afterwards,
King Edward's Chair stood in the Confessor's Chapel
without the slightest semblance of protection.[1]  All and
sundry were allowed to seat themselves therein, provided
that they paid the necessary forfeit in the current coin of
the realm, a practice from which the Abbey guides must
have derived no small amount of benefit.  That people
should have recorded their worthless existences upon its
surface with the aid of a pocket knife was inevitable, and
precisely what was to be expected in an age of general
neglect.

It is something of a relief to learn, however, that one at
any rate of these vandals was distinguished by a certain
amount both of courage and humour.  Needless to say, he
was a product of Westminster School, in which famous sem-
inary of sound learning and religion an enthusiasm for the
Abbey is traditional, though it has sometimes manifested
itself in unorthodox ways and at inappropriate times.

One of these budding Englishmen made a bet that he
would secrete himself among the tombs after dark and
inscribe his name upon the monument of Henry Purcell.
He was as good as his word, as regards part one; but it
would seem that in the course of his nocturnal explorations,
ambition impelled him to aim at still loftier heights.
Purcell's monument escaped the attentions of the young
vandal, but the following inscription in the seat of King
Edward's Chair will recall his audacious exploit for many
a long year to come.

'Peter Abbot slept in this chair July 5, 1800.'[2]

Ill usage on the part of the unthinking multitude, however regrettable, is not altogether unintelligible in an age

[1] *The Spectator*, no. 329.    [2] Malcolm, *Londinium Redivivum*, p. 191.

when the standard of education was low and historical appreciation practically nil. It is difficult, however, to excuse the State officials whose duty it was to make the necessary preparations in the Abbey with the advent of each Coronation.

At some time unknown it became the custom to swathe King Edward's Chair on these occasions with costly hangings. The responsible authorities wholly failed to realize that the richest fabrics of the Orient would not, and could not, add one iota to its prestige. Alas! pins, tin-tacks, and all manner of devices were utilized for the secure fastening of these wretched draperies. They were driven mercilessly into the rich gesso work of Walter the Painter with results heart-breaking to contemplate. It was bad enough to cover this old throne with cloth of gold or 'a cover of gold tissue', which formed the procedure at certain Stuart Coronations, but it was in the nineteenth century that the vandalistic treatment of King Edward's Chair touched the very nadir of abomination.

The happenings at the Coronation of George IV, for instance, were so deplorable that it is difficult to speak of them with restraint even at this distance of time. According to Brayley, 'the old crockets and turrets at the back were sawn off and new ones substituted under the direction of the upholsterers employed by the Board of Works; the lions at the bottom were also repaired and gilded. Soon after the ceremony, however, the new crockets, &c., were taken away, and the Chair by that means left in a more dilapidated state than before, while the four shields on the ornamental tracery were subsequently stolen.'[1]

Sixty-six years later came the Golden Jubilee of Queen Victoria. The authorities connected with the Office of Works used their best endeavours to emulate, if not sur-pass, their late Georgian predecessors. On this occasion

[1] J. P. Neale and E. W. Brayley, *History of the Abbey Church of St. Peter, Westminster*, vol. ii, p. 384.

they selected varnish as the principal medium for their activities and succeeded in inflicting permanent damage upon the Chair. Every effort was made to undo the evil work so soon as it was discovered, but it was too late. 'Though the work of varnishing was stopped, irreparable harm was done, the old surface being destroyed and the remaining traces of the carvings and decorations, while the names and initials which have been cut in the wood were rendered more obtrusive.'[1] The wriggling of the unfortunate Minister responsible, when pressed in the House of Commons to explain the action of the staff of his department, would provoke peals of mirth were the subject less serious.[2] Such was the historical and artistic appreciation displayed by a Government Department in the year 1887. As Professor Lethaby has grimly remarked, two or three more varnishings will obliterate such decoration as has survived.[3]

Once and once only has King Edward's Chair fallen a victim to deliberate malice. It was one Saturday evening in the June of 1914. The last party for that day was being escorted through the Royal Chapels when a loud report rent the air. A bomb had been exploded against King Edward's Chair. There could be but little doubt as to the origin of this attack, for the outrages of the 'Militant Sisterhood' were being recorded almost daily. The damage wrought was less serious than might have been anticipated; but the remains of the fourteenth-century paintings and the woodwork were injured and a number of dints made in the panelling of the stone screen immediately behind the Chair, which can be seen to this day. It was a marvellous escape, and it was not the fault of the perpetrator of this outrage that the Chair and a portion of the fabric of the Abbey Church itself were not destroyed.

[1] Hutchings, *London Town Past and Present*, vol. i, p. 510.
[2] See note at the end of this chapter.
[3] Lethaby, *Westminster Abbey and the King's Craftsmen*, p. 266.

It may be well at this point to correct an inaccuracy into which every modern historian of the Abbey has fallen without exception. Their error is scarcely wonderful, for the actual facts are only known to a few.

Not once but many times has the statement been made that the Cromwellian Installation in Westminster Hall forms the *sole* occasion on which the enormity (it might more accurately be termed the sacrilege) has been perpetrated, of removing King Edward's Chair out of the Abbey. This is altogether wrong. The shameful deed has taken place *twice*.

The Office of Works did not hesitate in 1887 to follow this seventeenth-century precedent, and for the time being King Edward's Chair disappeared from its historic home in order to undergo the varnishing process already mentioned. This statement will doubtless be received with amazement; but it is absolutely true. People only recently dead were able to testify to the fact.

## NOTE

### *The Coronation Chair of Edward I*

Mr. Howorth (Salford, S.) asked the First Commissioner of Works, whether the Coronation Chair, which was originally made by order of Edward I, and which has since remained in its original state, except so far as time has injured it, was during the recent celebration in the Abbey covered with a brown stain which cannot be removed; whether this has not destroyed and irretrievably lost to us the original decoration of its surface, consisting of fine plaster covered with gold, and pricked out in pattern; if this be so, who is responsible for this act; and if it be possible to place objects so precious beyond the reach of such disaster in future?

The First Commissioner (Mr. Plunket) (Dublin University): There is no foundation for the alarm expressed in the Question of my hon. Friend. The old Coronation Chair has not been in any way stained or disfigured, and not the slightest injury has been done to the traces which remain of the ancient gilded work. The misapprehension may possibly have arisen from the circumstance that it was necessary to fit in temporarily some few pieces of tracery which were missing, and to stain them brown to match the colour of the old work; but the colour of the old work was not touched, and remains exactly as it was before the ceremony.

Sir Thomas Esmonde (Dublin Co., S.) asked the First Commissioner of Works, if it is a fact that the missing portions of the Coronation Chair have been replaced with new work, the new parts painted brown, and the whole varnished with brown varnish; and, if so, whether the old painting and gilding of the chair have been injured; and, who is responsible for this restoration?

The First Commissioner (Mr. Plunket) (Dublin University): It is true, as I have already stated to the House, that certain missing portions of the Coronation Chair were, for the purposes of the recent ceremony, of necessity replaced by new work; but this was very carefully arranged, so that they could be again removed without any damage to the Chair, and they have been so removed. It is true, also, that a considerable portion of the Chair was slightly darkened with colour. On that point I was in error when I last spoke. That, too, was done so as to be equally capable of being undone; and the chair is now, both as to substance and colour, exactly as before it was given into my charge. There is no change whatever in the structure or the colour. I am glad to have this opportunity of assuring the House and the public that, after communication with the Dean of Westminster and the President of the Society of Antiquaries, I am so fortunate as to be able to state that they are well satisfied with the careful manner in which the monuments and the structure of the Abbey have been treated by the Office of Works. The hon. Baronet asks me who is responsible? Well, Sir, of course, I am responsible, and solely responsible, to this House for whatever has been done; but I am bound in justice to say that the whole of the credit is due to the permanent officials of my Department, and especially to my surveyor, Mr. Taylor, whose able and unremitting labours I cannot too highly commend.

Mr. Bradlaugh (Northampton) asked, whether, as a matter of fact, the Coronation Chair was not covered with a dark brown stain composed of gum and spirit; whether the decoration had not suffered from that staining; whether the stain was not rubbed off in the Abbey on Saturday last by the workmen pouring a large quantity of methylated spirit on the Chair, and then rubbing it off with their aprons until they were remonstrated with; and whether this process did not occur in the presence of several persons, one of them being the hon. Member for South Durham.

MR. PLUNKET: This is the most remarkable instance of trying to make a storm in a tea-cup that I ever heard of. The Chair is in exactly the same condition as to form, substance, and colour, as when it came into my charge.

(*Hansard's Parliamentary Debates*, 3rd Series, vol. cccxvi, col. 1785, July 5, 1887.)

# PART VI
# THE CHANTRY CHAPEL OF HENRY V

## 1. THE GATES

A NOBLE screen or grate of wrought-iron work gives access from the Confessor's Chapel to the platform on which rests the tomb of Henry V. It displays an almost bewildering complexity of design at first sight: but on closer examination it is seen to be a somewhat monotonous piece of work, consisting in the main of the endless repetition of one single pattern. Beautiful though it is, it suffers from its close proximity to one of the most wonderful specimens in the world of the art of the metal craftsman, viz. the thirteenth-century grate or closure attached to the tomb of Eleanor of Castile. If the two be compared, to quote the words of William Burges, 'we find that we have left art and arrived at mere architecture'.[1]

The grate is divided into three bays, the outer ones which serve as doorways containing three panels with rounded heads at the top, while the central portion contains six panels of similar character and design. At the springing head is a flat embattled rail, the tympanum of the arch being filled with open tracery. Below the rail the three bays are divided by means of buttresses. A kind of transom runs horizontally across the structure forming a middle rail. Above this the lights are open, while below they are closed, by means of thin sheet-iron, for the sake of greater security. The panels are all completely filled with a series of square diapers formed by means of a number of small horizontal and diagonal bars, each of them cusped in the centre. The general effect is extremely fine in spite of the constant repetition.

Originally the tomb of Henry V was entirely closed,

---

[1] Scott, *Gleanings from Westminster Abbey*, pp. 90 and 91.

F. Barlow Delin.      R. Gaywood fecit.

THE WESTERN FACE OF THE CHANTRY CHAPEL OF HENRY V, *c.* 1675

the grate forming a kind of cage; but the three sides which faced the ambulatory, were plain and solid, consisting simply of a series of vertical and horizontal bars. The costly silver-plated effigy of Henry V was doubtless responsible for this extremely elaborate and carefully thought-out scheme of protection. It was of no avail, however, during the dark and confused years which succeeded the fall of the monastery. The miscreants who are said to have 'broken in the night-season into the Church of Westminster' during the early days of January 1546 effectually ruined this remarkable work of art. To-day a mere oaken stump remains.

The grate was the work of one Roger Johnson, smith, of London. There is an agreement for its manufacture in the Patent Rolls of 1431. Without doubt it was originally decorated with colour. Barely a century ago it was possible to trace a number of coloured devices, consisting of rows of three fleurs-de-lis on a blue ground alternated with three gilded leopards on a red ground. Below these, near the middle of the gates, were fixed alternate rows of swans and antelopes.[1]

With the nineteenth century, tragedy in its most grievous form befell the grate, a tragedy in which the bulk of the metal-work belonging to the Abbey was involved.

Our forefathers down to relatively recent times made a point of protecting every tomb by means of an iron fence with the object of disappointing the relic-hunter and the vandal so far as such a thing was possible. These grilles or railings varied greatly in character and value, ranging from a simple palisade of metal bars to wrought-iron work of incalculable complexity and elaboration.

The older histories of Westminster Abbey, those of Ackerman and Neale in particular, with their copious

[1] J. P. Neale and E. W. Brayley, *History and Antiquities of the Abbey Church of St. Peter Westminster*, vol. i, pp. 86, 87, and Scott, *Gleanings from Westminster Abbey*, p. 92.

illustrations, show that there was scarcely a single tomb in the church which was devoid of this protection.

The eighteenth century, needless to say, was wholly incapable of appreciating such a treasure as the grate of Henry V's Chantry Chapel.  The opinion of one of its artistic authorities is illuminating.

'There is at the end of this place a sort of gate to the tomb of Henry V which was intended for a piece of magnificence; and no cost was spared to make it answer that design, but the taste of it is so unhappy and the execution so execrable that it has not the least claim to that character.'[1]

Wrong-headed ideas of this description were still potent at the commencement of the nineteenth century and may have carried some weight in the minds of the Dean and Chapter.  Early in the reign of George IV that body embarked upon a policy unfortunate to a degree.  They were not altogether to blame.  The real culprit was none other than the famous sculptor, Sir Francis Chantrey, who in those days enjoyed a kind of general commission from the Abbey authorities to maintain the numerous monuments in a clean and decent condition.  His word seems to have been regarded as law, if we may judge by Dean Ireland's encomium, 'knowing from long experience how delicate and honourable his judgment is in all matters relating to the Abbey'.[2]  Chantrey deluded himself into the belief that the iron railings were useless where the pedestal of a monument was concerned; that, so far from being a protection, they formed an actual temptation, in that they led people to clamber on top of them, in order to play tricks with the upper and more elaborate portions, and that, if removed, this temptation would automatically cease.

During the preparations for the Coronation of George IV a number of the railings underwent temporary removal, and the Dean and Chapter, under the influence of

[1] John Ralph, *Critical Review of Public Buildings in London and Westminster*, p. 86.                    [2] Chapter Book.

Chantrey, decided not to replace them. Unfortunately
they did not stop at this point. Not content with abolishing the simpler railings attached to the monuments which
lined the walls of their church, the interest of which was
comparatively small, they even removed such priceless
treasures as the beautiful grate of Queen Eleanor's tomb
(presumably because Chantrey failed to realize that it
formed part of the general composition, as much as the
effigy itself), and likewise those surrounding the tombs of
Henry V, the Lady Margaret Beaufort, Mary Queen of
Scots, and Queen Elizabeth, every one of them possessed
of great beauty and historical value. How the still more
elaborate grate attached to the tomb of Henry VII
managed to escape remains a mystery.

The sorry tale was revealed some years later in the evidence given before the Select Committee on National
Monuments and Works of Art, published in 1841.

By that time almost all those concerned in this deplorable vandalism had disappeared. The old Dean, Dr.
Ireland, was bedridden and had delegated his responsibilities into the capable hands of the Sub-Dean, Lord
John Thynne. Nine new Prebendaries had been installed. Chantrey was dead, Benjamin Wyatt had been
dismissed by the Dean and Chapter from the office of
Surveyor, and his place had been filled by Edward Blore,
a high-minded man of a very different stamp.

The Chapter were represented at the inquiry by the
Treasurer, the Rev. H. H. Milman, of historical fame,
the future Dean of St. Paul's, but neither he nor Blore
could throw much light upon the happenings of nearly
twenty years before. It was reserved for an old man of
seventy-nine, Samuel Tansley by name, formerly smith
to Westminster Abbey, to make, in a somewhat rambling
manner, a series of perfectly amazing statements.

From the information furnished by this witness it
appeared that he had received orders to remove all the

railings surrounding the monuments, ancient and modern
alike; that he had purchased from the Clerk of the Works
a quantity of the metal-work surrounding the royal tombs
at so much per hundredweight; that part of it was 'worked
up' by him, and another portion sold to a member of the
firm of Rundell and Bridge, the well-known goldsmiths
of Ludgate Hill. Fortunately, 'there was at that time
some stir in the House of Commons respecting the taking
down of the rails from the royal tombs'. The Dean and
Chapter had been roused to a sense of their responsibility
and in a moment of penitence repurchased, before it was
too late, some of the metal-work which they had shortly
before consigned so cheerfully to the scrap-heap.

Further evidence was laid before the Committee by
Edward Hedlake Brayley, who with John Preston Neale
had been responsible for the monumental history of
Westminster Abbey. Needless to say, he criticized the
vandalism of twenty years earlier in no measured terms,
and together with Blore urged that where possible the loss
be made good.[1]

Thus, although much had perished, including the
priceless grate of Queen Elizabeth's tomb, the Dean and
Chapter still possessed some valuable pieces of metal-work,
including the grate of Henry V's Chantry, which during
the early forties of last century was lying about in the
triforium or elsewhere utterly neglected. There would
not have been the slightest difficulty about replacing it
*in situ*, then and there, and it seems strange that the
advice given before the Select Committee by men of such
high standing as Blore and Brayley should have been
disregarded.

Nearly ten years were allowed to slip away, but still
nothing was done. In 1849, however, Sir Gilbert Scott
succeeded Blore as Surveyor. He at once replaced the

[1] *Report of the Select Committee on National Monuments and Works of Art*,
pp. 49, 59, 80, 82, 86, 87, 106, 113, 114.

neglected grates of the tombs of Queen Eleanor and Henry V, a prodigious undertaking in the case of the latter. He found that it had been 'broken up into a thousand pieces', and was lying scattered about the Chapel of St. Faith, for which the Dean and Chapter of those days could devise no better use than to be a lumber room![1] Unfortunately, those portions of the grate which formerly surrounded the northern, eastern, and southern sides of Henry V's tomb had perished. We can only be thankful that so much was saved from the wreck.

Harsh words are often uttered, not without justice, about the work of Sir Gilbert Scott all over the country; but in his restoration of this beautiful work of art and the grate of Queen Eleanor's tomb to their original positions he has laid posterity under a permanent debt.

In 1874 he designed the existing oak staircase, by means of which additional access is gained to the Chapel of St. Edward from the east. Up to that time it could only be entered from the north ambulatory.

## 2. THE CHANTRY CHAPEL

In order to reach this chapel which spans the ambulatory like a bridge, it is necessary to ascend the newel staircase in one or other of the great octagonal turrets of openwork, one for ascent, the other for descent, which face the Confessor's Chapel.[2] The nail-studded doors are original, and likewise the steps, but the latter have been in places almost worn through by the feet of countless worshippers in pre-Reformation times.

According to the terms of Henry V's will,[3] made at Southampton in 1415, every day were 'iii masses perpetually to be sungen in a fair chapel over his sepulchre' and 'thirty poor persons' were to recite in this place for a

---

[1] Scott, *Personal and Professional Recollections*, pp. 152–3.
[2] The influence is apparent here of the Sainte Chapelle at Paris, where the structures on which the relics were exposed were reached by means of spiral stairs in openwork turrets.　　　[3] Rymer's *Foedera*, vol. ix, p. 289.

whole year the Psalter of the Virgin with a special petition for the King.

The inaccessibility of the Chantry Chapel has proved its salvation. It has ensured its wholesale neglect, for only an infinitesimal number of people have in past times ever taken any interest in it at all, and for this reason any desire to be commemorated therein by tablet or monument has been effectively quenched. Obscurity has its advantages!

The reredos is still intact save for the loss of its central figure and a few statuettes. The base of this structure consists of a moulded cornice containing a series of groups of figures, viz. the swan and the antelope chained to the beacon, badges always associated with Henry V. The altar is surmounted by a blank panel which was probably covered with some rich hanging. Of the three carved trefoils over the altar, that in the centre, which is much perished, is adorned with a seated, irradiated figure bearing a cross. On each of the flanking trefoils are placed an irradiated Virgin and Child seated on a moon, and below, a maiden with a unicorn. Above the cornice rise seven large canopied niches extending beyond the chapel over the ambulatory. Each niche has a carved and pierced traceried pedestal and is flanked by pinnacled buttresses. It is surmounted by a semi-octagonal, vaulted canopy with ogee, crocketted heads, and a pierced, traceried tabernacle with moulded and carved cornice and cresting. Moving from left to right, the figures represent: (1) St. George of England in plate armour destroying the dragon; (2) a King in long robes, possibly St. Edmund of East Anglia; (3) the Archangel Gabriel kneeling; (4) the empty niche; (5) the Blessed Virgin seated with her hands crossed on her breast; (6) a bearded King in a long robe, probably St. Edward the Confessor; (7) St. Denys of France, arrayed in the mass vestments of a bishop and holding his mitred head in his hands. Figures Nos. (3)

N° I. The Head is not ill carved in Wood and the Cloth Drapery it is dressed in, is probably what originally belonged to the Figure.

N° II. Is entirely of Wood painted over.

N° III. The Head and Breast are carved in Wood, the Body is only a Wooden Post, the Thighs are canvas stuffed with Arms, and the Legs are carved in Wood.

N° IIII. The Head and Neck are finely modelled in Clay, the Body is composed of Plaster half an Inch thick, and covered with a kind of fine Cloth incorporated with the Plaster.

N° V. The Head is well carved in Wood, it is stuffed with Straw, and partly dressed in its original Drapery.

N° VI. Is a figure in complete drapery, the head is lost.

N° VII. Seems to have its original Clothing.

N° VIII. Is an whole Figure carved in Wood.

N° IX. Is a stuffed contrivance for Hips, exactly similar to what is worn by the Women of to-day. N.B. The Remains of the Robes of those Royal Personages are battered

about the pavement of the Chapel which is in a scandalous dirty and neglected condition.

N° X. Is the Shield and Helmet of Henry V.

N° XI. Is the Saddle of Henry V.

The Image of Elizabeth of York, Queen of Henry VII. is preserved in Westminster Abbey among those curious but mangled figures of some of our Princes which were carried at their Interments, and now called the Ragged Regiment. WALPOLE's Anecdotes. Edit. I. P. 54.

# THE INTERIOR OF THE CHANTRY CHAPEL OF HENRY V IN 1786

and (5) clearly relate to the altar which bore the dedication title of the Annunciation of the Blessed Virgin.
The larger niches are separated by groups of smaller ones
ranged one above the other. Five only out of the twenty-
four figures are missing. Those which survive in the
middle rows include St. John the Evangelist holding a
chalice and St. Paul wielding a sword. The figures in the
top row are wearing long robes and scrolls; but it is difficult to identify them. Some slight traces still remain of
medieval painting on the six shields which form part of
the cornice. The general ensemble is magnificent.

The reredos is not the only survival in this remarkable
little chapel. Almost the whole of the medieval pavement
remains intact. The western portion consists of plain red
tiles set square at the sides and diagonally in the middle.
Farther east the tiles are yellow and dark green, while the
footpace of the altar retains its marble step. The original
stone benches remain *in situ* on either side, and likewise
four recessed lockers at the east end with fragments of
their iron hinges. Two of these lockers possess carved and
crested cornices together with ogee-headed crocketted
panels, flanked and divided by pinnacled buttresses. The
shelves and other woodwork were intact two centuries ago,
according to Dart. 'On the walls are Presses of Wainscot
with Shelves and folding Doors, very neat, six in all, viz.
four on each side wall, and one each side of the altar.'[1]
Later in the century, in 1786, John Carter found a portion
of them still in being and made the sketch here reproduced.

Before the building of Henry V's Chantry the aumbry
containing the Relics (of which the Abbey possessed
many), and probably an altar also must have filled up the
eastern portion of the Confessor's Chapel. The Relics
were now transferred to the Chapel upstairs and were
possibly placed in these lockers.[2]

[1] Dart, *Westmonasterium*, vol. i, p. 63.
[2] Lethaby, *Westminster Abbey Re-examined*, p. 275.

## 3. THE ALTAR OF THE ANNUNCIATION
## AND ALL SAINTS

The altar slab was dedicated in 1448 by Nicholas Ashby, Bishop of Llandaff, a former monk of Westminster. The executors of Henry V, upon whom the responsibility devolved of erecting the chantry, would have been astounded beyond words could they have foreseen the strange vicissitudes which this simple piece of marble, undecorated save for a hollow-chamfered underedge, and its five consecration crosses was destined to experience.

John Carter found this relic of the past 'laying upon the side of the altar, and forming part of the pavement'.[1] Desecration of this kind has been so frequent since the Reformation that it occasions no surprise.

This outrage was matched by another, below, on the ground floor, which evoked indignant comment even in the middle of the eighteenth century, an epoch which could hardly be described as given to over-fastidiousness. To quote the sarcastic words of John Ralph:

'One thing we meet with in this place which merits a particular regard: that is a wooden chest of bones said to be the remains of Catherine daughter of the King of France, and consort of Henry V. If this account is authentic I think that nothing can be of greater violation of decency or more injurious to the memory of such illustrious personages than to expose their reliques in so licentious a manner, and make a show of what once commanded respect and adoration.'[2]

These words recall an extraordinary story, in the last phase of which the desecrated altar-slab figures with considerable prominence.

The Queen Consort of Henry V was Katharine of Valois, daughter of the unfortunate Charles VI, King of

[1] *Gentleman's Magazine*, 1799, p. 860.
[2] John Ralph, *A Critical Review of Public Buildings in London and Westminster*, p. 86.

France. So charming and attractive was she in the eyes of the doughty Englishman that the latter protested to one of his rivals, the Duke of Burgundy, that 'he would either enjoy the Lady Katharine or drive the King of France out of his Kingdom and the Duke out of his Dukedom'. Such was the beginning of the courtship, which preceded a married life of only two years.

Left a widow, in the full flush of youth, Katharine proceeded without much delay to take unto herself a second spouse in the person of a young Welsh squire, Owen Tudor by name, 'the most beautiful personage of that age'. The mésalliance was ill calculated to commend itself to Court circles, and the blue-blooded princess, 'the daughter and the mother of kings', sank into almost total oblivion. Her burial in 1437 was conducted in a manner which was hardly decent. She was not denied the privilege of a last resting-place in the Abbey, it is true, but her grave was placed in the Lady Chapel, a building which up to that time had witnessed no royal interment at all.[1] Her body was laid in a rude coffin, in a 'badly apparelled state'.

The years passed away and the time arrived when Katharine's grandson, the founder of the Tudor dynasty, was seated on the throne of the realm. Circumstances were now altogether changed. The Queen Consort, ignored and despised both in life and in death for three generations, was projected into a position of first-rate importance. In the remarkable will, in which he set forth at great length the various considerations impelling him to embark upon the task of rebuilding the Lady Chapel of the Abbey, Henry VII laid special stress upon the presence within that building of 'the body of his granddame of right noble memory Queen Katharine, wife to King Henry V and daughter to King Charles of France'. With the obvious exceptions of St. Edward the Confessor

[1] Agnes Strickland, *Queens of England,* pp. 103 and 209.

U

and Henry VI, Katharine alone is mentioned by name among the new Tudor sovereign's 'noble progenitors and blood'.

With the destruction of the thirteenth-century Lady Chapel in 1502 Queen Katharine's body underwent a kind of translation, intended at the outset to be only temporary. It could hardly be called a change for the better, neither was it consistent with the flattering expressions contained in her grandson's will. The corpse was wrapped in a sheet of lead taken from the roof and laid unburied beside the tomb of her husband on the ground-floor of his chantry chapel. It must, of course, be remembered that the place where lies the body of Henry V possessed in the sixteenth century a privacy wholly unknown to-day. The wooden staircase now connecting it with the ambulatory did not exist. The space was barred off on all four sides by the heavy iron grate. The one and only approach would normally be kept locked. Still, even after making every possible allowance, and bearing in mind the original temporary character of the proceedings, this method of handling the body of a departed Queen of England was irreverent in the extreme.

Time wore on. The temporary passed into permanence. No one troubled his head about the poor lady. Even such a Dean as Lancelot Andrewes, to whom the subject must surely have seemed revolting, allowed things to drift. No less than two hundred and seventy-four years passed by, during which time the 'wooden chest or coffin, wherein part of the skeleton and parched body of Katharine Valois his Queen (from the waist upwards) was to be seen'.[1] Dart has bequeathed to us a gruesome account of these poor, despised relics of humanity, which 'continued to be seen the bones being firmly united, and thereby clothed with flesh, like scrapings of fine leather',[2] while

---

[1] Keepe, *Monumenta Westmonasteriensia*, p. 155.
[2] Dart, *Westmonasterium*, vol. ii, p. 39.

THE VESTIBULE OF HENRY VII's CHAPEL, THE AMBULATORY, AND THE METAL BARRIER
ENCLOSING THE TOMB OF HENRY V

the ghastly birthday treat with which Pepys regaled himself on the Shrove Tuesday of 1668 fills us with nausea:

'Here we did see by particular favour, the body of Queen Katharine of Valois; and I had the upper part of her body in my hands, and I did kiss her mouth reflecting that this was my birthday, thirty-six years old, that I did first kiss a Queen.'[1]

A picture of the lower portion of Henry V's chantry in Sandford's *Geneaological History of the Kings and Queens of England* gives a faint indication of Queen Katharine's coffin lying on the right of her husband's tomb just where the passage–way is to-day.[2]

Not until George III had sat on the throne for some years did the powers that be wake up to this abominable state of things. Just before Christmas, in the year 1776, Elizabeth Percy, the first Duchess of Northumberland, was interred in the Chapel of St. Nicholas hard by, and it seems to have occurred to some one that the vault appropriated to this great north-country family would form a more seemly resting-place for this hapless lady. The interment, overdue for centuries, was therefore carried out, and the Queen was interred beneath the Villiers monument.

Just one hundred years later, in 1878, the final translation of the poor remains[3] took place. A tomb was erected on the site of the old Altar of the Annunciation and All Saints. The desecrated mensa was taken up from the floor and placed thereon by order of Queen Victoria. This graceful and appropriate action, inspired possibly by the example of Charles II in the case of the two

---

[1] *Diary and Correspondence of Samuel Pepys*, vol. v, p. 475.

[2] Sandford, Francis, *Genealogical History of the Kings and Queens of England*, p. 289.

[3] During their sojourn of a century in the Northumberland vault the Queen's remains had undergone a great change. 'The body i.e. ribs and vertebrae, was entirely wanting, also a clavicle and some part of the bones of the right limbs. Quicklime had entirely destroyed the face; but the hinder part of the skull remained unimpaired. The jaw had disappeared, and no vestige of teeth remained.'

murdered Princes, has been duly recorded by the following inscription sculptured upon the western face of this altar tomb:

Sub hoc tabula
(Altari Olim Hujusce Sacelli)
Qui Prostrata, Igne Confracta
Requiescit tandem Varias post Vices
Hic Demum Jussu Victoriae Reginae Deposita
Ossa Catherine de Valois
Filiae Caroli Sexti Franciae Regis
Uxoris Henrici Quinti
Matris Henrici Sexti
Aviae Henrici Septimi

During the palmy days of the fifteenth century the Chapel of Henry V must have been one of the most prominent and important in the Abbey. No other served such a remarkable variety of purposes, viz. the Chantry Chapel of the Warrior King, the Chapel of the Annunciation and All Saints, a Relic Chamber, and a Watching Loft. In the dark days which followed, it was despoiled of its treasures and pushed down into utter degradation. Thick with dust, the receptacle of odds and ends, and hardly ever opened, it was clean forgotten that it was a gem of fifteenth-century art, the common resting-place of Plantagenet and Valois, in which England and France join hands.

Those days are gone, it may be hoped, for ever. To-day chapel and altar are furnished in a simple but comely fashion. An atmosphere of prayer and devotion once more pervades the place, despite the sad losses inflicted by insensate bigotry and neglect.

His indenture made betwene the moost excellent and moost cristen Prince kyng Henry the seuenth by the grace of godd kyng of Englonde and of ffraunce and lorde of Irelande the sixtene day of July the xviiietene yere of his moost noble reigne of the oon partie And John Abbot of the monastery of Seynt Peter of Westm and the Priour and Convent of thesame monastery of the oder partie Witnesseth that Where thesaid Abbot priour and Convent by other Indentures made betwene theym and thesaid kyng oure Soueraigne lorde berying date thesaid day and yere Where vnto these Indentures be annexed haue conuenuanted and graunted emonge other thinge and bounden theym and thair Successours to thesaid kynge oure Soueraigne lorde his heires and Successours that thesame Abbot priour and Convent and their Successours aboue the noumbre of the pore men that they nowe fynde or be bounde or ought to fynde in thesaide monastery or without thesame shall from the date of thesame Indenture fynde thretene poore men of good and virtuose disposicion within the precincte of thesaide monastery perpetually whill the worlde shall

HENRY VII BESTOWING THE INDENTURES OF HIS NEW FOUNDATION
UPON ABBOT ISLIP AND THE CONVENT OF WESTMINSTER

# PART VII

# THE CHAPEL OF KING HENRY VII

## I. THE GREAT SCHEME OF HENRY VII AND ITS OVERTHROW BY HENRY VIII

THE story of this chapel forms no exception to that of other portions of Westminster Abbey. It has suffered in varying degrees at the hands of the Reformer, the Puritan, and the Restorer, but it still retains a remarkable number of its original ornaments and treasures, all of the deepest interest. In our own day an attempt has been made, not without success, to recall some of the ideals which inspired its royal founder when he embarked upon his prodigious undertaking.

Henry VII can hardly be called an attractive character. Perhaps he has not always received full justice at the hands of the historian, but, even after making every allowance, no one could possibly style him a lovable man. His Will, which fortunately has been preserved, displays another side of his character, to which posterity has so far given but little heed. It deserves to be read from end to end. Some of the expressions in which the royal piety finds an outlet will fail to commend themselves to the twentieth-century mind. None the less, taken as a whole, the Will is a beautiful and touching document, breathing a spirit of sincere devotion, and throws a flood of light upon the ideals by which the King was inspired. It displays the outlook of the later Middle Ages at its best. It was not drawn up until he lay upon his death-bed; but it plainly indicates the ideals and motives by which he was actuated from the first.

From the very beginning Henry VII kept three objects steadily in view.

In the first place, it was his eager desire to show all possible honour to the Blessed Virgin, in whom, next to

the Holy and Undivided Trinity itself, he had ever reposed his 'moost singulier trust and confidence'.[1] In the
funeral sermon delivered by his friend Thomas Fisher,
Bishop of Rochester, the preacher stressed this outstanding feature of the King's spiritual life. 'On the daye of his
departynge he herde Masse of ye gloryous Virgyn ye
moder of Cryste, to whom alwaye in his lyfe he has a
synguler and specyall devocyon.'

The King determined therefore to rebuild, upon a
magnificent scale, the thirteenth-century Lady Chapel,
erected a quarter of a century before our third Henry
commenced work upon the choir of the Abbey. The
question of expense was a minor consideration altogether.
Alike from the point of view of construction and of decoration, the King strove to bestow upon the world a building
which should be one of the noblest creations ever con-
ceived by the mind of man.

In the most prominent position of all was to stand the
'high Aultre within our said Chapell called our Lady
Aultre', upon which Henry determined to bestow a
special token of his devotion, viz. the greatest 'image of
Our Lady that we now have in our Juelhouse' and 'a
crosse of plate of gold upon tymber to the value of C$^{li}$'.

The King's second object was the erection of a chantry,
or, as it was termed in an indenture drawn up with Abbot
Islip, 'a closure of metall in maner of a Chapell'. Within
the said closure at the east end was to stand an altar
dedicated to the Holy Saviour, the remaining space being
set apart for the sumptuous tomb of the royal founder and
his Consort, Elizabeth of York. This chantry was to stand
in 'the myddes of the same chapel before the high aultier',
a direction defined yet more clearly by another passage in
the Will:

'also we Wol that by a convenient space and distaunce from the

---

[1] Several quotations in this and subsequent chapters are taken from *The Will
of Henry*, edited by Thomas Astle (1775).

grees of the high Aultier of the said Chapel, there be made in length and brede about the said tombe, a grate in maner of a Closure of coper and gilte, after the faction that we have begoune, which we Wol be by our said Executours fully accomplished and p'fourmed. And within the same grate, at owre fete, after a convenient distaunce from our tombe, bee maid an Aultier, in the honour of our Saviour Jhu Crist stright adionyng to the said grate.'

The chantry chapel, then, was intended to be a masterpiece of bronze metal, designed upon a most elaborate scale and furnished with buttresses, window traceries, and pinnacles, like a structure of stone. It is important, too, to note that according to the extremely precise terms of the Will, the closure was to stand between the two rows of stalls on either side, an arrangement which obviously had a most important bearing upon the general planning of the new chapel. A large amount of floor-space was imperatively demanded, and this in its turn compelled the erection of somewhat narrow sets of stalls, pushed right up against the arches, and approached by unusually steep flights of steps. Unless the stalls had been constructed on these somewhat inconvenient lines it would have been impossible for their occupants to see over the grate standing immediately in front of them. Again, the great breadth of the latter in a similar way came to exercise an influence upon the dimensions and proportions of what may be termed the nave. It was the undoubted intention of the King to erect the principal altar of the chapel east of the site occupied by its modern successor, otherwise the huge grate, occupying such a large portion of the nave, would have completely frustrated any clear and uninterrupted view of the officiating clergy from the stalls.

Last of all, and this was perhaps the primary motive by which he was inspired, it was the ardent desire of the King to provide an honourable resting-place for his Lancastrian predecessor, the 'bodie and reliques of our Vncle of blissid memorie King Henry VIth' which he intended 'right shortely to translate' from St. George's Chapel, Windsor, to Westminster. That monarch's figure, set up in scores of churches all over the land, had already begun to attract pilgrims, and Henry VII evidently had good hope at the outset of securing his canonization from the Papacy.

In order to carry out this pious purpose, Henry proposed to utilize the easternmost chapel of the building, thus following the precedent already set in the Chapel of St. Edward the Confessor. The tomb of Henry VI was to stand a little distance to the east of the altar of the Blessed Virgin, the reredos of which would have been kept quite low. The ground floor was to be occupied by a table tomb supporting the customary effigy, while above, approached by staircases, was to be built a chantry chapel, not altogether unlike that of Henry V.

With great good fortune, a sketch drawn about the year 1500 of the chapel proposed as the last resting-place of Henry VI has been preserved in the Cottonian Collection at the British Museum.[1] It would have been a work of remarkable beauty had it ever been erected.

From the angles rise slender octagonal turrets, terminating with ogee, curved cappings cut into scales, similar to those on the exterior of the chapel. Arches spring from turret to turret, while above them appears a tier of niches intended to accommodate about twenty statues, supported upon pedestals after the fashion of pillars.

Let us endeavour to picture to ourselves the spectacle which would have met the eye of a person sitting in one of the upper stalls. He would have looked directly upon the chantry chapel of Henry VII, the altar of the Holy Saviour, and the splendid tomb of the Royal Founder and his wife, surrounded by the magnificent bronze grate.

[1] Cottonian MSS., Aug. 11, vol. i, 'The Monument intended for Kinge Henry the Sixte.'

The Monument intended for Kinge Henry the sixte.

THE PROPOSED CHANTRY CHAPEL OF HENRY VI

Farther to the east he would see the altar of our Lady with the gorgeous hangings and ornaments provided by the terms of the King's Will. Last of all, and still farther eastward, he would have descried the chantry chapel of Henry VI, with its delicate architecture, towering up in the background and forming a wondrous canopy over the tomb of that monarch beneath.

Thus, had the intentions of Henry VII been carried out in their entirety, Westminster Abbey, already one of the noblest churches in Europe, would have been graced with a superb addition, filled with works of art costly beyond words. It was to be stamped from the outset with the hall-mark of royalty, being a great mausoleum chapel with the sumptuous tomb of the Founder enclosed in its brazen chantry, and with the remains of Henry VI (duly canonized) reverently preserved in the easternmost of the five radiating chapels.[1]

Provision was also made for the burial of the mother of Henry VII, the Lady Margaret Beaufort, in the south aisle chapel, where a statue of St. Margaret appears among the imagery over the altar.

In the same way, the northern aisle chapel, where to-day lie the two Tudor sisters, Mary and Elizabeth, was intended to become the receptacle of yet another royal tomb. Possibly the Founder had it in mind to set apart this portion of the building as the last resting-place of his son and successor.[2]

Whether the apsidal chapels were ever dedicated or not is doubtful. It has been conjectured that three of them bore the titles of St. Denys, St. Ursula, and St. Giles, but the evidence is not altogether convincing.[3]

---

[1] There is an empty niche in the wall of this chapel, on the pedestal of which can still be seen the letters H.R. Evidently it was intended to fill this place with a statue of Henry VI.

[2] Lethaby, *Westminster Abbey Re-examined*, p. 159.

[3] Westlake, *The Story of Westminster Abbey*, p. 47, and *Westminster Abbey*, vol. ii, p. 364.

Nothing in the nature of a congregation or congregational worship could have been contemplated for one moment. The fact that so large a portion of the central space was to be filled up with the great chantry would obviously have reduced the accommodation for worshippers to the smallest possible limits.

It must be noted that the stalls occupy one bay less than to-day. By this means direct communication was secured from the two aisle chapels into the central area, through curved screens similar to those which still survive in part in two of the apsidal chapels. Thus the whole building was intended to form one coherent whole, to which the two aisle chapels would have made an important contribution. To-day, unfortunately, they are demarcated off almost as much as if they were separate buildings. Again, the four unappropriated radiating chapels were undoubtedly intended to be similarly utilized as time went on for additional royal tombs and chantries. Thus no less than eight royal chantry chapels would ultimately have been grouped together round the splendid high altar dedicated to the Blessed Virgin.

What an astounding conception has Henry VII bequeathed to the world!

It is clear, too, that the vast exuberance of ornament, no less than the actual structure, was due to his own emphatic commands. His Will leaves no room for doubt. He insisted in that document that the chapel should be 'painted, garnished and adorned in as goodly and rich a manner as such a work requireth and as to a King's work apperteyneth'. Again, when speaking of the furnishings of the various altars, he laid down that the question of expense should be wholly disregarded: 'as for the price and value of them our mind is that they be such as apperteyneth to the gift of a Prince; and therefore we will that our executors have a special regard to the laud of God and the weal of our soul and our honour royal'.

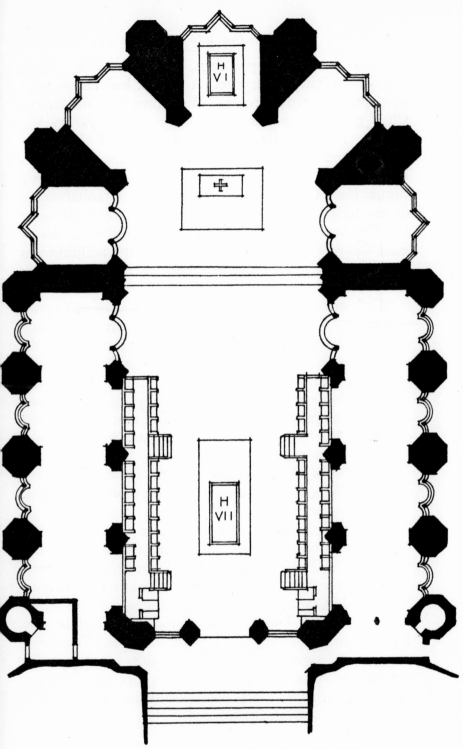

GROUND PLAN OF HENRY VII'S CHAPEL

(*a*) AS INTENDED BY THE FOUNDER

With these high hopes, then, did Henry VII embark upon his mighty enterprise. A contest had taken place between the three churches of Westminster, Windsor, and Chertsey for the possession of the remains of Henry VI. The decision of the Lord Chancellor and the Privy Council had been given in favour of the first-named and the King lost no time in getting to work. During 1502 the old Lady Chapel was demolished, and on January 24th of the following year the foundation stone of the new building was laid by Abbot Islip.[1] Six years of strenuous work followed, at the end of which time the building was complete. Within a week of making the last payment the King died.

Much still remained to be done. The task of equipping the chapel with the costly furnishings, intended to enhance its charm and wonder yet further, was one of untold magnitude, almost, if not quite as great as the erection of the beautiful fabric itself. The responsibility of carrying out his father's wishes passed of necessity into the hands of the son, who made no secret of the fact that he definitely 'misliked' some of those splendid projects. The result was closely akin to tragedy.

The scheme for the translation of the remains of Henry VI from Windsor to Westminster was soon abandoned. The canonization proposal had already collapsed, probably because it was too costly. A new site considerably to the east of the original choice was now selected to be the burial-place of Henry VII and his Consort, above which their tomb and the surrounding grate were ultimately to be erected. Consequently, it became impossible to set up the altar of our Lady in the position intended by the Founder in the eastern portion of the chapel. There was no alternative save to bring it a bay or more forward, to the west of the royal tomb. Thus, the empty nave with its undue breadth has a sadly disproportionate effect. To the

---

[1] Holinshed, *Chronicles*, vol. iii, p. 529.

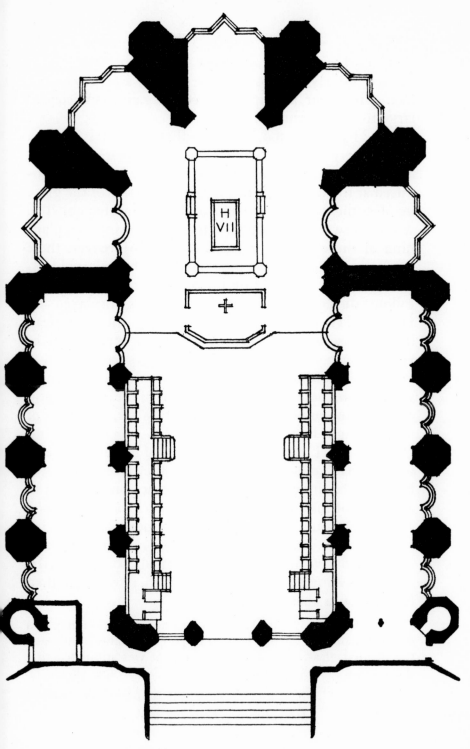

H VII

GROUND PLAN OF HENRY VII'S CHAPEL

(*b*) AS COMPLETED BY HENRY VIII

mind of Henry VII all this vacant space would have seemed utterly purposeless, so much waste ground in fact. He never anticipated a congregation sufficiently large to occupy this extensive area.

The High Altar, too, is awkwardly placed. It is jammed up so closely as almost to touch the bronze grate surrounding the Founder's tomb. Thus a crowded effect is produced at the east end, while the immense size of the grate involves the masking of several of the apsidal chapels. The word 'awkward' is a mild term to use for the internal planning of the chapel as it exists to-day. Moreover, these arrangements are wholly inconsistent with the lofty idealism by which the building itself has been inspired. The callous disregard of his father's wishes displayed by Henry VIII, when he consigned them to the scrap-heap in this unscrupulous fashion, was from every point of view utterly indefensible. His changes constituted a veritable revolution, with the result that the chapel, notwithstanding its exquisite beauty, 'one of the stateliest and daintiest monuments of Europe',[1] falls far, far short of what it might have been.

Henry VIII during the early years of his reign appears to have had some idea of utilizing the nave as his own burial-place; indeed, he even gave some consideration to a design for his tomb therein. Had this idea materialized the chapel would have reproduced to some extent the intentions of his father. The disproportionate effect, at any rate, would have been somewhat modified. Long before the end of the King's life, however, this plan, never more than tentative, was abandoned.

'Reinstate St. Saviour's Chapel, Our Lady's Altar, Henry VI's tomb and chantry chapel, each in its proper position: put back the painted glass, once so glorious that it was stipulated that the windows of King's College Chapel, Cambridge, should be made in its likeness, restore the magnificent images, crucifixes,

---

[1] Bacon, *History of Henry VII*, p. 417.

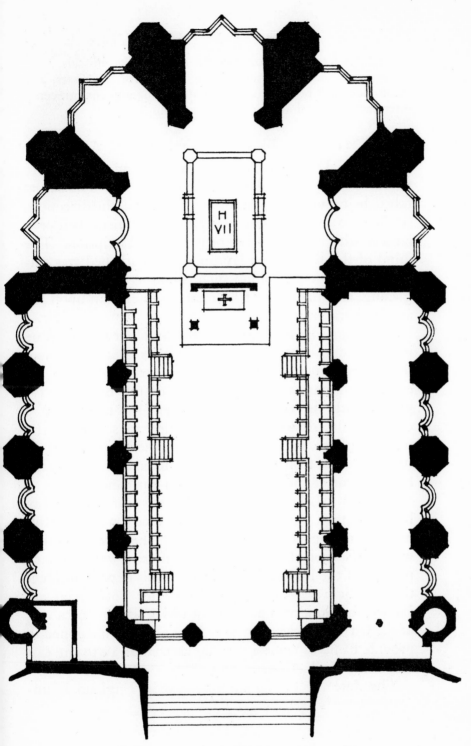

GROUND PLAN OF HENRY VII'S CHAPEL

(c) AS EXISTING TO-DAY

chalices, cruets, bells, corporasses, candlesticks, missals, vestments, altar cloths, bequeathed by Henry for the altars, and
some idea may be formed of the splendour and magnificence
intended by the pious and generous King.'[1]

## 2. THE ERECTION OF THE HIGH ALTAR

Henry VII passed away on April 22nd, 1509, only
twelve days after the drawing up of his Will. The actual
fabric being virtually complete at the time, the directions
set forth in this intensely interesting document deal very
largely with subjects of an ornamental description. The
mind of the King as he lay upon his death-bed was evidently concentrated upon such things as the furnishing,
glazing, and painting of his chapel rather than upon the
architectural framework.

The huge sum of £5,000 placed by Henry at this time
in the hands of Abbot Islip was doubtless intended to meet
the heavy expense involved in the carrying out of his
extensive plans for the decoration of the building, together with the cost of 'the grate in the manner of a
closure', already started and destined to stand 'in the
myddes of the same chapell, before the high aultier, in
such distaunce from the same as is ordered in the plat made
for the same chapell and signed with our hande.'

Henry VIII allowed upwards of three years to slip away
before he took practical steps for the erection of a worthy
monument over the grave of his sire. The latter, together
with his Consort, had already been interred in the eastern
portion of the building in defiance of his express instructions, which seem to have counted for nothing at all.
Hence, the wondrous monument which 'Peter Torrisany,
of the City of Florence, graver,' was now commissioned to
provide came of necessity to be erected away to the east
*behind* the High Altar.

The date of Torrigiano's arrival in England is un-

[1] F. Bond, *Westminster Abbey*, p. 150.

known, though the reason is not far to seek. It does not reflect over-much credit upon the character of this brilliant Florentine.

Some time previously, probably in the year 1492, Torrigiano, most fiery of youngsters, had succeeded in disfiguring for life no less a personage than Michel Angelo. With an unlucky blow, delivered in a moment of violent passion, he 'broke the cartilage of his enemy's nose, as if it had been paste'. The cause of the affray is unknown, but its after results were of a sufficiently serious character to compel the pugilist to beat a hasty retreat from Florence. A long interval then ensued, the greater portion of which was spent on active service in the army. Disgusted at length with military life, Torrigiano repaired to his native city, things having blown over during the interim. He promptly returned to an artistic career and was found fashioning a number of small figures in bronze and marble for certain Florentine merchants. The latter after a time ended by bringing their gifted compatriot to England,[1] in which country he soon found employment in the service of the King.

On October 26th, 1512, he entered into a contract with the executors of Henry VII's Will for the fashioning of a tomb of white marble and black touchstone at a cost of £1,500, for the commemoration of that Sovereign and his Consort. The construction of this marvellous piece of work occupied a little over six years. One of the finest monumental structures in Europe, it survives to-day almost intact.

While the tomb was gradually taking shape, there came an important new development. On the eleventh day of March 1516 Torrigiano entered into a further contract to build the High Altar. An indenture and a bond were drawn up between the artist and the executors of Henry VII, under the terms of which the former bound himself

---

[1] *Archaeological Journal*, vol. li, pp. 130, 131.

to provide a number of objects therein set forth. One of these was an altar, which he engaged 'at his owne propre costs clerely to set up w'in the new Chapell which the forsaid late King caused to be made at Westm'; before November 1st, 1519, in return for the sum of £1,000 which was duly paid over to him.[1]

Another two years passed away. The sumptuous royal tomb was by now completed, but it would seem that Torrigiano had not even started work upon the altar. On the other hand, a letter is extant addressed by the artist to Cardinal Wolsey in which he urged the all-importance of his paying a visit to Florence if he were to complete certain works still remaining unfinished *pro illustrissimo defuncto rege*.[2] At the same time Torrigiano seized the opportunity of reminding the Cardinal of a promise previously made by him to place further royal commissions in his hands.

These overtures proved fruitless, however, and the artist, evidently in a state of high dudgeon, took French leave and forthwith departed for Italy. He had reckoned without his host. A veritable tempest burst about his head. A communication couched in the most indignant terms followed from the Florentine Consul in London, Rinaldo de' Ricasoli, recounting the fact that the sum of £1,000 had been paid over to him no less than two years previously, for work upon which he had not made even the pretence of a start. Moreover, the sculptor had left England, *insalutato hospite*, and without the royal permission. The Florentine Signory took vigorous measures. The truant was compelled to return to the country he had deserted at the end of 1519, or possibly at the beginning of 1520. Accompanying him were three brilliant craftsmen, who solemnly bound themselves to work under him as their

---

[1] J. P. Neale and E. W. Brayley, *History of the Abbey Church of St. Peter Westminster*, vol. ii, part ii, p. 58.

[2] *Archaeological Journal*, vol. li, p. 142.

chief during the following four years and a half in any part of the world. In return for their services they were to be paid a salary of three gold florins a month. Thus our land remains to this day permanently indebted to the Florentine Signory.

Torrigiano commenced operations, then, upon the High Altar just about the time when it ought to have been completed, according to the terms of the original contract. Another three years passed by before his task was finished. The Florentine then disappeared from the country which he had so splendidly adorned with the fruits of his genius; but which, if report is to be believed, had never occupied even a small corner of his heart. He died several years later, probably in 1528, in Spain.

Torrigiano's personal reputation has never stood very high. The prejudice aroused in men's minds by his unfortunate affray with Michel Angelo hung about his head like a cloud for ever after, while Benvenuto Cellini's vivid but highly unflattering description has conferred immortality upon his evil renown.

'About that time there came to Florence a sculptor named Torrigiano: he arrived from England where he had resided several years. . . . This man had a splendid person and a most arrogant spirit, with the air of a great soldier more than of a sculptor, especially in regard to his vehement gestures and his resonant voice, together with a habit he had of knitting his brows enough to frighten any man of courage. He kept talking every day about his gallant feats among those beasts of Englishmen.'[1]

The work of setting up our Lady's Altar in our Lady Chapel 'at Westminster'[2] was entrusted to Benedetto da Rovezzano, and in the year 1526 it stood in its appointed place. The Abbey was enriched by another priceless work of art. Three extremely beautiful fragments of Torrigiano's genius still survive, together with a quantity of

---

[1] J. A. Symonds, *Life of Benvenuto Cellini*, p. 27.    [2] W.A.M. 30626.

valuable testimony, written and pictorial. The combined aid of these different pieces of evidence enables us to gain an extremely clear idea of this masterpiece.

The documentary evidence may be summarized as follows: (1) The original contract made between Torrigiano and the executors of Henry VII; (2) a report as to the State of the Royal Tombs made to Lord Burleigh in the reign of Elizabeth; (3) a curious early Stuart broadside, depicting a session of the Upper House of Convocation, which, in the years preceding the Great Rebellion, was wont to assemble in the Chapel of Henry VII; (4) an elaborate engraving, somewhat similar in character, which first appeared in the *Genealogical History of the Kings of England* by Francis Sandford, Lancaster Herald, the well-known antiquary; (5) the descriptions given by certain historians writing not long after the Great Rebellion, when the circumstances connected with the demolition of the altar were still relatively fresh in the public mind.

From the original contract[1] (1) we learn that the height of this imposing structure from the pavement to the cornice of the canopy was nine feet, and the width of the western front from north to south the same. The altar table was six feet long, three feet high, and three feet four inches wide. The canopy and its four supporting columns rested upon square bases of black and white marble one foot square and eighteen inches high. The columns, composed of copper gilt, were 'wrought with bases, capitells and other garnishments,' above which was 'a vault of white marble, with archytraves, and frese and crests'. The base upon which the actual altar stood was made of black touchstone, while the mensa of similar material rested upon 'four square pillars of white marble with levys and crests, with their proportions all coloured as app'teyneth to the work'. Additional support was provided for the

[1] W.A.M. 6638*.

mensa by means of sixteen balusters of gilded bronze, five of which are very distinctly indicated in Sandford's picture. Beneath the altar, though no pictorial evidence of the fact exists, is said to have been placed a 'bakyn image of erthe coloured of Christ dede'. Behind stood a reredos or dorsal of gilded bronze, adorned with marble inlay and carving, set in a frame between two square pillars of similar material. On its western face was represented Christ rising from the tomb, while the back of the panel was decorated by a picture of the Nativity. The thoroughness with which the work was carried out is evidenced by this dorsal. Although its position prevented this representation of the Nativity from being seen save with considerable difficulty, it seems to have been as costly and elaborate as the western face. At each corner of the canopy was a kneeling figure of an angel, two feet high, holding one of the instruments of the Passion, and fashioned out of 'erthe bak'd in an oven after the colour of white marble', possibly a kind of glazed terra-cotta. The canopy was decorated with the royal arms, the arms of Henry VII and his Queen, the arms of England and the arms of Spain, placed upon 'scochyns of white marble surmounted by a Crown Imperiall' and having rose branches in marble at the sides, the marble of 'oon p'fite colour'; the copper 'good, pure, fayre and clene'; and the gilding done with 'fyne golde'.

The description of the altar contained in the Report on the Royal Tombs (2) forwarded to Lord Burleigh at a later date in the same century is of an extremely abbreviated character, but it fully agrees with the directions of the original contract. It bears on its fourth and last leaf the docket '. . . embrances for the Righte . . . rable the Lorde Trer^r . . . ouching Kinge Henry . . . gte Tome at Wyndsor'. The description of the altar is as follows:

'At the hedd of the said Tombe standeth an aulter upon 4 pyllasters of white marbell and balesters of metle and gylte.

The back of the said aulter both the sydes stories metle and gylte, two pilasters metle and gylte with either end of the said backe, 4 pillars bearing the Roofe w$^{th}$ petistales, vazes of metle and gylte and white marbell, the rofe also white marbell and gylte the arms about the said Aulter white marbell and gylte and the west end of the garnishment about the Roofe is metle and gylte.'[1]

The engraving of the altar contained in Sandford's work (4) is particularly striking. Studied side by side with the terms of the original contract it throws a flood of light upon the somewhat archaic language of that document, though it can hardly be regarded as a wholly authoritative guide to all the decorative details.

Again, Sandford's *History* was not published until more than a generation had elapsed after the destruction of the altar in 1643. Obviously, then, its historical value stands upon a decidedly lower level than that of the rare and charming broadside (3).

The latter takes us back to the reign of James I. It dates from the year 1623 and indicates Archbishop Abbott occupying the president's seat in the Upper House of Convocation. The various details depicted in this print fully harmonize with the information derived from other sources, though the introduction of the members of Convocation is for the present purpose unfortunate. The large table and the seats provided for the Right Reverend Fathers in God have the effect of concealing the whole of the lower portion of the structure. None the less, the historical and antiquarian value of this piece of direct contemporaneous evidence cannot be over-estimated.

It proves how eager was Torrigiano to bring his masterpiece into due relation with the closure surrounding the tomb of the first Tudor monarch. The height of the cornice of the closure governed to an inch that of the baldacchino. A similar precision governed the width.

---

[1] Lansdowne MSS. CXVI, No. 13.

THE TWO HOUSES OF CONVOCATION IN SESSION AT WESTMINSTER
ABBEY

On no account whatsoever must the altar and its immediate surroundings obscure the beautiful towers adorning each angle of the closure. The eastern portion of the chapel was badly crowded up as a result of Henry VIII's disregard of his father's wishes; but it is impossible to withold our admiration from the brilliant success achieved by Torrigiano, who by his meticulous attention to proportion welded the splendid ornaments of the east end into one coherent whole.

It was the intention of Henry VII to provide furnishings and hangings both for the High Altar and

'eny other Aulter being within our said Chapell of our Lady, bee thei of the sids of the same, or in any other place within the compasse of the same, two suts of Aultier clothes, two paire of Vestiments, two corporas with their cases, oon Masse booke, oon Chalice of silver and gilte, oon peire of Cruetts silver and gilte, oon belle silver and gilte, and two peire of Candilstikks silver and gilte, oon of theme for high Aulter, and thoder for the Aulter of our said Vncle of blessed memorie, King Henry the VIth, and we wol that the said Vestiments, Aulter clothes, and other ornaments of our said Aultres, bee soo embroidred and wrought with our armes and cognisaunts, that thei may by the same be knowen of our gifte and bequeste.'

To what extent these injunctions were carried out we can only conjecture.

At first sight it would seem surprising that this magnificent structure should have weathered the stormy years which followed the accession of Queen Elizabeth. It escaped the miserable fate of its companions at the hands of that detestable Prebendary John Hardyman, thanks either to the summary curtailment of his career at Westminster, or to the fact that Edward VI, most Protestant of Kings, had been interred 'under the high altar of brass'[1] only a few years before.[2] The latter is perhaps the more

[1] Sandford, *Genealogical History of the Kings of England*, p. 472.
[2] Camden described Edward VI's burial-place as being 'ad caput avi Henrici Septimi Requiescit, sub altari ex aere deaurato et artificiose elaborato'. *Reges, Reginae et Nobiles in Ecclesia Beati Petri Sepulti*, 1600.

probable explanation; indeed, after a time the altar came to be popularly known as King Edward's Tomb.

It is clear beyond all doubt that this altar always occupied a prominent position in the public mind. Despite the up-heaval of the seventeenth century and its own destruction, a long time elapsed before the tradition of its beauties wholly faded away. Thus Dart, writing three-quarters of a century after the débâcle, waxes enthusiastic over the 'large altar of black touchstone of one piece admirable and un-equalled for its curiosity which stood at the head of King Henry VII's tomb, upon which formerly was placed four wax tapers, of twelve pounds each, perpetually burning'.[1]

Henry VIII has received unsparing condemnation, and deservedly, for the havoc he made of his father's wishes and intentions, but in his selection of Torrigiano as his principal artist and in the glorious works of art with which that genius has enriched the chapel, common justice demands that posterity should not withold from him the very highest praise.

## 3. THE ALTAR OF THE HOLY SAVIOUR

The tomb of Henry VII and his Consort, Elizabeth of York, is surrounded by a lofty grate or closure which, although it has suffered severely, still retains no small amount of its original beauty. Bishop Hacket, writing in the middle of the seventeenth century, went so far as to say, 'this brazen impalement looks like work, not of our moderns but of Bezaleel'.[2]

This 'grate in the manner of a closure of coper and gilt after the faction that we have begoune' falls outside the scope of this volume, seeing that it forms part of one of the royal tombs; but a word must be said about the Altar of the Holy Saviour, explicitly enjoined in the King's

[1] Dart, *Westmonasterium*, vol. i, p. 41. The four sconces have once more (1939) been filled with great candles twelve pounds in weight, to the immense improvement of the structure.

[2] John Hacket, *Life of Archbishop Williams*, p. 46.

THE ALTAR AND BALDACCHINO IN HENRY VII'S CHAPEL ERECTED BY
PIETRO TORRIGIANO

Will, which the grate formerly enclosed, and such traces of the same as still survive.

It was undoubtedly Henry's intention, had he lived, to add to this altar a reredos portraying the Crucifixion, together with figures of the twelve Apostles and other saints. He further directed that all this complicated work was to be fashioned of 'tymbre cou'led and wrought with plate of fyne golde', and he undertook to bestow upon this altar, so specially dear to him, 'our grete pece of the Holie Crosse', also 'the preciouse relique of oon of the leggs of St. George' set in a panel of parcell and gilte brought from Milan and adorned with jewels'. Lastly, the plate, hangings, and other ornaments were to be provided utterly regardless of cost.

It is not easy to determine the extent to which these particular provisions of his father's Will were carried out by Henry VIII. Certain traces, however, survive from pre-Reformation times, sufficient to indicate that the altar of Our Saviour was almost certainly set up and that it must have been a structure of some dimensions. The step upon which it rested remains unchanged. A moulded bar running across the east end from parapet to parapet of the grate evidently formed part of a canopy or tester, while certain mortices remain, intended presumably for the reception of cross bars. The fact, too, that the lengthy black letter inscription commemorating the career of the Founder terminates just at the point where a reredos or dorsal would have been placed clearly suggests the former existence of an altar.

By degrees the pre-Reformation altars of the Abbey have been replaced, save in those chapels where the sites are already filled up by monuments. So soon as the Altar of the Holy Name in the lower story of the Islip Chapel shall have been re-established, this task will be virtually complete, save for the Altar of the Holy Saviour. More than one of our English cathedrals have ventured, not without success, to restore their chantry chapels. Although in this particular case the majesty and the unique character of the surroundings would obviously demand the utmost delicacy of treatment, the task is assuredly not one of which to despair.

## 4. THE STALLS

The two rows of stalls on either side of the chapel are magnificent specimens of sixteenth-century carved wood-work, and are calculated almost to challenge comparison with the glories of Amiens itself. They display a good deal of Germanic influence; in fact some of the carvings have actually been identified with work depicted on engravings by Albert Durer and other German artists.[1]

The three western bays are ancient, so far as the upper rows are concerned, save for a certain amount of restoration. They are furnished with moulded divisions and elbow-rests, from which spring the oak shafts supporting the canopies. The decoration of the shafts is extraordinarily rich; for, in addition to their moulded capitals, bases and bands, they are cut into a number of facets displaying a great quantity of detail. The backs are panelled, being divided into two bays with traceried heads. Above each of the cusped and vaulted soffits rises a tabernacle, divided into three main stages. The lowest of the three displays a semi-hexagonal projection, with ogee, cusped heads with foliated cresting. From the pinnacles spring a number of crocketed buttresses. The second stage follows, square in plan, with a triangular projection in front, each of the faces being decorated with pierced tracery. The semi-hexagonal shape is reproduced in the third stage, at the angles of which appear pinnacled buttresses once more, while the whole structure is finished with an ogee cupola. The detail is almost bewildering in its variety and beauty, for no two canopies are entirely alike.

[1] Lethaby, *Westminster Abbey and the King's Craftsmen*, p. 239.

The upper range is furnished with a wide bookboard, the front edge of which is ornamented with an embattled moulding. The soffits beneath, with their fine traceried decorations, form a rich cusped vault for the lower tier. This vault springs from attached shafts with moulded capitals and bases. Between each pair are two open lights containing four-centred traceried heads, and at the base a succession of quatrefoils terminating in an embattled moulding. The actual stalls display little or no variation from those in the upper tier. The shafts which originally supported the bookboard above have, at some time or other, most regrettably disappeared.

At the outset no such thing as a lower tier existed save in the western bay, and for an extremely practical reason. The tomb of the royal Founder, had it occupied the centre of the nave, as originally intended, would have filled up a very considerable space. Hence it was essential to secure sufficient room for an ample passage-way north and south of the tomb, and with this end in view it was decided to omit the lower tier of stalls from the second and third bays.

The two returned stalls are decorated with richly panelled fronts and sides. Their heads are adorned with traceries and foliage, while the bases consist of rows of quatrefoils charged with roses and leaves, a castle, and a pomegranate. At the angle stands a pedestal, hexagonal in shape. That on the north is surmounted by a regal figure, somewhat injured, wearing a crown and arrayed in a long mantle with a deep collar. The fact that an antelope is seated at the back suggests that Henry VI is here represented.

The flights of steps by which the returned stalls and those immediately adjoining them are approached are original. They are made of solid oak with moulded bases and were originally furnished on their western sides with an ogee rail, springing from a hexagonal post which supports a winged dragon. Unfortunately, the rail has been broken away on the northern side. The remainder are all modern work, save for the pedestals on the western side of the middle pair.

The standards to the bookboards form another most beautiful feature. The four westernmost are original, though they have undergone a certain amount of reparation.

The extension of the stalls eastward took place during the reign of George I. It was due to the establishment of the Most Honourable Order of the Bath upon a fully organized basis and the selection of Henry VII's Chapel as its head-quarters. The powers that be decided to make the stalls the official seats of the Sovereign, the Great Master, and thirty-six Knights, each stall to be distinguished by the customary metal plate with its heraldic insignia, while a banner bearing the same arms floated above each canopy. The Statutes of the Order further laid down that to each one of these K.B.s there should be assigned three Esquires. The authorities at once found themselves involved in a deadlock, owing to a shortage of seating accommodation. What, then, was to be done? The answer was precisely that which might be expected in such an age as the eighteenth century. King, Premier, Dean, and all parties concerned, realizing that they were confronted by a somewhat knotty problem, discovered a solution in a policy of hopeless vandalism.

It was decided, then, to fill up the whole of the next bay eastward on either side with stalls, at a sacrifice of the two noble screens, and to continue the lower range, hitherto confined to the western bay only, along the entire length. From that time onward all direct communication between the central portion of the building and the two aisle-chapels ceased to exist, owing to this blocking up of the bay.[1]

Unfortunately, the tragedy did not end here, for the whole atmosphere was permeated with the spirit of cheap-

[1] See pp. 157 and 159.

ness. The additional stall accommodation must be secured, somehow or other, if the regulations enacted for the
organization of the new Order were to be carried out in
their entirety. That was clear enough; but the authorities
while accepting the responsibility determined not to spend
one single penny more than they were positively obliged.
The methods which they adopted were reprehensible beyond words, and will never fail to arouse deep indignation.

They decided, then, to provide the canopies required
for the new sets of stalls by mercilessly bisecting a number
of the magnificent ancient pieces. The halves which faced
the north and south aisle chapels having been expedi-
tiously removed, they were re-erected above the new stalls
in the fourth bay, facing the nave. By this means a general
impression of uniformity throughout the entire range of
stalls on either side is conveyed to the minds of observers
in the nave; but the spectacle in the aisles baffles belief.
Wicked ingenuity and shameless irreverence could hardly
go farther. This disgraceful performance for which
George I, Sir Robert Walpole, and, it is to be feared, the
Dean and Chapter of Westminster also, must be held
responsible, stares every one in the face who, when visiting
the north or south aisle chapels, happens to turn his gaze
upwards. Nor again will he fail to notice at the same time
the dull, uninspired panelling affixed to the backs of the
early Georgian stalls in the eastern bay. Contrasted with
the rich ornamentation which graces their beautiful companions, as a result of the munificence of Henry VII and
the genius of the sixteenth-century craftsmen, the effect
is almost complete bathos. Little did the founder of the
Tudor dynasty dream of the miserable fate awaiting the
precious stalls, erected for the staff of his new foundation,
who were directed to sing their offices therein 'as long as
the world shall endure'.[1]

---

[1] J. P. Neale and E. W. Brayley, *History and Antiquities of the Abbey Church
of St. Peter, Westminster*, vol. ii, part ii, pp. 47 ff.

As at present constituted, then, there are two complete tiers of stalls on either side. In the upper row there is one large returned stall at the west end, together with fifteen smaller ones, facing north and south. In the lower tier they are arranged in three divisions, seven in the first and five in each of the others, separated by flights of steps.

The misericordes, though occasionally marred by the coarseness of their subjects, are of the greatest possible interest. Even those specimens which can claim no greater antiquity than the first quarter of the eighteenth century surprise us with their execution, which is, to say the least, quite passable work. Generally, though not invariably, they consist of three separate compartments in high relief, viz. a large one in the centre, flanked by a smaller one on either side. The latter are for the most part bordered by wreaths of foliage branching out from the centre. The various sculptured figures, which are extremely numerous, are depicted either sitting or in inclined positions so as to accommodate them to the space available.

### North Side. Upper Row. Ancient

(1) On the large returned stall a group of Bacchanalians: one of the party is seated upon a barrel, another endeavouring to push him off with his foot, two other men are looking on.

(2) Two malignant looking devils, one carrying off a monk, another beating a drum: a woman uplifting her hands in horror.

(3) Male and female figures arrayed in sixteenth-century costume, the former searching in his pouch for money. Flanked on the left by a dragon, on the right by a sow playing on a pipe.

(4) Male and female figures playing upon musical instruments: at the sides clusters of water flowers.

(5) Large winged dragon, magnificently carved. On the left a smaller dragon, wingless; on the right a reptile, or possibly a hedgehog, gazing fixedly at a serpent.

(6) Two monsters chained and padlocked to a stump on which is a falcon. One resembles a dog: the other has a long tail and is covered with scales. On one side a fox arrayed in armour, riding a goose, on the other a goose riding a fox: both figures much injured.

(7) Forest scene containing a group of apes whose heads have perished. On the right, man astride a unicorn; on the left, man riding a goat.

(8) Forest scene with figures of

THE STALLS AND GATES OF HENRY VII'S CHAPEL

a man and an ass, almost wholly destroyed. On one side a beast holding a winnowing fan: on the other a windmill on the steps of which is another beast.

(9) A remarkable representation of the Judgement of Solomon. In the centre the King seated upon a canopied throne supported by three councillors: the two quarrelling mothers on either side, and the dead baby lying in the foreground: a soldier about to cut the other infant in half. Two smaller scenes: (*a*) a house in which one of the women is exchanging the dead for a living baby, (*b*) the women, one holding a dead baby in her arms.

(10) A vigorously carved bearded monster whose heads are destroyed, grasping a club in the left hand. On the sides clusters of foliage, flowers, and fruit.

(11) Mermaid holding a mirror in one hand and a comb in the other with rocks and coral for a background: on the sides conventional flowers and foliage.

(12) Foliated corbel springing from a moulding; clusters of water flowers at the sides.

(13) Foliated corbel: on the sides circular bosses of holly leaves.

### North Side. Upper Row. Modern

(14) Cluster of foliage: on either side a boar encircled by a snake.

(15) Collection of snakes and animal heads.

(16) Monster, surrounded by foliage, flanked by snakes and dragons.

(17) Grotesque mask.

(18) Groups of dragons surrounded by foliage.

### North Side. Lower Row. Ancient

(1) Two savages, one wearing a helmet, fighting with clubs: at the sides bosses of acanthus leaves.

(2) This is one of the most striking of all the misericordes. In the centre (*a*) David standing beside the headless body of Goliath, (*b*) returning in triumph bearing the giant's head. On the right Goliath peering over the walls of a castle; on the left David discharging his sling, a man and a woman looking on from a castle.

(3) Head swathed in foliage: bosses of conventional foliage at the sides.

(4) A fine representation of the Tudor Royal Arms, surmounted by a crown. The dragon, or left-hand supporter, is perfect: its companion has disappeared: on the right a Tudor rose: on the left a pomegranate.

(5, 6, 7) Various types of foliage springing from moulding: bosses of conventional foliage on either side.

### North Side. Lower Row. Modern

(8) Two boys at play: clusters of conventional foliage.

(9) Monsters' heads.

(10) Two dragons piping: conventional foliage.

(11) Grotesque heads surrounded

by foliage: flanked by flowers entwined with snakes.

(12) Grotesque mask in the midst of foliage.

(13) Grotesque head flanked by dogs.

(14) Phoenix rising from its ashes, flanked by dragons encircled with snakes.

(15) Group of dragons and snakes.

(16) Bear and lion and clusters of fruit.

(17) Bunch of foliage flanked by roses.

### South Side. Upper Row. Ancient

(1) Beneath the returned stall a savage family, two parents and four children, all nude, with a quantity of vines in the background. On either side clusters of conventional flowers.

(2) Spirited representation of a grotesque fiend seizing a tonsured clerk for the sake of the bag which he carries. On the right a pair of fighting cocks, on the left a monkey beating a drum.

(3) Woman giving a man a box on the ear: flanked by clusters of conventional flowers.

(4) Samson tearing asunder the lion's jaws: on the right a lion licking itself, on the left a lion slaying a lamb.

(5) In the centre a striking carving of a large winged dragon: on the right a hedgehog gazing fixedly at a serpent, on the left a wingless dragon coiled up.

(6) Cluster of foliage springing from a moulding.

(7) Man with club fighting two dragons, one of them headless: on the right Samson astride a lion, tearing asunder its jaws, on the left a small boy assailed by three turkeys.

(8) Naked and bearded savage attacked by a bear: at the sides conventional flowers.

(9) This misericorde, a cluster of late-thirteenth-century foliage, is of the greatest interest, being one of the two fragments which alone survive of Henry III's choir. How it came to be inserted in the middle of this later woodwork will always remain a mystery.

(10) Couchant lion flanked by arum lilies.

(11) Flogging scene. A boy undergoing chastisement from a birch wielded by a second boy, a third holding him down: flanked by clusters of conventional foliage.

(12) Battle between two winged dragons: flanked by clusters of foliage.

(13) Grotesque face surrounded by foliage: at the sides bosses of fruit and foliage.

### South Side. Upper Row. Modern

(14) Monster in the midst of foliage.

(15) Elaborately foliaged corbel, flanked by heads representing Age and Youth.

(16) Scaly monster: flanked by lions' heads devouring snakes.

(17) Foliated corbel with clusters of fruit and foliage.

(18) Snake entwining a dragon.

*South Side. Lower Row. Ancient*

(1) Woman knocking down a man with her distaff, the latter trying to protect his head: on the right man making a grimace, on the left jester wearing a cap with ears.

(2) Man thrashed by a woman with a birch rod, apparently for having broken her distaff: at the sides clusters of foliage.

(3) Man and a woman seated: on the right boy with bird, on the left laughing child.

(4) Savage shielding himself from another savage shooting at him with a bow and arrows: at the sides conventional flowers.

(5) Two boys, their hands tied over their knees, fighting: on the right boy riding a hobby horse, on the left boy holding a shield.

(6) Two monsters, one of them winged: at the sides clusters of nuts and foliage.

(7) Group of monkeys, one feeding a female with her young: on the right chained monkey drinking from a flask, on the left chained bear playing on bagpipes.

*South Side. Lower Row. Modern*

(8) Foliage entwined by a snake with monsters on either side.

(9) Winged dragon with foliage.

(10) Lion with foliage.

(11) Grotesque mask swallowing leaves, flanked by clusters of foliage.

(12) Clusters of foliage.

(13) Eagle grasping a snake.

(14) Wild boar and grotesque animal playing together.

(15) Group of snakes and monsters surrounded by foliage: on the left head of Hercules, on the right monster entwined by a snake.

(16) Monster's head devouring foliage: flanked by dragons.

(17) Cluster of foliage and grotesque heads: flanked by two monsters, one grasping a snake, the other devouring foliage.

A very cursory examination will suffice to show that the carvings, which are coeval with the building itself, are enormously superior to their eighteenth-century companions, although the latter are far from despicable.

## 5. THE GATES

The splendid gates beneath the three great archways through which access is gained to the chapel are fashioned out of massive oak and plated with burnished bronze of the most elaborate description. The large pair in the centre are separated from a smaller pair on either side by means of octagonal pillars surrounded by triplicated bands.

The central pair are divided up into no less than sixty-two perforated panels, almost square in shape, together with six additional panels, slightly incomplete, at the turn of the four-centred arch above. Various badges have been repeated over and over again, associated for the most part with the newly established House of Tudor. They include the leopards of England, the fleurs-de-lis of France; the initials HR conjoined by a knot and a crown; a falcon perched upon an open fetter-lock (a badge of Henry's father-in-law, Edward IV); a portcullis chained and crowned; a daisy plant crowned; and a rose spray crowned. The framework enclosing this great mass of squares has been studded at the intersections with bronze representations of the Tudor rose and winged dragons, a quaint allusion to the Welsh descent of the King. Between these badges appear small foiled studs, also in bronze.

The smaller pairs of gates each contain eight and twenty of these pierced divisions, filled with heraldic insignia similar to those adorning the central pair. Nor, again, must mention be omitted of the richly traceried locks.

It is a marvel that these beautiful works of art have survived. Their merciful escape from the order given by the Long Parliament to the effect that all work in iron and brass contained in Henry VII's Chapel should be destroyed has never been explained.

The assaults of fanaticism were, however, one thing; but the corroding effects of the London atmosphere were quite another. Against this insidious foe the gates were powerless. As time went on their lustre came to be dulled, their general appearance tarnished, and their brilliant gilding disappeared altogether.

An attempt was made, apparently not without success, during the reign of George II to rescue them from decadence, for in 1736 they were carefully cleansed and renovated. The cost incurred by the Dean and Chapter appears to our ideas almost ludicrous even after allowing for the change in the value of money. According to the Treasurer's accounts for that year, a bill amounting to the small sum of half a guinea was paid to the smith for 'cleaning and setting up the brass gates in Henry VII's Chapel'.

Some extremely interesting evidence is also forthcoming from the well-known *Memoirs of the Reign of George II* by Lord Hervey. The story is so graphic that it deserves to be quoted in full, though not without a strong protest against Hervey's unjust and most uncalled for criticism of Dean Wilcocks. The administration of the Abbey by the latter during his long decanate forms an outstanding landmark in its eighteenth-century history. In an age, too, when self-aggrandizement was regarded as the most natural thing in the world, the Dean had sufficient strength of character to decline all offers of further preferment, not excluding the northern Primacy itself.

It would seem that a discussion had been taking place between the King and Queen and Lord Hervey regarding that not very attractive personality, Bishop Hoadley, during which the temperature had risen considerably. In order to turn the conversation, Lord Hervey informed the tiresome King how he had the same day been in the company of a bishop of very different stamp,

'who would never, he dared answer for him, disturb his Majesty's Government with writing. The man he meant was one Wilcocks, Bishop of Rochester, the dullest branch of Episcopacy and the most ignorant piece of orthodoxy in the whole kingdom.'

'As soon', continued Lord Hervey, 'as Lord Wilmington, Lord Chancellor, and I had to-day discharged your Majesty's commission in proroguing Parliament, my Lord of Rochester carried us to Westminster Abbey to show us a pair of old gates in Henry VII's Chapel, which were formerly overrun with rust and turned quite black, but are now new cleaned, as bright as when they were first made, and the first things of the kind I ever saw in my life.'

Whilst Lord Hervey was expressing his admiration of the

gates, the Queen asking many questions and apparently much pleased with the description, the King stopped the conversation short by saying, 'My Lord, you are always putting some of these fine things into the Queen's head, and then I am to be plagued with a thousand plans and workmen'. . . . Lord Hervey, hoping to remove the King's fears, replied that it was the sort of work that if His Majesty were to give all the money in his exchequer, he could not have more.[1]

As time went on, the deterioration reappeared again. Tarnished and even rusty in places, the gates hung there upon their hinges, like huge pieces of black iron, presenting a perfectly deplorable appearance at the commencement of the twentieth century, despite their wealth of heraldry. Fortunately a process of scientific cleansing has met with wonderful success, a success fully equal to that achieved a few years earlier with the Sedilia and the Sanctuary Tombs. It almost deserves the word 'resurrection'.

### 6. HENRY VII'S CHAPEL IN POST-REFORMATION TIMES

Henry VII's Chapel escaped to a great extent the perils of the Reformation period. Stow has recorded a serious burglary in the year 1569 when 'a certain lewd fellow stole away divers parcels of brass and copper' which adorned the tomb of Henry VII, subsequently receiving condign punishment at the hands of the Common Serjeant,[2] but of official destruction comparatively little took place. Some of the statues were destroyed; but the great bulk of its glories, its stained glass, and the altar with its baldacchino remained untouched.

Dean Stanley has characteristically commented upon the strange fact that Edward VI, of all people, should have

[1] Lord Hervey, *Memoirs of the Reign of George II*, vol. ii, p. 221.
[2] Strype's Stow, *Survey of London and Westminster*, vol. ii, p. 582.

been buried on this spot by his bigoted half-sister, and that 'the tomb under which he reposed should have been the altar built by Torrigiano for the chanting of masses, which he himself had been the chief means of abolishing'.[1]

During Elizabethan and early Stuart times Torrigiano's altar is said to have stood here unused. It was regarded by the Dean and Chapter as a remarkable ornament and nothing more, according to Bruno Ryves.[2] The latter was not, however, entirely accurate. The altar must almost certainly have been in use on one memorable occasion which must not pass unrecorded.

It was the early morning of Trinity Sunday, in the year 1626. Three people had met together by appointment in the chapel. One of these was William Laud, recently elevated to the episcopate, but still retaining his stall at the Abbey, and during his sojourns in the metropolis residing in his official house on the north side of the nave. The second was his friend, Augustine Linsell, Dean of Lichfield, who was destined to occupy in succession the Bishoprics of Peterborough and Hereford. The third was that splendid son of England's Church, Nicholas Ferrar, whose ordination to the diaconate was about to take place. Laud, needless to say, was more than willing. When approached by Linsell, who in former years had acted as tutor to Ferrar, he stated his readiness to 'receive him there with very particular esteem and with a great deal of joy that he was able to lay hands on so extraordinary a person. So he was ordained deacon and no more for he protested that he durst not advance one step higher'.[3]

Ferrar kept his intentions under lock and key. Even to his near relations the announcement of his ordination, which took the form of a solemn vow, carefully recorded on parchment, came as a surprise. He stated that he had

---

[1] Stanley, *Historical Memorials of Westminster Abbey*, p. 150.
[2] Bruno Ryves, *Mercurius Rusticus*, p. 155.
[3] Mayor, *Cambridge in the Seventeenth Century*, vol. i, p. 24.

only decided to take this step in order that he might be 'legally authorized to give spiritual assistance to his family or others with whom he might be concerned'.[1]  The ordination over the Ferrar family returned almost immediately to Little Gidding.

Whether occasionally used for the celebration of the Holy Eucharist (as was probably the case on this Trinity Sunday) and at an infrequent consecration of a bishop, or whether reduced to the position of a tomb or monument, the days of Torrigiano's altar were numbered.  In less than twenty years the storm broke.  So soon as the Long Parliament had settled down into its stride, it directed its unhallowed gaze to the Abbey.

On April 24th, 1643, a Commission was appointed under the chairmanship of Sir Robert Harley, 'a hot-braned zealot of those times', to whom the agreeable duty was assigned of demolishing all 'monuments of superstition and idolatry' in the chapel.[2]  Harley had already distinguished himself as a member of another parliamentary committee which had been responsible for the destruction of the time-honoured crosses of Charing and Cheapside.  A structure such as Torrigiano's altar, with its wealth of statuary and other decorations, would receive but short shrift at the hands of such a man.  Without one moment's delay he carried out his instructions, culminating in an act of sublime folly and unmitigated knavery.

We are indebted to Professor Lethaby for the discovery of an interesting minute in the Report of the Historical Manuscripts Commission relating to the commercial side of the wretched business, viz.

'1644, April 19, Receipt for six[s] by Thomas Gastaway from Sir Robert Harley for taking down the High Altar of Henry VII's Chapel.'[3]

[1] H. J. K. Skipton, *Nicholas Ferrar*, p. 86.
[2] Dart, *Westmonasterium*, vol. i, p. 41.
[3] Lethaby, *Westminster Abbey Re-examined*, p. 176; *Historical Manuscripts Commission, Fourteenth Century*, Appendix II, Welbeck Abbey MSS.

1644. May 21st. 'Henry Wilson, ffreemason. Working in taking downe the Altar in Henry VII Chapel. Item for rassing out the painted images. £7. 16s.'

Even Dean Stanley, whose criticism of the Puritan oppressors of the Church is always of the gentlest, cannot refrain from commenting upon the strange paradox that 'the only royal memorial destroyed by the Puritans should have been that of the only Puritan Prince who ever sat on the English throne'.[1]

Bruno Ryves, who became Dean of Windsor at a later and happier epoch, has recorded the terrible story under his pseudonym of Mercurius Rusticus. Sir Robert Harley, the chief culprit, is branded by him with infamy unspeakable, for he 'breaking into Henry VII's Chapel, pulled down the Altar Stone which stood before the goodly Monument of that King (Edward VI) it was a curious Touchstone, a rarity, not to be match'd; that we know of, in any part of the World: there it stood for many years, not for Use, but only for Ornament; yet it did not escape the Frenzy of this Man's ignorant Zeal, for he break it into Shivers'.[2]

Thus perished one of the noblest works of art produced by the sixteenth century; the 'brazen altar, artificially wrought and gilt with gold', 'the work of Peter, a painter of Florence',[3] 'admirable and unequalled for its curiosity'.[4] Many a long year passed away before the recollection of its glories wholly disappeared from the minds of men. We must be thankful that certain portions have survived to perpetuate its memory in our own day and generation.

The destruction of Torrigiano's altar was the first of the great changes wrought by fanaticism in the interior of Henry VII's Chapel. The disappearance of this imposing structure, the centre-piece of the building, represented the

---

[1] Stanley, *Historical Memorials of Westminster Abbey*, pp. 150, 151.
[2] Crull, *Antiquities of St. Peter's*, ii, Appendix II, p. 14.
[3] Dart, *Westmonasterium*, vol. i, p. 41.
[4] Keepe, *Monumenta Westmonasteriensia*, p. 87.

infliction of a grievous wound. The Puritans, with eager delight, did their work only too well. As they gloated over the sad spectacle they must have realized with unfeigned satisfaction that the beauty of this incomparable chapel had been marred for ever.

But the miserable tale is still far from complete; Henry VII in his Will had laid special stress upon the windows. He directed that they be 'glased with stories, ymagies, armes, bagies and cognoisaunts, as is by us redily devised and in picture delivered to the Prior of Sainct Bartelmews besides Smythfeld, Maister of the Works of our said Chapel in as goodly and riche maner as suche a work requireth, and as to a King's werk app'teigneth'.

Such was the beauty of these windows that they were selected a few years later to be the model of those which, fortunately, still grace another chapel of almost equal renown. An indenture drawn up in 1516 between Dr. Robert Hacombleyn, Provost of King's College Cambridge, on the one side, and certain 'Glasyers', on the other,[1] laid down that the windows of that chapel were to be filled with 'good, clene, sure and perfyte glasse, and oryent colors and imagery of the story of the olde lawe and of the former maner, goodenes, curiosytie and clenelyness in every point of the glasse windowes of the Kynge's newe Chapell at Westminster, and also accordyngly and after suche maner as oon Barnard Flower late deceased by Indenture stood bounde to do'.[2]

To the jaundiced eyes of the Puritan majority in the Long Parliament this dream of beauty was an anathema. Accordingly, in this dark year, 1644, the 'cleaning out the pictures' took place after which they were carried to Harley's house. On June 9th of the following year John Rutland received from the latter £10, followed by a

---

[1] J. P. Neale and E. W. Brayley, *History and Antiquities of the Abbey Church of St. Peter Westminster*, vol. ii, part ii, pp. 43, 44.
[2] Walpole, *Anecdotes of the Arts*, vol. i, App.

*A Prospect of the inside of King Henry the vii.th Chapel.*

AT THE BEGINNING OF THE EIGHTEENTH CENTURY

further sum of £30 for substituting white glass in place of
the coloured glories which had disappeared.[1]

It is probable that irreparable damage was at the same
time inflicted upon the floor. The immense expense of
laying down the present pavement—a work carried out
after the Restoration—would never have been incurred
had it not been absolutely necessary. The original pavement would have remained good for many years. Wanton
injury alone could have demanded its replacement after a
short life of a century and a half.

The name of the donor of the existing pavement is
recorded upon a battered brass near the west end of Henry
VII's chantry on the north side. The inscription runs as
follows:

'Henricus Killigrew STP Hujus Collegii Prebendarius
Marmoreum Pavimentum Dedit. Obiit Martii 14$^{to}$ 1699.'

Curiously enough, the inscription has been repeated for
some reason unknown in the corresponding position on
the south side, where it has been incised on the step. There
is, however, a strange variation in the date, which in this
second place is given as 1669.

Henry Killigrew was one of the eight Prebendaries appointed immediately after the Restoration of Charles II.
Dying in the year 1699, he occupied his stall for nearly
forty years. He combined his office at the Abbey with the
Mastership of the Chapel Royal, Savoy, the revenues of
which he is said to have dissipated right and left and in a
manner not altogether free from scandal. Possibly the
earlier of the two dates represents the year of his gift to the
chapel.

The pavement consists of squares of slate and white
marble laid for the most part diagonally, thus conveying a
lozengy effect. In all probability the design was at the
outset uniform over the entire area. In the centre of the
nave, however, the pavement is divided up into three

[1] Lethaby, *Westminster Abbey Re-examined*, p. 182.

B b

large square sections by means of bands. The lozenge-shaped slabs, too, are smaller in size, while those in the central space are laid square. This break in the symmetry probably dates from the reign of George II, when the construction of the royal vault must have necessitated an extensive rearrangement.

Some portions of the original sixteenth-century flooring may still be seen in the two aisles, the eastern chapel and within the brazen chantry. It consists of small slabs of grey marble laid in alternate strips, square and diagonally. It is infinitely more attractive to look upon than Killigrew's monotonous blue and white lozenges.[1]

By degrees the wretched legacy which the eighteenth century inherited from its two predecessors was still further developed. The first Hanoverian joined hands with the second Tudor and the Cromwellians and proceeded to set at naught, though, for different reasons, the intentions of the Royal Founder, and yet another injury was inflicted upon 'the wonder of the world'.

As already stated, the existing stalls were found insufficient for the accommodation of the Knights of the newly established Order of the Bath. It was decided, therefore, to secure the extra space required by utilizing a bay on either side of the chapel, and smashing to pieces the pair of remarkable stone screens which had from the first occupied these positions. The vandalism then committed was deplorable, and John Carter's furious invectives in a later generation were more than justified.

'It is believed the several screens filling in the lower portions of the five recesses, or small chapels at said east end have on the like occasions been at various times knocked down piecemeal, or otherwise got rid of: the extremities of surrounding screen of Henry's tomb, so extraordinary and so beautiful, torn away and disfigured.'[2]

[1] Lethaby, *Westminster Abbey Re-examined*, p. 173.
[2] *Gentleman's Magazine*, 1817, part ii, pp. 33–4.

These screens were lofty structures, curved in plan and somewhat resembling the bow windows in the aisles. Their general design was unusual but wonderfully beautiful, consisting of three segments of circles of which that in the centre was the larger. Each was divided horizontally into three stages. The two upper formed ranges of open lights and terminated with a moulded and embattled cornice. The middle segment was divided into three main and six sub-lights, the side segments into two main and four sub-lights with moulded mullions. To-day only a few mutilated fragments of the upper portion remain. The lower stages of the screens, though not free from injury, are virtually intact. They consist of a series of richly decorated panels with trefoiled, subcusped, and traceried heads, eight in the middle and five in the side segment. The rail is embattled and adorned with a quantity of bosses consisting of carved foliage, animals, and heads of beasts. On the base is a row of quatrefoils carved with fleurs-de-lis and roses. In one of the side segments is a doorway with moulded panels and a four-centred arch in a square head, with carved spandrels. Thus, of the four screens with which the chapel was originally graced, two alone survive, and even these have lost their upper portions, the result probably of the erection of tiers of seats at the east end of the chapel at successive Installations of the Order of the Bath.

After the death of Ludovic Stuart, Duke of Richmond, in 1623, an immense monument was raised to his memory by his widow and placed in one of the southern chapels. The Duchess had the audacity to appeal to Charles I's good offices, since she desired to remove the stone screen and substitute 'an iron grate in lieu thereof'. The King displayed the most excellent taste and referred the matter to the Dean and Chapter. Although 'ready to do anything that may add to the honour of the Duke', he was 'careful not to command anything that may give an injury and blemish to the strength and security of that Chapel'. Nothing more was heard of the outrageous proposal. Would that subsequent generations had displayed the same tender care as Charles I![1]

After the Restoration the Dean and Chapter, once more in their rightful position, set to work to provide a humble substitute for the noble altar which had perished so miserably. Thus, in the Inventory of 1661 allusion is made to 'a plane purple cloth and two cushions for ye table in Henry VII's Chapel'.[2]

In those days an early morning service was read in this chapel. It continued without a break into the second half of the eighteenth century, though it was subsequently removed first to the south transept and then to the Consistory Court. The Treasurer's Accounts for the year 1689 record the payment of a fee of £8 to the Precentor, Stephen Crespion, *pro Matutinis Precibus in Sacello*.[3] Again, in 1738, the sum of £1. 9s. was expended on providing a surplice and Book of Common Prayer for the Reader, who was not necessarily or invariably a member of the Collegiate body,[4] in 1782 two surplices costing £5. 9s.,[5] and a similar payment in 1800.

Consecration of bishops took place here with some frequency after the Restoration, for the majority of the sees had become depleted of their occupants during the troubles of the two previous decades. Four of these services took place within the first twelve months, after which they continued at irregular intervals down to the consecration of Sir William Dawes to the Bishopric of Chester in 1708. Nor, again, were Ordinations wholly unknown in this chapel during the years immediately succeeding the Restoration. An altar was obviously essential on these and other occasions. It is explicitly

---

[1] State Documents quoted in Stanley, *Historical Memorials of Westminster Abbey*, p. 196 note.
[2] W.A.M. 44026, A and B.     [3] Ibid. 33721.     [4] Ibid. 33770.
[5] Ibid. 33813.

mentioned in connexion with the funerals of General Monk in 1670 and the great Duke of Marlborough in 1722.[1]

This altar was probably a poor sort of an affair, though there is little evidence upon which to base a positive opinion. A late-eighteenth-century engraving represents an extremely ineffective table standing against the west side of Henry VII's chantry, and the monumental history of Westminster Abbey by Neale and Brayley, published in the reign of George IV, makes mention of a 'Communion Table of oak stoutly framed, and evidently of the Tudor period'.[2] On a great occasion, such as an Installation of the Knights of the Bath, this table was covered with a piece of rich velvet or other material, together with a dorsal.

Apart from actual services, the chapel continued to be used after the Restoration by Convocation, the Lower House taking the place of the Upper which now repaired to the Jerusalem Chamber. It may be said to have witnessed the birth of the Church overseas, for it was the action of the Lower House in 1701 which led to the granting of a Charter to the Society for the Propagation of the Gospel.[3] This arrangement might conceivably have continued indefinitely, had it not been for the 'Bangorian Controversy', which brought the meetings of the Church's Parliament to an abrupt end and flung an apple of discord into her life.

[1] *Atterbury's Letters*, vol. iv, p. 11; Stanley, *Historical Memorials of Westminster Abbey*, p. 226 note.

[2] J. P. Neale and E. W. Brayley, *History of the Abbey Church of St. Peter, Westminster*, vol. ii, part ii, p. 50. This table now forms part of the furniture of the Muniment Room.

[3] Atterbury, *Some Proceedings in the Convocation of 1705*, Preface, p. 13.

## 7. THE FOUNDATION OF THE MOST HONOURABLE ORDER OF THE BATH

Henry VII's Chapel with its magnificent architecture, its peerless tombs, and its august associations, was destined to receive a further accession of dignity during the early decades of the eighteenth century. Strangely enough, it fell to the lot of that unimaginative age, though devoid of the knightly and chivalrous ethos of the Middle Ages, to witness the revival and the permanent establishment of the Most Honourable Order of the Bath.

It is unnecessary to dwell upon the surrounding circumstances, the corrupt state of politics, and the prevalence of bribery, the remembrance of which will always cling to the personality of the Premier, Sir Robert Walpole. The establishment of the new Order evidently formed part and parcel of his general policy. It was, to say the least, an ingenious expedient for the securing of additional political support.

'No, nothing but the Garter', indignantly exclaimed that formidable veteran, the Duchess of Marlborough, when a stall in the new Order was suggested for her grandson. 'Madame', was the Prime Minister's frigid reply, 'they who take the Bath will the sooner have the Garter.' Subsequent events proved Walpole to be as good as his word.

The sarcastic remarks, too, of the Prime Minister's son throw an equally lurid light upon the subject:

'The Order of the Bath was an artful bank to supply a fund of favours in view of places and to stave off the demand for Garters, intending that the Red should be a step to the Blue.'[1]

In former generations the Knights of the Bath, though large batches had been created at coronations, royal weddings, and other occasions of national importance, had

[1] Nicolas, *History of the Orders of Knighthood of the British Empire*, vol. iii, p. 39 note, and p. 256.

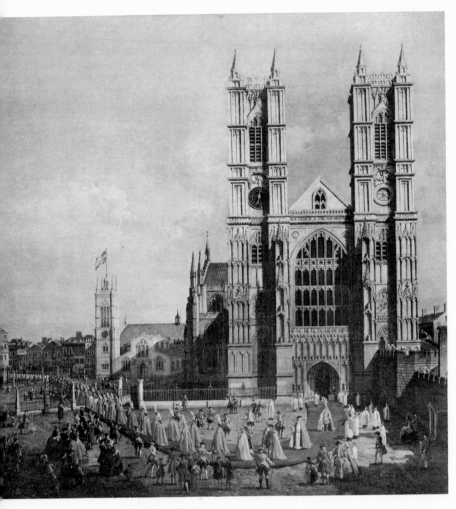

E PROCESSION OF THE KNIGHTS OF THE BATH ON JUNE 26th, 1749

been unable to claim any continuity of organization for their Order. At irregular intervals only did the country witness the dubbing of these dignitaries, who were generally characterized by youth, with the honour of knighthood; while the custom, if such it could be called, fell into complete abeyance after the Coronation of Charles II.

The powers that be now decided to create an Order, governed by its own statutes, in which due provision was made for the periodical performance of the ceremony of Installation, when the places vacated by death or other cause would be filled up in regular succession.

Accordingly, on May 18th, 1725, letters patent were signed by George I, in which were set forth with pompous grandiloquence the various considerations by which he had been moved in recreating this Order. This Monarch, as the Fountain of Honour, after calling to mind how his royal predecessors had 'upon divers wise and honourable considerations', on occasions of certain august solemnities conferred with great state, 'upon sundry deserving individuals' distinguished by birth, quality, and personal merit, 'the Knighthood of the Bath', now declared it his will to re-establish that order of knighthood and confirm it in 'its former lustre and dignity'. The letters patent further announced that the Order would include, in addition to the Sovereign himself, a Prince of the Blood Royal, a Great Master, and thirty-five Companions.

The Collegiate Church of St. Peter, Westminster, was selected to be the permanent home of the Order. The head of that foundation was to be for ever after the Dean of the Bath. Not long before the Scottish Order of the Thistle had come into being and the Presbyterian influences which surrounded its birth were made manifest by the absence of any episcopal office-holder therein. A period of slack churchmanship had commenced with the arrival of the House of Hanover upon the throne of

England. Hence, it would seem that the Order of the Thistle, rather than that of the Garter, was selected to serve as the model when framing the constitution, for here again was the episcopate conspicuous by its absence. Probably Dean Stanley was not far wrong in thinking that with Protestant influences so greatly in the ascendant it was natural to turn to the Dean of Westminster, 'as the most independent presbyter in the Church of England',[1] to be the permanent holder of the distinguished position of Dean of the Bath.

The central ceremony of the Order was the Installation of new Knights. It invariably attracted an immense amount of public attention. In the eyes of our eighteenth-century forefathers it was as a spectacle, more popular than any other, a Coronation only excepted. People came up from the country in large numbers on the chance of beholding some portion of the festivities. The notable personages of the land, from the Royal Family down-wards, vied with one another in conferring lustre upon the occasion, while the Knights' Ball and Supper, with which it became the custom to round off a day of brilliant splendour, were carried out regardless of expense. Pro-motion to the Order must have spelt bankruptcy to any one whose coffers were not thickly lined with gold.

Altogether eleven Installations took place in the course of the eighteenth and early nineteenth centuries. A con-temporaneous print which portrays the arrangements in Henry VII's Chapel at the first of these ceremonies, that of 1725, is quite astonishing. The entire east end of the building was filled with a 'large theatrical scaffold for the music and company',[2] at once gigantic and hideous. Boxes for the members of the Royal Family and the various ambassadors were erected against the western wall. The north and south aisle chapels were also filled with galleries,

[1] Stanley, *Historical Memorials of Westminster Abbey*, p. 84.
[2] *Gentleman's Magazine*, 1817, part ii, pp. 33–4.

THE PROCESSION OF THE KNIGHTS OF THE BATH ON JUNE 1st, 181

for numerous heads are visible of persons peering over the canopies of the stalls.[1] According to our twentieth-century ideas these arrangements must have been incongruous, unsightly, and irreligious. From a liturgical point of view, too, the 'Divine Service', as it was termed in the official documents, was utterly jejune and inadequate, while the music, judging by such records as survive, could have availed but little to save the situation. The following quotation from one of the Banks MSS. in the British Museum, containing a description of the Installation of May 19th, 1803, speaks for itself.

'The part of the Divine Service performed was: the Dean read, "Let your light so shine etc", and some more of the sentences; Dr. Bell, who acted as Sub-Dean, read the prayer for the Church Militant; the Dean the Blessing, "the Peace of God, etc.". No other part of Divine Service, except the Anthem performed, Psalm cxxxiii, Part 1.'[2]

The erection of the Banners and the remainder of the paraphernalia of the Knights of the Bath over the stalls undoubtedly introduced a welcome element of colour into the building, denuded of its stained glass, and afforded some compensation for the grievous losses of the seventeenth and eighteenth centuries. At the same time these furnishings detract seriously from the beauty of the remarkable canopies with their domical tops, considerable portions of which have ever since been hidden from view. In all probability the loss outweighed the gain and, as already explained, permanent wounds were inflicted upon the beauty of the chapel as a result of these developments.

The Installation which took place on June 1st, 1812, marked the conclusion of the Hanoverian epoch in the history of the Order of the Bath. A year or two later a disastrous mistake was made which had the effect of

[1] John Pine, *The Procession and Ceremonies observed at the Installation of the Knights Commanders of the Most Honourable Order of the Bath on June 17, 1725*, plate III.

[2] Jocelyn Perkins, *The Most Honourable Order of the Bath*, p. 91.

thrusting into the background almost the whole of its religious significance for many a long year.

Towards the close of the Napoleonic Wars, in which the country had been involved for so long, the desire was universally manifested for some signal favour to be bestowed upon the numerous sailors and soldiers who had covered their native land with glory. It was a grand opportunity for the establishment of some wholly new Order, and there is reason for thinking that an Order of the Royal Oak was at one time actually contemplated. Why other considerations were allowed to prevail it is difficult to say. At any rate, the authorities now proceeded to embark upon the impossible and always undesirable task of adapting an established institution to lines differing *in toto* from those upon which it had originally been framed. Worse still, these changes were carried through with a display of carelessness and ignorance which almost baffles belief. A warrant was issued under the Royal Sign Manual bearing the date January 2nd, 1815. In the Preamble mention was made of the desire of the Prince Regent to 'commemorate the auspicious termination of the long and arduous contest in which this Empire has been engaged, and of marking in an especial manner His gracious sense of the magnificent perseverance and devotion manifested by the officers of His Majesty's forces by sea and by land'. The Ordinance went on to state that for this reason it had been 'thought fit to advance the splendour and extend the limits of the Order of the Bath', to the end that 'those officers who have had the opportunities of signalizing themselves by eminent services during the late War might share in the honours of the said Order, and that their names may be delivered down to remote posterity accompanied by the marks of distinction which they have so nobly earned'.

The former arrangement by which the Order was limited to thirty-five K.B.s was therefore drastically re-

THE INSTALLATION OF THE KNIGHTS OF THE BATH ON JUNE 1st, 181

modelled. Three separate classes were now created, viz.
(*a*) Knights Grand Cross, limited to the number of
seventy-two, who were to be regarded as 'subject to the
same rules and ordinances and to have, hold and enjoy all
and singular the rights, privileges, immunities and advantages' of their predecessors; (*b*) Knight Commanders,
limited to one hundred and eighty; and (*c*) Companions.
The second class were informed that the privilege would
be duly accorded to them of having their banners suspended in Henry VII's Chapel in precisely the same
manner as the Knights Grand Cross. On the strength of
this wholly misleading statement, the Officers of Arms
forthwith hastened to secure as many fees as possible in
return for the said privilege, while the stall plates of
Knight Commanders unwise enough to pay up were
actually engraved. The situation was calculated to evoke
hard words and not a few of them.

A state of hopeless confusion was now brought into
existence. Where, for instance, would it have been possible to suspend one hundred and eighty additional
banners in the already overcrowded chapel? So long as
the Order had remained a comparatively small body
things were relatively simple. The policy of expansion
now set on foot by the Prince Regent was almost farcical
in its results, for, in the head-quarters of the Order, it was
wholly impossible to provide even standing-room for the
members. Thus the stately ceremony of Installation
automatically came to an end. The religious aspect, in
which had been set forth the true ideals of Knighthood,
sank into the background to the general loss of the members of the Order and, indeed, of the whole country.

The lowness of ideal characteristic of the early decades
of the nineteenth century is illustrated by a letter written
by the Duke of Wellington to his brother, Sir Henry
Wellesley:

'I congratulate you upon being made Knight of the Bath.

You must be introduced by some Knight of the Order to the person who is to invest you carrying in your hand the Insignia of the Order. The authority who invests you is then read; and the person who is to invest you must Knight you by passing his sword over your shoulder. He then puts the Ribband over your right shoulder and the Star on your left breast. The ceremony here generally ends in eating and drinking.'

No religious ceremony in connexion with the Order of the Bath took place for upwards of a century. The banners inherited from the Installation of 1812 remained suspended in the chapel, becoming more and more decrepit every year. A familiar object to three generations and more of sightseers, their faded and dilapidated condition evoked frequent criticism and small wonder. The years went by, but no move was made by the authorities, and there the banners continued to hang, a standing witness to the policy of muddle and ineptitude inaugurated by the Prince Regent.

## 8. THE NINETEENTH-CENTURY ALTAR

In the year 1870 a permanent altar of stone and marble was set up. Very likely it would never have come into existence at all had it not been for certain extraordinary happenings which attended Dean Stanley's historic search for the coffin of James I. The story of that remarkable adventure may be read in full detail in the Appendix to the last edition of the great Dean's well-known volume. A more thrilling tale has never been given to the world. Moreover, it led to several highly interesting discoveries, with one of which this chapter is directly concerned.

In the course of his lengthy search Stanley made an exhaustive examination of the site of Torrigiano's altar, traditionally believed to be the last resting-place of Edward VI. In the vault beneath the pavement he unexpectedly came upon a piece of white marble frieze three feet eight inches in length. Its elaborate Italian decoration, a kind of arabesque, proclaimed with absolute certainty that it must have formed part of the 'matchless' altar of former times.

What precise position, then, did this precious fragment occupy in Torrigiano's masterpiece? There is more than one theory. The Dean hastily jumped to the conclusion that it had belonged to the entablature of the baldacchino. A second theory assigned to it a place at the base of the picture in bronze relief which served as a dorsal, while a third suggested that it had served as the plinth supporting the Royal Arms which, depicted in marble, formed a head-piece to the canopy.[1]

The design consists of a number of heraldic badges, the roses of the Tudors and the lilies of France alternating with one another, while connecting them are a number of pleasing floral designs, arranged in a pattern of scroll-work.

Not long after this important discovery the Dean and Chapter decided to incorporate their new treasure, this waif from the tomb, in an altar. Sir Gilbert Scott was entrusted with the responsibility of providing Henry VII's Chapel with this additional piece of furniture, and a deplorable failure was the result.

A slab of black marble was laid upon a cedarwood structure, consisting of some eight pillars, richly wrought with motifs derived from Torrigiano's ornamentation, with Corinthian bases, shafts, and capitals, together with a frieze. Of the thirty-two faces of these eight pillars, eighteen were decorated with Renaissance foliage in a highly finished manner. On the remaining fourteen these designs were simply carved in outline. The cedar frieze bore the following inscription in gold lettering:

'In Honorem Dei et In Piam Memoriam Edvardi Sexti Regis Infra Sepulti Hanc Sacram Mensam In Mitiori Saeculo Instaurandum Curavit Arturus P. Stanley S. T. P. Decanus

[1] *Archaeological Journal*, vol. li, p. 148.

Westmonast. MDCCCLXX, Pro Antiquo Altari Inter Civilia Odia
Vi Diruto.'

Resting upon the mensa, and regardless of form and
function, Scott, without the slightest justification, now
placed here the fragment of Torrigiano's beautiful work
to serve as a species of gradine, typical of the age.

But the conclusion of the story has not yet been reached.
Dean Stanley, whose historical imagination occasionally
played tricks with him and led him into developments
savouring strongly of pedantry, was not content. In a
manner hardly distinguishable from the relic worship he
detested, he caused fragments of three other ruined altars
to be inserted into this gradine, thus incorporating them
with Torrigiano's sixteenth-century work.[1]

The first of these fragments was an altar slab from some
Abyssinian church unknown. It had been lying together
with a quantity of similar slabs, preserved as trophies in
Magdala, until the conflagration which destroyed that
town in 1866. The great church was burnt and a number
of the slabs disappeared. Four, however, were conveyed
to England, and one of these, presented to Dean Stanley
by Captain Arbuthnot, now found a home in this curious
gradine.

The second fragment was a piece of mosaic from the
great church at Damascus, the head-quarters of the Greek
Patriarchate of Syria. In the terrible massacre of 1860 the
Christians who had fled for safety within its walls were
massacred by thousands, while of the treasures of the
church only one mosaic escaped, together with portions
of the sanctuary pavement. Two years after the massacre
the late King Edward VII visited Damascus, Stanley
being a member of his suite; hence the removal of this
fragment from Damascus to Westminster.

The third relic is a piece of jasper from the old high altar
of 'Conrad's glorious choir' in Canterbury Cathedral,

[1] Stanley, *Historical Memorials of Westminster Abbey*, p. 473 note.

THE ALTAR IN HENRY VII'S CHAPEL FROM 1870 to 1935

which building was burnt down in 1174, four years after the Becket tragedy. The fragment still displays distinct marks of the fire.

The new permanent altar was duly set up, and although public opinion was at that time running high, Stanley had the pluck, some perhaps would say the temerity, to erect a structure consisting almost entirely of solid marble. Stone altars had been erroneously declared illegal by the Judicial Committee of the Privy Council, but the Dean continued upon his way unmoved, despite the atmosphere of clerical prosecutions through which the Church at that time was passing.

On the other hand, he made not the slightest attempt to provide adequate furniture for the new altar. A pair of metal gilt candlesticks of the most commonplace description represented the sum total of his efforts in this direction.

The altar was completed by the summer of 1870 and used for the first time at a celebration of the Holy Communion on the twenty-second day of June. It was a highly memorable occasion. The company of scholars entrusted with the task of revising the Old and New Testaments was about to hold its first meeting in the Jerusalem Chamber, and the members now gathered together at this service by Stanley's invitation. The Dean had just entered upon his sixth decade. During his long and varied career he had become more than familiar with the proverbial hornets' nest, but the hubbub which naturally arose as a result of his extremely comprehensive invitation must have surpassed all his previous experience. The tale had best be told in his own graphic words.

'In front of this table, itself a monument of the extinct strifes of former days, and round the grave of the youthful Protestant king, in whose reign the English Bible first received its acknowledged place in the Coronation of the sovereign, as well as its free and general circulation throughout the nation, knelt together the band of scholars and divines consisting of representatives of almost every form of Christian belief in England. There were Bishops of the Established Church, two of them by their venerable years connected with the past generation; there were delegates from our historic Cathedrals and Collegiate churches, our Universities, our parishes and our chief ecclesiastical assembly; and with these, intermingled without distinction, were ministers of the Established and of the Free Church of Scotland and of almost every Nonconformist Church in England—Independent, Baptist, Unitarian. It is not to be supposed that each one of those present entered with equal agreement into every part of the service; but it is not without a hopeful significance, that, at the time, such various representatives of British Christendom partook, without difficulty, on such an occasion, in the sacred ordinance of the Christian religion.'[1]

A tradition has survived to the effect that Stanley, when officiating at this remarkable celebration, seized the opportunity of indulging in some curious vagaries. To gratify some strange whim, he thought proper to celebrate on the eastern side of the new altar, facing the congregation. Stanley being what he was, it is unlikely that he was actuated by any ecclesiastical considerations!

During the next ten years the Dean and Chapter had the satisfaction of recovering two more specimens of Torrigiano's genius. The two square piers or posts of white marble indicated in Sandford's engraving as supporting the original mensa were identified among a collection of marbles in the Ashmolean Museum at Oxford by Dr. J. H. Middleton, subsequently Director of the Victoria and Albert Museum.[2] A comparison of the details of their decoration with those depicted in Sandford's engraving left no doubt as to their identity. They were ultimately restored to the Abbey and placed in positions analogous to those for which they had originally been designed by Torrigiano.

[1] Stanley, *Historical Memorials of Westminster Abbey*, pp. 505, 506.
[2] Loftie, *Westminster Abbey*, p. 52.

They are perfectly lovely examples of Italian decorative carving, their four panelled faces displaying a quantity of Renaissance ornament consisting of conventional foliage and vases in low relief, with a portcullis at the base.

As a result of this welcome addition, eight of the slender pillars of cedarwood, provided some ten years before, were displaced. There was no longer any function for them to fulfil. A happy thought then occurred to the Dean. Only a few months before the Right Rev. Acton Windeyer Sillitoe had been consecrated to the missionary bishopric, newly established in the little city of New Westminster in British Columbia, the daughter, in a sense, of our own venerable city on the Isle of Thorns.[1] The Dean now presented the pillars, together with an altar cross fashioned out of wood of the Abbey, to the young Bishop. The latter in his turn bestowed these gifts upon his own Cathedral dedicated to the Holy Trinity, standing on the banks of the Fraser River, where they may be seen arranged so as to form a credence table surmounted by a canopy.[2]

Distant six thousand miles from the heart of the British Empire, these precious links with the historic Abbey Church, from which both diocese and city derive their name, are preserved with reverent and loving care.

These three specimens of Torrigiano's genius are of such signal beauty that they cannot fail to confer distinction upon any structure with which they are incorporated. At the same time, it is wholly impossible to gainsay the fact that the Abbey authorities and Sir Gilbert Scott threw away a grand opportunity. It was hardly perhaps to be expected that they would venture to embark upon such an heroic undertaking as the reproduction of the great 'altar of brass' and its costly adjuncts; but they might at least have followed the precedent of the original altar, as regards proportions. Nor, again, need they have stulti-

[1] The name of this city was chosen by Queen Victoria.
[2] H. H. Gowen, *Church Work in British Columbia*, pp. 82–4.

fied themselves by following the debased art of the day, and converting Torrigiano's exquisite frieze into a meaningless gradine. The net result was poor and insignificant, in spite of the presence of three noble relics of the past which, though redeeming the altar from complete bathos, only served to accentuate its lack of dignity. The latter remained *in situ* for upwards of sixty years, a terrible blot upon the beauty of the chapel.

## 9. THE REINAUGURATION OF THE MOST HONOURABLE ORDER OF THE BATH

Towards the close of the nineteenth century a keener historical sense began to manifest itself, coupled with a general revival of the spirit of beauty. Criticisms of the condition of Henry VII's Chapel, with the dusty, worn-out banners which our Victorian predecessors had accepted, almost as a matter of course, waxed year by year louder and more severe. The Honourable Order of the Bath was by no means unique in this respect. Great Britain's Orders of Knighthood were all, in a sense, under a cloud. The time was long overdue for bringing them into closer harmony with the demands of a new age.

By degrees a change came to pass over the scene. It dated from the accession of King Edward VII. Within little more than a decade the Garter ceremonial was revived in all its ancient glory at Windsor. The modern Order of St. Michael and St. George was officially attached to St. Paul's Cathedral, though it can scarcely be maintained that the tiny chapel at the west end forms a worthy home. A splendid addition was made to St. Giles' Cathedral, Edinburgh, in order to compensate the Knights of the Thistle for the loss of their beautiful ruined chapel at Holyrood. The next step was the rehabilitation of the Order of the Bath, together with its adaptation to twentieth-century needs and conditions, in which the late Dean Ryle played a prominent part.

First and foremost it was found imperative to apply the pruning-knife with a drastic hand. It was clearly essential to retain Henry VII's Chapel as the official head-quarters, but considerations of space rendered it necessary to confine the participants in the time-honoured ceremonial to the Knights Grand Cross. There was no other alternative, and even this extremely radical change did not afford a complete solution to the problem. The building still remained too small even after this very considerable reduction of the demand made upon its capacity. This body of distinguished public servants numbered upwards of four score, exclusive of the Officers of the Order, whereas the Chapel contained less than seventy stalls.

The next step, then, was the abolition of the Esquires, three of whom had been assigned to each of the Georgian Knights of the Bath. From an historical point of view this represented a distinct loss; but under the circumstances it was inevitable. By this means the whole of the sub-stalls were set free and a considerable addition made to the much needed floor-space.

But, even when this process of elimination was completed, stalls and sub-stalls were still too few to accommodate each one of the Knights Grand Cross simultaneously, while the suspension of the Banners constituted yet another difficulty. A certain number were bound to be left out in the cold and relegated to a position neither enviable nor edifying. Very wisely, therefore, it was laid down that for the purpose of Installation, the upper tier of stalls should alone be employed and that they should be assigned to the six-and-thirty senior members of this section of the Order. At the same time, the privilege of entering the Chapel and assisting at the official Bath ceremonies within its walls was accorded to the junior Knights Grand Cross.

The ground having been at length cleared and the task of reorganization accomplished, the next step was to prepare the building for the ceremony of reinauguration. The canopies of the stalls were carefully cleaned. The decaying Banners, suspended above them ever since the Installation of 1812, were formally handed over to the descendants of their original owners, though a few, for whom no claimants were forthcoming, are still preserved in the side aisles. The stall plates of the eighteenth and early nineteenth centuries which, though interesting, were not possessed of great antiquarian value, were removed to a lower position beneath the misericordes. Banners and stall plates thus gave place to others, designed for the approaching installation, infinitely more accurate and effective. A set of copies of the Book of Common Prayer, dating from the commencement of the reign of George III, magnificently bound in crimson morocco, hand-tooled with gilt, were unearthed from the chests in which they had lain untouched for upwards of a century and once more placed in front of each stall.

The solemn reinauguration took place on July 22nd, 1913. Save for the two coronations in 1902 and 1911, it was quite the most brilliant spectacle witnessed either by the Abbey or by any other building during the first decade and a half of the twentieth century. Thanks to a wider liturgical knowledge, and a deeper sense of the claims of things spiritual, the stately service was rendered in a manner far more uplifting than anything of which our eighteenth-century forefathers could have dreamt. As the crimson-mantled Knights filed with slow and stately steps round the Abbey, the blaze of crimson relieved by the surplices of the choir and the white mantles of the Canons and Officers of the Order, followed by the Sovereign whose long train was borne by two Pages of Honour with the Yeomen of the Guard in their splendid uniforms bringing up the rear, the effect was indescribably magnificent.

So, too, with the brilliant scene in Henry VII's Chapel

A TWENTIETH-CENTURY INSTALLATION OF THE KNIGHTS OF THE BATH

itself. The old historic Order had at last come into its own after the lapse of more than a century, as King George V reinaugurated the Order and placed his uncle in the stall of the Great Master.

Then this goodly company repaired once more to the choir to offer up their praises and thanksgivings, while, with the clergy grouped together in front of the High Altar, the Cross of Westminster in their midst, the *Te Deum* was solemnly sung.

On that eventful day another link was forged by the historic Church of Westminster in the chain uniting the British Empire to the most venerable and sacred of all the many sanctuaries which grace our island home.

Installations have taken place four times since 1913, viz. in 1920, 1924, 1928, and 1935. That of 1928 was marked by a revival, with some variation, of one of the most picturesque and popular features of the eighteenth-century ceremony, namely, the outdoor procession through St. Margaret's Churchyard.

This ceremony has been recorded in an extremely interesting picture by Canaletto painted in 1749 and preserved in the Deanery at Westminster. It represents the members of the Order on their return journey from the west door of the Abbey to the Prince's Chamber in the Palace of St. Stephen, after an Installation in the reign of George II.[1] In 1928 it was arranged that after the Bath ceremonial had been duly performed in Henry VII's Chapel, the Abbey clergy, together with the members of the Order, should pass from the north transept through the churchyard, re-entering the building by the great west door.

It was an extremely happy thought to revive this attractive outdoor feature. Thousands of people for whom seats could not possibly have been found in the building were thus enabled to participate in a great and notable occasion.

[1] See illustration facing p. 190.

## 10. THE REPLACEMENT OF THE HIGH ALTAR IN 1935

An early-nineteenth-century writer has written a vivid description of Henry VII's Chapel in the heyday of its beauty and glory, when

'the windows were filled with painted glass and the light, which streamed through them, was tinged with a warm glow of colours that heightened the brilliancy of the gold and silver utensils of the various altars and the embroidered vestments of the priests, at the same time touching one pendant of the roof with purple, another with crimson and a third with yellow. The burning tapers waving with every current of air varied the strong shadows on the exquisite statues above them and showed their features in every lineament. In the centre stood . . . the High Altar. Behind it the polished, brazen screen and within it the tomb and altar, glowing with the light of tapers. The sculptured walls and exquisite minutely carved roof bounded this unparalleled view and, thanks to the skill of its architect, still enchants us though all its accompaniments are buried in irretrievable gloom.'[1]

Malcolm wrote these glowing words in an unsympathetic age, when only a limited number of people were capable of appreciating the full wonder of Henry VII's Chapel. If he were living to-day he would scarcely believe his eyes, though even now the *miraculum orbis* is far from displaying the sumptuous intentions of its Royal Founder in their entirety. That, however, which has already been accomplished, in our own generation, justifies the hope that those who come after will one day behold a chapel which would move Henry VII himself to unqualified joy and pride.

During the late summer of 1932 consternation was caused by the fall of a piece of masonry from the elaborately sculptured roof of the chapel. A portion of one of the cusps had become detached and without the slightest

---

[1] Malcolm, *Londinium Redivivum*, vol. i, p. 229.

warning descended on to the marble floor close to the altar. Had this accident taken place at a time of day when the place was full of visitors, the consequences might have been terrible.

The chapel was at once closed and an exhaustive investigation took place. Did the fracture of this cusp indicate the presence of decay in the wondrous roof? Was the development of modern traffic, with its constant vibration, about to effect a collapse of one of the loveliest creations of man? Such were some of the questions which were anxiously asked.

For nearly three years the chapel remained in the hands of the masons. Little save a forest of scaffolding met the eye all through that long period. Inch by inch the marvellous stone tapestry was laboriously scrutinized and strengthened where necessary, while from end to end of the building the dust and grime of many generations were swept away. The whole of the structure was made fair and beautiful and reappeared virtually the same as it left the hands of the Tudor craftsmen, save for the loss of its glass and the screens of the apsidal chapels. Europe displays no fairer spectacle than the interior of Henry VII's Chapel to-day.

As the great work of renovation proceeded and the matchless beauty of the place came to be realized in increasing measure, the painful contrast between the glorious work of the sixteenth-century craftsmen and the meanness of the altar erected in 1870 by Dean Stanley and Sir Gilbert Scott was still further accentuated. Always a poor thing, save for the fragments of Torrigiano's work, it now became a positive eyesore.

Hence, it was a happy thought on the part of the members of the Order of the Bath to crown the work of renovation by reproducing Torrigiano's masterpiece, so far as circumstances permitted.

Ample evidence as to the general character of the

famous altar and its baldacchino was available, both pictorial and documentary, and the Surveyor of Westminster Abbey, the late Sir Walter Tapper, R.A., in designing the new structure adhered to the ancient lines with scrupulous exactitude.

The proportions of the sixteenth- and the twentieth-century structures are identical. The two beautiful piers or posts, Torrigiano's own handiwork, are once more carrying out their original function of supporting the mensa of black marble, together with two modern replicas of the ancient work. As before, the great canopy with its coffered ceiling rests upon four elaborately decorated Corinthian columns. The beautiful arabesque work of the frieze has been carefully reproduced, though with a pleasing and appropriate addition consisting of the Badge and Star of the Order of the Bath. At each angle of the entablature has been placed a kneeling figure of an angel, holding one of the instruments of the Passion, viz. a pillar surmounted by a cock, a cross, a spear, and a reed with a sponge at the end. In the centre facing westwards is a shield bearing the Royal Arms of the Tudor dynasty, supported by a lion and a dragon and surmounted by an Imperial Crown, while, in the corresponding position on the eastern side, supported by two black eagles, are the arms of the monarchy of Spain, viz. in the first and fourth quarters Castile and Leon, in the second and third Aragon and Sicily with the pomegranate of Granada in the base.

This splendid work was carried out by Mr. Lawrence Turner, F.S.A., and his accomplished school of craftsmen with the utmost delicacy and skill.

As explained elsewhere, Torrigiano's great structure included an altar-piece of gilded bronze depicting on its western face a somewhat realistic representation of the Resurrection and on the eastern face, the Nativity. The reproduction of anything at once so costly and so beautiful could only be regarded as a counsel of perfection

THE HIGH ALTAR OF HENRY VII'S CHAPEL ON CHRISTMAS DAY, 1938

in such difficult times as the thirties of the twentieth century. At the last moment, however, the gap was filled, and in a manner fully equal to the original arrangement. The Right Hon. Viscount Lee of Fareham, himself a Knight Grand Cross of the Bath, presented to the Dean and Chapter a glorious picture of the Madonna and Child by the Venetian master Bartolommeo Vivarini (*c.* 1480). Alike in size and general character this splendid work of art fills the position to perfection.

The renovated chapel with its new altar was reopened on July 3rd, 1935, by the Dean of Westminster acting in the capacity of Dean of the Bath, when the traditional ceremonies of the Order were once more performed and a number of new Knights Grand Cross installed. No such ceremony had taken place in Henry VII's Chapel since 1928.

The occasion was, however, not untinged by sadness. The great Christian architect under whose superintendence all this work had been carried out, though present and able to take part in the ceremony, was a dying man. He was never seen again in his much-loved Abbey, and in less than three months his remains were laid to rest in the west walk of the Great Cloister.

The altar set up by Dean Stanley and Sir Gilbert Scott was so hopelessly inadequate that its replacement by a worthier structure could only be a matter of time. It was fortunate that this great enterprise was deferred to an age characterized by a real development alike of artistic feeling and of the historical sense, and placed in the hands of a man capable of doing full justice to this unique opportunity.

Henry VII laid down in his Will that the 'high Aultre' and 'every other Aulter' in the chapel were to be equipped with 'two sets of Aultier clothes, two pairs of Vestiments, two Corporacs with their cases, oon Masse booke, oon Chalice of silver and gilte, oon paire of Cruetts, silver and gilte, oon Belle, silver and gilte, and two pairs of Candle-sticks silver and gilte,' all of which were to 'bee soo em-browdered and wrought with our arms and cognisaunts that thei may by the same be knowen of our gifte and bequests'.

It can scarcely be maintained that even the restored altar wholly reflects to-day the spacious ideals of the Royal Founder, for the majority of the ornaments which were to be 'such as apperteigne to the gifte of a Prince' have still for the most part to be provided; but this generation is at least entitled to claim that a grievous wrong has been re-paired and that the wound inflicted by Sir Robert Harley, nearly three centuries ago, has at last been healed.

## 11. MY LADY MARGARETTE'S CHAPEL

It would seem that the work of erecting the south aisle of Henry VII's Chapel must have been pushed forward from the outset with considerable vigour, for it was in actual use so early as 1505.

The memory of the Lady Margaret Beaufort is in-separably linked with this part of the building, and for more reasons than one. Following the example of her much loved son, she did not hesitate to pour forth her wealth upon 'oure Chapell of Westminster', its furniture and endowment. In her last will and testament this de-voted daughter of the Church laid down that her executors should 'make in the chapel a convenient tomb, and one altar or two in the same chapel for two chantry masses there perpetually to be said'. She survived her son a bare three months, but for some considerable time before her death masses were being said here, beneath the statue of St. Margaret of Antioch, by Thomas Elfride and others of the monks.[1]

It was not for long. The hand of the iconoclast soon fell with heavy weight upon the chapel. The empty niche

[1] *Church Quarterly Review*, vol. lxiv, p. 71.

which once contained the central figure of the magnificent reredos, probably that of the Blessed Virgin, tells an eloquent tale. Still, save for this loss, the smashing of the beautiful windows and the introduction of the huge and almost terrifying monument of General Monk in the eighteenth century, the east end of this chapel displays comparatively few traces of the upheavals witnessed by subsequent generations.

From Elizabethan days onwards, the filling up of the numerous chapels belonging to the Abbey with monuments, good, bad, and indifferent, proceeded apace. No doubt the central positions formerly occupied by the altars smashed by the Prebendary, John Hardyman, and other miscreants at the beginning of that reign formed a temptation, as being the first and most obvious space upon which to erect a tomb. The Chapel of My Lady Margarette stands almost unique among its companions, for, although the altar perished, yet the step remained untouched and has never been equipped with the customary monument, perpetuating the memory of some departed public servant or aristocrat.

Hence, when the opportunity arrived it was a comparatively simple matter to fill the space left vacant so long and to refurnish the east end. The offer was made by the late Countess Grosvenor so far back as the year 1916. It was accepted by the Dean and Chapter and the work placed in the hands of Mr. Detmar Blow. Many years, however, came and went before the task was completed. Not until the Feast of St. Margaret in the year 1929 was it found possible to dedicate the new altar and its other treasures to the glory of God, when the Holy Communion was celebrated here, presumably for the first time since the Reformation, by Dean Norris.

The altar[1] consists of a slab of black marble supported

---

[1] The altar bears the date 1924, but it was placed *in situ* a long time before the remainder of the ornaments.

by two massive pedestals of similar material. The following inscription carved upon the south side of the mensa sets forth the reasons which inspired this generous gift:

'Capellam Istam Qua Requiescat Domina Margerita Beaufort Mater Regis Henrici Septimi Restituit Sibell Comtessa Grosvenor in Cultum Dei et In Piam Memoriam Filii Sui Dilectissimi Percy Wyndham Pro Rege et Patria Mortui Necnon Herberti Comitis Kitchener de Khartoum Militis Illustrissimi Anno Sal. Nostrae MCMXXIV, Architecto Detmar Blow Amico.'

The eastern wall of the chapel is covered with a mass of sculpture. The lower stage contains two rows of perpendicular panelling surmounted by a frieze, consisting of angels supporting the customary Tudor emblems, the rose, the portcullis, and the fleur-de-lis. Above stand two fine figures of St. Catherine of Alexandria and St. Margaret of Antioch occupying pedestals and surmounted by richly decorated canopies. The central niche is empty.

A large plain slab forms the centre-piece of the lower stage. In pre-Reformation days it must have been covered with sculpture, subsequently defaced, or perhaps with some rich fabric. To-day the empty space has been filled by a splendid piece of Flemish tapestry dating from the last half of the sixteenth century, woven in silk, wool, and gold thread, on which is depicted the Descent from the Cross. It is surrounded by a border of flowers and fruits with the Four Evangelists bearing their distinctive emblems at each corner, St. John and St. Matthew at the top, St. Luke and St. Mark at the bottom.

The tapestry is enclosed in a frame of metal gilt to which are attached a number of shields and lozenges decorated with the arms of various personages, either buried in the chapel or associated with its refurnishings.

The arms of the Lady Margaret Beaufort engraved upon a lozenge occupy the central position above the tapestry, flanked by those of Grosvenor and Kitchener. Two shields are placed on either side of the frame, viz. those of Henry VII, Charles II, William III, and Queen Anne, all of whom lie in the chapel. On the lower side are the arms of the medieval convent and those of St. Edward the Confessor. The subject of the latter shield is, however, an error. It ought to bear the arms of the Collegiate Church.

## 12. THE BRONZE MEDALLION

In the south aisle of Henry VII's Chapel, and hard by the tomb of that Sovereign's mother, there hangs a splendid medallion containing a portrait bust surrounded by a scroll bearing the motto of the Order of the Garter. The fine, strongly-moulded face has been cast in bronze. It is clearly the work of a sculptor whose technique was as perfect as his grasp of character was unfaltering.

Neither the name of the artist nor that of his subject is discoverable anywhere upon the bronze, but there is good reason for thinking that the former was none other than 'Peter Torissany of the City of Florence'. The figure is believed to be that of a prominent statesman of early Tudor times, viz. Sir Thomas Lovell, K.G., Speaker of the House of Commons, Chancellor of the Exchequer, and Chancellor of the Universities of Oxford and Cambridge. During the course of his life, which terminated in 1524, he was always found in close association with the new Tudor dynasty, becoming the recipient of marks of special confidence, for he was executor both to Henry VII and to the Lady Margaret Beaufort.

Sir Thomas sprang from a Norfolk county family of strong Lancastrian predilections, he himself being the fifth son of Sir Ralph Lovell of Barton Bendish. He entered at Lincoln's Inn, where his shield is still visible upon the ancient brick gateway, surrounded by the scroll of the Garter. Attainted in the first Parliament of

Richard III, he was destined to experience a striking change of fortune after the victory of Bosworth Field, in which he himself played a part.

Before the year 1485 had drawn to its close, he was created Chancellor of the Exchequer for life, and received at the same time more than one valuable Court appointment. For three years he served as Speaker, while on June 9th, 1487, he received the honour of knighthood, and was appointed to the important positions of Treasurer of the Household and Lord President of the Council. The much prized distinction of the Garter followed sixteen years later.

His official duties and his close connexion with the Royal Family brought him, almost of necessity, into constant communication with Torrigiano while the latter was at work in Henry VII's Chapel between 1509 and 1519. Under these circumstances it was not unnatural for Sir Thomas, himself a great builder, to seek the aid of this distinguished Florentine in the erection of his own monument in the Nunnery of Holywell in Shoreditch. In this respect he was but following the contemporary fashion.

Further, he arranged for the making by Torrigiano of 'a brass bust of his own likeness surrounded with the Garter', and placed it above the archway of the gatehouse of East Herling in Norfolk, the great mansion built out of his accumulated wealth.

Unfortunately, one of his descendants, Gregory Lovell by name, allowed this magnificent house to fall into ruin towards the close of the seventeenth century. The bust found its way to another Norfolk country residence, Weeting Hall, where it remained till 1895, when it figured in a sale of articles contained in this house. It was described as 'a bronze medallion with a portrait bust of an elderly man, wearing a cap, encircled by the Garter, 17¾ inches in diameter, recently obtained at a sale of miscellaneous works of art from Weeting Hall, Norfolk, being the residue of collections made during a long series of years by Mr. Angerstein'. The bronze relievo was soon recognized as being the work of Torrigiano, but the subject remained uncertain for some years. It is so full of life and vigour as to justify the belief that it was taken from the living model.

During the early years of the present century the bust was presented to the Dean and Chapter of Westminster by Sir J. Charles Robinson, K.C.B., sometime Keeper of Queen Victoria's pictures. It was suspended in the south aisle of Henry VII's Chapel, immediately above Torrigiano's masterpiece, the tomb of the Lady Margaret Beaufort. No happier position could have been found for this notable addition to the treasures of Westminster Abbey. Long may it continue to remain in close proximity to the tomb of the distinguished lady, to the interests of whose family Sir Thomas Lovell gave some of the best work of his life.

PRINTED IN
GREAT BRITAIN
AT THE
UNIVERSITY PRESS
OXFORD
BY
JOHN JOHNSON
PRINTER
TO THE
UNIVERSITY

THE ALCUIN CLUB exists in order to encourage and assist in the practical study of ceremonial, and the arrangement of Churches, their furniture and ornaments, in accordance with the rubrics of the Book of Common Prayer, strict obedience to which is the guiding principle of the work of the Club.

The Club shall consist of Members and Associates, to be elected by the Committee.

The Subscription for *Members* shall be 20s. per annum, entitling them to current publications *gratis*; and for *Associates*, 5s. per annum, entitling them to such of the Tracts *gratis* as the Committee may determine. There shall be no Entrance Fee, nor Composition for Subscriptions.

---

Application for election and for the List of Publications should be sent to Miss DUNCAN-JONES, The Deanery, Chichester, as well as all Subscriptions.

---

A complete set of Alcuin Club publications, formerly belonging to the Society, is now in the Library of King's College, Strand, and may be consulted by members of Alcuin Club on application to the Librarian.

A number of lantern-slides illustrating Church ceremonial, furniture, architecture, &c., formerly belonging to the Society, are now the property of the Press and Publications Board of the Church Assembly. Members of Alcuin Club, who wish to make use of such for the purpose of lectures, may have the loan of any of the above on application to the Secretary, The Church House, Westminster.

# PUBLICATIONS

*All prices are net*

## COLLECTIONS

*Published by* OXFORD UNIVERSITY PRESS

I. **English Altars.** A large folio volume with 14 pp. of Collotypes. Explanatory Notes by Sir W. H. St. JOHN HOPE, Litt.D., D.C.L. [*Out of print.*]

II. **Exposition de la Messe.** A large folio volume containing a Treatise on the Mass from a French Version of the Legenda Aurea of Jacobus de Voragine, now in the Fitzwilliam Museum at Cambridge, and 22 plates from Illustrations in this MS. Together with four Tracts from ' The Lay Folks' Mass Book ', ' Merita Missæ ', &c. Edited by the Right Rev. WALTER HOWARD FRERE, D.D. Price £1 10s. [*Out of print.*]

III and IV. **Pontifical Services,** vols. i and ii. Two large folio volumes containing Descriptive Notes and a Liturgical Introduction by the Right Rev. WALTER HOWARD FRERE, D.D., and 20 plates of 62 Illustrations from Miniatures of the fifteenth and sixteenth centuries. Price £1 10s. each. [*Out of print.*]

V. **Dat Boexken van der Missen** (The Booklet of the Mass). By GHERIT VANDER GOUDE, 1507. 34 woodcuts illustrating the Celebration of the Holy Communion, described, and the explanatory text of the Flemish original translated, with illustrative excerpts from contemporary missals and tracts by the Rev. PERCY DEARMER, D.D. Price £1 1s. [*Out of print.*]

VI. **The Edwardian Inventories for Bedfordshire.** Edited by F. C. EELES, F.R.Hist.S., F.S.A.Scot., from transcripts by the Rev. J. E. BROWN, B.A. Price 5s.

VII. **The Edwardian Inventories for Huntingdonshire.** Edited by Mrs. S. C. LOMAS, Editor of ' State Papers Charles I Addenda ', &c., from transcripts by T. CRAIB. Price 10s.

VIII. **Pontifical Services,** vol. iii. Descriptive Notes and 143 Illustrations from woodcuts in pontificals of the sixteenth century. Edited by F. C. EELES, F.R.Hist.S., F.S.A.Scot. £1 1s.

IX. **The Edwardian Inventories for Buckinghamshire.** Edited by F. C. EELES, F.R.Hist.S., F.S.A.Scot., from transcripts by the Rev. J. E. BROWN, B.A. Price £1 1s. [*Out of print.*]

X. **Fifty Pictures of Gothic Altars.** Descriptive Notes and 50 Illustrations. Edited by the Rev. PERCY DEARMER, D.D. Price £1 1s. [*Out of print.*]*

XI. **The Sarum Missal in English.** Two volumes, containing a translation of the complete Sarum Missal by the Rev. F. E. WARREN, B.D., F.S.A. Price £1 2s. 6d. [*Out of print.*]

* This work has been reprinted by Messrs. Mowbray, and can be purchased by members of the Club on application to the Secretary.

iii

XII. **Pontifical Services**, vol. iv. Descriptive Notes and 134 Illustrations from woodcuts in pontificals of the sixteenth century. Edited by ATHELSTAN RILEY, F.S.A. £1 1s. [*Out of print.*]

XIII. **A History of the Use of Incense in Divine Worship.** xx +404 pp. 60 Illustrations. By E. G. CUTHBERT F. ATCHLEY, L.R.C.P., M.R.C.S. Price £3.

XIV. **Visitation Articles and Injunctions of the Period of the Reformation**, vol. i. An Introduction on the theory, history, and practice of Episcopal and other Visitations. By the Right Rev. WALTER HOWARD FRERE, D.D. Price £1. [*Out of print.*]

XV. **The Same**, vol. ii (1536–58). Edited by the Right Rev. W. H. FRERE, D.D., with the assistance of W. M. KENNEDY, Litt.D. Price 30s. [*Out of print.*]

XVI. **The Same**, vol. iii (1558–75). Edited by the Right Rev. W. H. FRERE, D.D. Price 30s. [*Out of print.*]

XVII. **Traditional Ceremonial and Customs connected with the Scottish Liturgy.** By F. C. EELES, F.R.Hist.S., F.S.A.Scot. Price £1.

XVIII. **The Rationale of Ceremonial**, 1540–3, with Notes and Appendices and an Essay on the Regulation of Ceremonial during the Reign of King Henry VIII. By Sir C. S. COBB, K.B.E., M.V.O. Price 10s. [*Out of print.*]

XIX. **Illustrations of the Liturgy.** Thirteen drawings of the Celebration of the Holy Communion in a parish church. By CLEMENT O. SKILBECK. With Notes descriptive and explanatory, an Introduction on ' The Present Opportunity ', and a Preface on the English and American Uses. By the Rev. PERCY DEARMER, D.D. Price 4s. 6d. [*Out of print.*]

XX. **The Edwardian Inventories for the City and County of Exeter.** Edited by Miss B. CRESSWELL, from transcripts of the original documents in the Guildhall, Exeter. Price 10s.

XXI. **The Sacrament Reserved : being a History of the Practice of Reserving the Eucharist up to the IVth Lateran Council.** By the Rev. W. H. FREESTONE. Price £1.

XXII. **The Ornaments of the Ministers as shown on English Monumental Brasses.** Illustrated. By the Rev. H. J. CLAYTON, A.K.C. Price £1 5s.

XXIII. **The Chantry Certificates for Oxfordshire.** Edited and transcribed by ROSE GRAHAM, F.R.Hist.S., formerly of Somerville College, Oxford, and **The Edwardian Inventories of Church Goods for Oxfordshire.** Edited by ROSE GRAHAM from transcripts by T. CRAIB, of H.M. Public Record Office. Price 10s. 6d. [*Out of print.*]

XXIV. **Illustrations of the Occasional Offices of the Church.** Taken from Medieval pictures and miniatures. Edited by H. S. KINGSFORD, M.A. Price £1 5s.

**XXV–XXVII. Elizabethan Episcopal Administration.** An Essay introductory to a further Collection of Visitation Articles, by Professor W. M. KENNEDY, Litt.D. Vol. i: The Essay. Vol. ii: Articles, &c., 1575–83. Vol. iii: Articles, &c., 1583–1603. Price £3 3s. the set. Vol. i: The Essay, can be bought separately. Price £1 5s.

**XXVIII. Studies in the Early Roman Liturgy.** I. The Kalendar. By the Right Rev. WALTER HOWARD FRERE, D.D. Price £1 1s.

**XXIX. Historical Survey of Holy Week: its Services and Ceremonial.** By the Rev. JOHN WALTON TYRER, M.A. Price £1 5s.

**XXX. Studies in the Early Roman Liturgy.** II. The Roman Gospel-Lectionary. By the Right Rev. WALTER HOWARD FRERE, D.D. Price £1 5s.

**XXXI. On the Epiclesis of the Eucharistic Liturgy and in the Consecration of the Font.** By E. G. CUTHBERT F. ATCHLEY, L.R.C.P., M.R.C.S. Price £1 1s.

**XXXII. Studies in the Early Roman Liturgy.** III. The Roman Epistle-Lectionary. By the Right Rev. WALTER HOWARD FRERE, D.D. Price £1 1s.

**XXXIII. Westminster Abbey, its Worship and Ornaments.** By Jocelyn Perkins, M.A., D.C.L., F.S.A., Sacrist of Westminster Abbey. Illustrated. Vol. i. Price £1 5s.

**XXXIV. The Same,** vol. ii. Price £1 5s.


## TRACTS (i.e. SMALLER BOOKS)

*Published by* A. R. MOWBRAY & CO. LTD.

**I. Ornaments of the Rubric.** (Third Edition.) By J. T. MICKLE-THWAITE, F.S.A. Price 5s.

**II. Consolidation.** (Second Edition.) By the Rev. W. C. E. NEWBOLT, M.A., Canon and Chancellor of S. Paul's. Price 1s.
[*Out of print.*]

**III. Liturgical Interpolations.** (Second Edition.) By the Rev. T. A. LACEY, D.D. [*Out of print: see Pamphlet I.*]

**IV. The Parish Clerk and his right to read the Liturgical Epistle.** By E. G. CUTHBERT F. ATCHLEY, L.R.C.P., M.R.C.S. (Second Edition.) Price (in boards) 2s. 6d.

**V. A First English Ordo : A Celebration of the Lord's Supper with one Minister, described and discussed by some members of the Alcuin Club.** Price 2s. [*Out of print.*]

**VI. The People's Prayers : being some considerations on the use of the Litany in Public Worship.** By E. G. CUTHBERT F. ATCHLEY, L.R.C.P., M.R.C.S. Price 1s. 6d. [*Out of print.*]

**VII. The Sign of the Cross in the Western Liturgies.** By the Rev. E. E. BERESFORD COOKE. Price 1s. 6d. [*Out of print.*]

VIII. The 'Interpretations' of the Bishops and their Influence on Elizabethan Policy. By W. M. KENNEDY, Litt.D. Price 1s. 6d. [Out of print.]

IX. Prayer Book Revision : The 'Irreducible Minimum'. Edited by ATHELSTAN RILEY, F.S.A. Price 2s. [Out of print.]

X. The Bread of the Eucharist. By the Rev. R. MAXWELL WOOLLEY, D.D. With 11 Illustrations. Price 4s. 6d.

XI. English or Roman Use ? By E. G. P. WYATT, M.A. Price 3d.

XII. Russian Observations upon the American Prayer Book. Translated by WILFRID J. BARNES, and Edited with Notes by the Right Rev. WALTER HOWARD FRERE, D.D. Price 2s. 6d.

XIII. A Directory of Ceremonial. Third edition (revised). Price 3s.

XIV. Ceremonial Pictured in Photographs. A Collection of Pictures, with Explanatory Notes, forming a companion volume to A Directory of Ceremonial. Price (in boards) 3s. and (in paper covers) 2s.

XV. The Mozarabic and Ambrosian Rites. Four Essays in Comparative Liturgiology. By the Rev. W. C. BISHOP, M.A. Arranged from his papers by the Rev. C. L. FELTOE, D.D. Price (in boards) 5s.

XVI. The Uniats and their Rites. A paper read before the Alcuin Club on November 20, 1924, by Sir STEPHEN GASELEE, K.C.M.G., C.B.E., F.S.A. Illustrated by nine photographs. Price (in boards) 3s. and (in paper covers) 2s.

XVII. Linen Ornaments of the Church. By the Rev. PERCY DEARMER, D.D. With seven illustrations. Price 2s. 6d.

XVIII. Cassock and Gown. By the Rev. H. J. CLAYTON, A.K.C. With six illustrations. Price 2s. 6d.

XIX. A Directory of Ceremonial. Part II, for services not included in the first Tract XIII. Price 3s.

XX. Processions. By the Rev. COLIN DUNLOP, M.A. A dissertation, together with practical suggestions. Four illustrations. Price 3s.

XXI. A Server's Manual. Directions for one server at the Holy Communion (1662 and 1928). Price 1s. 9d.

XXII. Anglican Liturgies. The full texts of the English Eucharistic Rites of 1662 and 1928, the Scottish, American, South African, Indian, and Ceylon Liturgies, together with notes on the divergences of the Irish and Canadian Rites from the English of 1662, and 'An Essay in Liturgical Construction', being comments on the South African revision by the Right Rev. W. H. FRERE. Price 10s. 6d.

## PAMPHLETS

*Published by* A. R. MOWBRAY & CO. LTD.

I. Liturgical Interpolations and Prayer Book Revision. By the Rev. T. A. LACEY, D.D. Price (in boards) 1s. and (in paper covers) 6d.

II. **The Liturgical Gospels.** By the Right Rev. W. H. FRERE, D.D. Price (in paper covers) 1s.

III. **A Century of Collects.** Selected and translated by the Rev. ATWELL M. Y. BAYLAY. [*Out of print.*]

IV. **The Manual Acts.** By the Rev. VERNON STALEY. [*Out of print.*]

V. **The Eucharistic Prayer.** By E. G. P. WYATT, M.A. Price 1s. 6d.

VI. **Memorial Services.** Extracted by permission from 'A Prayer Book Revised', as issued in 1913 with a Preface by the Right Rev. CHARLES GORE, D.D. Price 1s.

VII. **The Burial Service.** By E. G. P. WYATT, M.A. Price 2s.

VIII. **The Primitive Consecration Prayer.** A Lecture given at the Annual Meeting of the Club, June 7, 1922, by the Right Rev. W. H. FRERE, D.D. Price (in boards) 2s. 6d. and (in paper covers) 1s. 6d.

IX. **'He that Readeth the Epistle.'** A cheap reissue with frontispiece of Tract IV, by E. G. CUTHBERT F. ATCHLEY, L.R.C.P., M.R.C.S. Price 6d. [*Out of print: see Tract IV.*]

X. **Reservation : its Purpose and Method.** By D. L. MURRAY, M.A. Price (in boards) 2s. 6d. and (in paper covers) 1s. 6d.

XI. **What is the English Use ?** An enquiry into the principles underlying the conduct of public worship in the Church of England. By the Rev. COLIN DUNLOP, M.A. Price (in boards) 2s. 6d. and (in paper covers) 1s. 6d.

XII. **A Survey of the Proposals for the Alternative Prayer Book.** (Second Edition.) By a group of members of the Alcuin Club. Part I: The Order of Holy Communion. Price (in boards) 2s. 6d.

XIII. **The Same.** Part II : Occasional Offices. Price 2s. 6d.

XIV. **The Same.** Part III : The Calendar, &c., The Collects, Epistles, and Gospels, and The Ordination Services. Price 2s. 6d.

## OCCASIONAL PAPERS, LEAFLETS, ETC.

**Why Change the Communion Service?** By the Very Rev. A. S. DUNCAN-JONES, B.D., Dean of Chichester. A paper upon the content of the Eucharistic Prayer of Consecration, with special reference to that of 1928. S.P.C.K. Price 6d.

**Liturgy in the Parish.** Six cheap tracts for popular use, by members of the Club, bound in a single volume. Mowbrays, price 2s.

This comprises the following:—

**Praying with the Church.** Price 2d.

**The Consecration of the Eucharist.** Price 2d.

**'English Use'.** Price 1d.

**The Parish Eucharist.** Price 1d.

**The Catholic Altar.** Price 2d.

**Processions.** Price 2d.

The next series has opened with:—
  **Simple Eucharistic Ceremonial.** Price 2*d.*
  **Eucharistic Ceremonial in One-priest Parishes.** Price 2*d.*
and will include leaflets on
  **The Offertory.**
  **Standing, Kneeling, and Sitting.**
  **The Music of the Parish Eucharist.**
  **The End of the Communion Service.**

*Clerical Members of the Club who find themselves in agreement with these leaflets are asked to keep their parish tract-cases stocked with them. By so doing they will help forward the cause which the Club is designed to serve.*

---

*Publishers*

HUMPHREY MILFORD, OXFORD UNIVERSITY PRESS,
Amen House, Warwick Square, London, E.C. 4.
and
A. R. MOWBRAY & CO. LTD.,
28 Margaret Street, London, W. 1.

PRINTED IN GREAT BRITAIN AT THE UNIVERSITY PRESS, OXFORD
BY JOHN JOHNSON, PRINTER TO THE UNIVERSITY